CHEAP SLEEPS IN PARIS

SECOND EDITION

The Savvy Traveler's Guide to the Best Accommodations at the Best Prices.

SANDRA A. GUSTAFSON

CHRONICLE BOOKS
SAN FRANCISCO

Printed in the United States of America.

SEVENTH EDITION

ISBN 0-8118-0858-0

ISSN 1074-505X

Cover design: Robin Weiss
Cover photograph: Alain Choisnet/THE IMAGE BANK
Book design: Words & Deeds
Original maps: Françoise St. Clair

Distributed in Canada by Raincoast Books,
8680 Cambie Street, Vancouver, B.C. V6P 6M9

10 9 8 7 6 5 4 3 2 1

Chronicle Books
275 Fifth Street
San Francisco, CA 94103

For Gina

Contents

To the Reader

You, who have ever been to Paris know;
And you who have not been to Paris—go.

John Ruskin, A Tour through France, *1835*

La Belle France continues to beckon us no matter what. Paris is one of the most popular travel destinations in the world. Each year Parisians play host to more than 15 million visitors. The American passion for Paris has now entered its third century: it has continued through wars, riots, occupations, and the rise and fall of hemlines and the dollar. Whether seen for the first or the tenth time, Paris is a never-ending love affair for most of us. Walk a block, turn a corner—in Paris there is always something interesting, something beautiful and new, or something that has been there forever which you never noticed until now. No matter what time of year you visit, it is impossible to keep from falling in love with the city, its grand boulevards, the beautiful women, the breathtaking monuments and museums, the glorious food, the famous art, and the sweeping views from place de la Concorde up the Champs-Elysées or from the steps of Sacré-Coeur over the entire city.

The first priority for visitors to Paris is a roof over their heads. In Paris, despite its reputation for high prices, there is an abundance of hotels in all price ranges, so even travelers on very tight budgets can enjoy a stay in the city.

The essence of any Parisian hotel is its individuality, and no two are alike. They vary from the most luxurious pleasure palaces in the world to those few people would consider. It is always possible to check into the Hilton or any other big-name chain hotel, but only in Paris can you sleep in a romantic hideaway in Montmartre and be served breakfast in bed while looking out the window and seeing all of Paris below you; or rent a houseboat docked along the banks of the Seine; or check into a suite in a renovated hotel a block from the Ritz, but light-years away in price.

It is certainly true that a trip to Paris will cost more today than it did a few years ago, but what doesn't? Europe—or Paris—on $5 or $10 a day no longer exists for any traveler. Most of those romantically threadbare hotels of our youth are gone for good. More and more smaller hotels are being renovated—adding bathrooms, fluffy towels, fax machines, and buffet breakfasts served in 16th-century stone-walled basements. This, of course, means higher prices. Yet, there are still many ways to save money and maximize the buying strength of the dollar without feeling *nouveau pauvre* in the process.

If you are looking for a book about the cheapest beds in Paris, *Cheap Sleeps in Paris* is not for you. What you will find here is a highly selective guide to the hotels that I have discovered to be the best value in their category, be it a no-star with the shower and toilet down the hall, or an antique-filled, three-star Left Bank hotel with a Jacuzzi in the marble bathroom. The purpose of this book is to offer fail-safe advice for the first-time visitor and the Paris veteran on finding the hotel that is in keeping with their daily needs, tastes, and budgets. The selections include hotels—from the center of Paris to the fringes—for lovers and honeymooners, nostalgia buffs, backpackers, and families. Other options include camping, renting an apartment, exchanging your home for one in Paris, staying in a B & B, or living in a student dorm or hostel. Each listing has been included because I feel it has something special to offer. Some represent a particular style or era; others have been beautifully restored. Some are in nontourist neighborhoods where people like you and I live and work, send their children to school, get their cars repaired, each lunch, shop, and go to the dentist. Some accommodations are basic, many are charming, and a few are starkly modern. Many are cheap, others not so cheap, and a few fall into the Big Splurge category for those with more flexible budgets and demanding tastes. All have one vital feature in common: the potential for providing a memorable stay that will make you feel you have discovered your own part of Paris.

It is important for readers to know that no hotel can purchase a listing or ask to be included in this book. I do all the research and writing for *Cheap Sleeps in Paris* myself; the buck stops right here. In reviewing the hotels, I pull no punches and call the shots as I see them . . . including telling you the pluses and minuses you can expect to find so that you will have the best idea of what to expect of your major travel investment for your Parisian holiday.

On my last trip to Paris, I inspected every hotel and shop in this edition, along with hundreds that did not make the final cut for one reason or another. In so doing, I walked 487.5 miles and climbed 33,264 steps up and down to my fourth-floor walk-up flat. That figure represents 88 steep steps up and down, three times a day for nine weeks.

What are the guidelines I use for selecting a hotel? The two primary concerns are value for money and cleanliness, followed by pleasant surroundings in the room, location, and management attitude and service. On my visits to the hotels, which are always unannounced, I wipe my fingers across the door tops, check closets, turn on the showers, look for mold, flush toilets, spot thin towels and waxed or sandy toilet paper, open and close windows, bounce on the beds, look under them for dust, and visit the dining room where breakfast is served. I have stumbled along dimly lit corridors, climbed endless flights of stairs, and been squeezed into miniscule cage elevators that seem to have been in operation since the fall of the Bastille.

In addition to giving the value-conscious traveler the inside track to the best hotel prices in Paris, *Cheap Sleeps in Paris* offers insider information on shopping. If you are like I am, and believe the eighth deadly sin is paying full retail price for anything, then you will love the Cheap Chic shopping section beginning on page 215. There you will learn where to find everything from designer discount shops and big-name cosmetics to the latest models of shoes—all sold for less than their regular cost.

My goals in *Cheap Sleeps in Paris* are to show you how to cut corners in style, so traveling on a budget will not make you give up the good life by lowering your standards, and to give you enough information on the hotels listed to help you select the one that will make your stay in Paris truly special and set the stage for many return visits. If I have been able to do this, I will have done my job well. I wish you *bonne chance* and *bon voyage.*

General Information

Tips for Cheap Sleeps in Paris

1. Unless you enjoy standing in long lines in French government tourist offices or rail stations, or wandering the streets looking for a hotel, never arrive in Paris without confirmed hotel reservations *in writing.*
2. If a hotel has a toll-free 800 number to call from the U.S. and Canada, do call and ask about special package deals for senior citizens, weekends, families, etc. Then call the hotel directly and see if you can better the price. Chances are good that you can.
3. The two weeks in mid-January and mid-February, and the months of May, June, September, and October are the hardest times to find a hotel room in Paris. Try to go during the off-season when rates and air fares are at their lowest.
4. Twin beds cost more than a double, and any room with a private shower will be less than one with a bathtub.
5. Back rooms often face blank walls or dreary courtyards and are usually smaller, but they cost less and are quieter.
6. Inquire about the hotel's refund policy in case you send a deposit and then have to cancel at the last minute. Some smaller hotels have draconian ideas about refunds.
7. If you have booked an apartment and paid a chunk of money in advance, are flying charter, or have a nonrefundable and non-changeable airline ticket, seriously consider purchasing trip insurance. If you have to change dates, interrupt travel, or cancel altogether, you will be grateful to have trip insurance. The Automobile Club of America has a list of carriers. Some are Access America, Inc., 1-800-284-8300; Carefree Travel Insurance 1-800-323-3149; and Travel Guard International 1-800-782-5151.
8. Always check out the room before you check in. Confirm the rate and discuss the cost of any extras (e.g., telephone calls, both local and long distance) ahead of time, not when paying the bill. All hotels must clearly post their rates by the reception desk.
9. Avoid eating breakfast at your hotel if you want to save money. Instead, join the Parisians standing at the bar at the corner café. Be sure to tell the hotel at the beginning of the stay that you will not be eating breakfast, and see that the cost is deducted per person, per day, from your hotel bill if it is included in the original room

rate. Only a few hotels refuse to deduct breakfast, but you must ask; it is never done voluntarily.

10. Do not drink the beverages from the mini-bar. Remove them and put in your own, purchased from the corner grocery store.
11. Do major laundries at the local laundromat and take your cleaning to the neighborhood dry cleaner yourself. Laundry and dry cleaning sent from the hotel can blow a budget to shreds. If you do wash out a few things, be sure they do not drip over carpeting or fabric. And please, do not hang things in the windows!
12. Notify the hotel if you expect to arrive after 6 P.M. Even if you paid the room deposit, the hotel can technically resell your room to someone else if they do not know your arrival time.
13. Change money at a bank, *never* at a hotel.
14. In France, the ground floor (*rez-de-chaussée*) is what Americans call the first floor; the French first floor (*premier étage*) is our second floor.
15. Paris is a very noisy city both day and night, making it heaven for night owls and a nightmare for insomniacs. Traffic, sirens, motor scooters, and voices magnify on the narrow streets, echoing throughout the night. Street cleaning crews and trash trucks start their rounds at zero-dark hundred, never thinking someone might still be sleeping, or wishing they could. If noise is a problem, ask for a room away from the street, in the back of the hotel, or facing an inner courtyard. For added insurance, buy or bring earplugs (*boules de quièss*).
16. Savvy travelers always check with airlines or their travel agents for package deals that include airfare coupled with a car rental and/or a hotel at a fraction of the cost if paid for separately. If you are willing to take a chance and really lock yourself into a ticket that cannot be changed without an act of Congress, investigate discount air ticketers who advertise on Sundays in most major metropolitan newspaper travel sections. The fares are low, but the restrictions are many, so be sure you understand all the fine print and are able to live with it. Another great deal is to fly as a courier.

When to Go

High and Low Seasons

How wonderful it would be to be able to drop everything and fly to Paris whenever the spirit moved us! If such romantic impulses do not quite fit into your schedule or budget, then the high and low seasons must be taken into consideration. These times of the year affect not only the availability of hotel rooms and the rates, but airline fares as well. The best time to go to Paris is in the early spring or late autumn, when most of the other tourists have gone home and everything is easier to come by, including Métro seats, café tables, and good-natured waiters.

For about two weeks in mid-January and mid-February, fashion showings fill the city to the bursting point, and many hotels charge their highest rates. Dates vary slightly from year to year, so the best bet is to check with the French Government Tourist Office in New York or Los Angeles for the latest information. During most of July and all of August, you will be sharing your Parisian holiday with many other tourists and very few French. Despite government pleadings and tourist demands, August is still the traditional vacation month for most Parisians, and many restaurants and shops are closed for at least a week or two. The good news is that hotels are always open, and during August they may be willing to negotiate lower rates, especially for longer stays.

French Holidays

Holidays (*les jours fériés*) are vital dates to bear in mind when planning any trip to Paris. Banks and stores are all closed, and museums that are open may run on different time schedules. In addition, banks may be closed a half day before each holiday as well as the day after in some instances. The traffic is horrendous, especially if the holiday falls on a Tuesday or Thursday, since many French will take off Monday or Friday to make it a long weekend. Restaurant holiday policies vary with the rise and fall of the economy. *Always* call ahead to make sure, because even if they say they are open, they may change their mind and be closed. Skeleton or third-string crews man the hotel desks, and there is often a laid-back attitude during a holiday period, resulting in quick excuses for things not working. It can all add up to some very frustrating times for a traveler.

New Year's Day (January 1)	*Jour de l'An*
Easter Sunday and Monday	*Pâques et Lundi de Pâques*
Labor Day (May 1)	*Fête du Travail*
VE Day (May 8)	*Armistice 1945*
Ascension Day (40 days after Easter)	*Ascension*
Pentecost (seventh Sunday after Easter and Pentecost Monday)	*Pentecôte et Lundi de Pentecôte*
Bastille Day (July 14)	*Quatorze Juillet/Fête Nationale*
Assumption Day (August 15)	*Assomption*
All Saints' Day (November 1)	*Toussaint*
Armistice Day (November 11)	*Armistice 1918*
Christmas Day (December 25)	*Noël*

For motorists, the time to avoid is the last weekend in August, when Parisians return *en masse* via the *autoroutes.* This *grand rentrée* creates traffic snarls of world-class proportions.

Reservations

People ask me, "Do I need advance hotel reservations in Paris?" The answer is yes, positively! In order to be assured of a room, you *must* reserve as far in advance as possible. Paris can be one of the worst hotel bottlenecks in Europe, and a confirmed reservation, even on the slowest day in the low season, will save you frantic hours spent searching for a room after arrival. It will also save you money, because without advance reservations, you will probably be forced to take something beyond your budget, perhaps in a part of the city that you do not like. Do not reserve for more nights than you think you will need. If you decide to leave before you intended, or if you want to switch hotels, you may not get back any money you have paid ahead of time.

The easiest way to reserve is to let your travel agent do all the work. However, it is not hard to do it yourself, and frankly, it is better because you will be able to ask questions, inquire about exact rates, and arrange just what you want without going through a middle person. Today the best way to reserve is by fax or telephone, followed by a guarantee with a major credit card, an international money order, or, in a few cases, a money order in French francs.

No matter how you decide to make your reservation, the following points should be covered:

1. Dates of stay, time of arrival, and number of persons in the party.
2. Size and type of room (double or twin beds, extra beds, adjoining rooms, suite, etc.).
3. Facilities needed: private toilet, shower and/or bathtub, or hall facilities if acceptable.
4. Location of room: view, on the street, on the courtyard, or in the back of the hotel.
5. Rates. Determine what the nightly rate will be, including the per person City of Paris tourist tax (1–7 francs per person, per night, depending on how many stars the hotel has; see page 33 for details on this new tax). Be sure to state whether or not you will be eating breakfast at the hotel, and remember you will save money if you do not.
6. Deposit required and form of payment.

7. Refund policy if you should have to cancel.
8. Request a written confirmation and take it with you to the registration desk.

Fax

All but the smallest budget hotels in Paris have joined the electronic age and have a fax machine. If you have a fax, or access to one, this is the best way to secure a confirmed booking. To fax a hotel in Paris, dial 011-33-1, and then the fax number in Paris.

Telephone

Always make the call during the hotel's weekday business hours to avoid talking to a night clerk with no authority to make price negotiations. Before calling, write down all your requests and questions. Ask the hotel to send you a written confirmation (or fax), and send them a letter (or fax) confirming your telephone reservation in turn. Send your letter by certified mail and keep a copy. In your letter to the hotel, cite the details of the conversation, the name of the person with whom you spoke, and the date and time of the call. You should also enclose a deposit if they do not accept a credit card as a room guarantee. To dial direct to Paris from the U.S., dial 011-33-1, and then the number of the hotel.

Letter

Transatlantic mail can take more than two weeks each way. If there is a strike, who knows how long mail will take to reach its destination. When you consider the entire cost of your trip to Paris against the cost of a fax or a telephone call made when the rates are low, it amounts to a *very* small percentage . . . and never mind the convenience. In today's world, writing for reservations is about as *au courrant* as the bustle. If you do insist on reserving by mail, allow sufficient time for the hotel to respond (and I mean weeks) and then to make alternative plans when they tell you they are fully booked.

The following letter should cover the bases.

Dear Sir or Madam:

I would like to reserve ___ room(s) that is/are quiet (on the garden/the street/the courtyard) with two beds (one big bed/one regular-size bed) with bath and toilet (with shower and toilet/without shower/bath and toilet) for ___ night(s) beginning on ___ to ___. I would like to have the room(s) include (without) breakfast. You will find attached ___F (my credit card number and expiration date) as a first night deposit.

Would you please be kind enough to confirm this reservation as soon as possible? Thank you for your assistance.

Yours sincerely,

If you want to write it in French . . .

Monsieur/Madam:

Je voudrais réserver ___ chambre(s) (tranquille) qui donne sur le (jardin/la rue/la cour) à deux lits (avec un grant lit/à un lit) avec salle de bains et WC (avec douche et WC/sans douche ou bain et WC) pour ___ nuit(s) à partir du ___ au ___. Je voudrais prendre la chambre(s) avec (sans) le petit déjeuner. Vous trouvez ci-joint ___f (mon carte de credit) à titre d'arrhes.

Auriez-vous le bonté de bien vouloir me confirmer cette réservation dès que possible? Je vous remercie de votre obligeance, et je vous prie de croire, Monsier, à l'assurance de mes sentiments distingués.

With your letter, be sure to enclose an international reply coupon sold at the post office, so the hotel will not have to worry about international postage. It is a courtesy on your part and appreciated on the other side.

Deposits

After making a reservation, most hotels will require at least a one-night deposit, even if you have been a guest there before. This is smart insurance for both sides. The easiest way to handle a deposit is with a credit card. If the hotel does not take credit cards, there are other options. You can sometimes send your own personal check, which the hotel will only cash if you are a no-show. They will return it to you upon arrival. The next best option is to send the hotel an international money order in U.S. dollars. This can be converted into French francs by the hotel and saves you from having to secure a deposit in French francs on this side of the Atlantic. While this option is more convenient for you, it is added work for the hotel, and some, especially in the lower price ranges, simply refuse. If your hotel insists on a deposit in French francs, you will have to purchase them through your bank.

Money Matters

If you carry traveler's checks, charge big items on your credit card, convert franks as you go, and use ATMs for incidental cash, you will do fine. Also, remember to carry a few of your own personal checks. If you suddenly run out of money, you can use them to get cash advances, provided the credit card you have allows this. Try to have a few francs on hand when you arrive. This gets you out of the airport faster and keeps you from having to wait in line to get enough francs to get into Paris. True, you may pay more for this convenience, but if you change $200 or so before you leave home, you will never miss the few cents extra it may cost. If you cannot get francs locally, order a *tip pack* by mail from Thomas Cook Currency Service, 630 5th Avenue, New York, NY 10101, Tel: 212-757-6915.

Automatic Teller Machines—ATMs

Automatic Teller Machines are all over Paris. You can use your bank ATM card, American Express, or a Visa or MasterCard (known abroad as Carte Bleu and Eurocard, respectively). There will be fees involved, but you will be getting a wholesale conversion rate that is better than you would get at a bank or currency exchange office. Naturally you are limited to the amount you can withdraw by the type of account you have and your cash advance balance. Please—and I cannot stress this enough—do not think your ATM card or credit card will work *as is* in Paris. It might, but chances are great that you will have to have a special pin (personal identification number) or enroll in a special program (American Express). For Paris Cirrus locations and details you will need to use your card there, call 1-800-4-CIRRUS (424-7787). For foreign Plus locations and information, check the Plus directory at your bank. To enroll in the American Express foreign ATM program, call 1-800-CASH NW (227-4669). Setting up an account takes several weeks but costs the card holder nothing.

Currency Exchange

Estimate your needs carefully. If you overbuy francs, you will lose twice, buying and then selling. Every time you change money, someone is making a profit, and, I assure you, it is not you. Your best currency exchange rate will always be at a bank. You will get a better rate for traveler's checks than for cash, but the real cost lies in what you spent to get the traveler's checks in the first place. If your bank gives free American Express traveler's checks, you can cash them commission free at the American Express office in Paris. The drawbacks here are that the exchange rates are not always the best, and the lines are slow and oh, so long. The office is at 11, rue Scribe (9th) Métro Opéra; open Monday–Friday from 9 A.M.–5 P.M. and Saturday, 9 A.M.–noon. The worst rates are at the airport. The second-worst rates are at hotels, restaurants, and shops. These places should be avoided at all costs when it comes to money changing. Banking hours are Monday through Friday, 9:30 A.M.–4:30 P.M. Many banks close at noon the day before a public holiday, and all remain closed on holidays and the day after Christmas, Easter, and Pentecost. The following banks either give commission-free rates or have longer hours:

Commission-free rates

Banque Libanaise, 7, rue Auber (9th); Métro: Opéra; Tel: 47-42-33-89; Open Monday–Friday 9 A.M.–5 P.M.

Comptoir de Change Opéra, 9, rue Scribe (9th); Métro: Opéra; Tel: 47-42-20-96; Open Monday–Friday 9 A.M.–5:15 p.m., Saturday 9:45 A.M.–4:15 P.M.

Later hours

Bureau de Change, 66, avenue des Champs-Élysées (8th); Métro: Franklin D. Roosevelt; Open Monday–Friday 9:30 A.M.–midnight, Saturday and Sunday until 10 P.M.

Societé Financiere de Change Lincoln, 11, rue Lincoln (8th); Métro: George-V; Tel: 42-25-22-57; Open Monday–Friday 9:30 A.M.–midnight, Saturday and Sunday until 10 P.M.

You can also exchange money at scores of authorized money-changers' offices, which are thick around tourist areas, especially along rue de Rivoli, the Champs-Élysées, and the Centre Pompideau (Beaubourg). Sometimes they advertise "commission-free" exchanges, but often you have to change large amounts, and usually the rates are lower than at a bank, or even at American Express. Your best bet with these is to use them only when all else fails, and then to shop around for the best deal.

Credit Cards

For the most part, I recommend using a credit card whenever possible. The benefits are many. It is the safest way because it eliminates the need for carrying large sums of cash that you have purchased by standing in line at a bank or at another money-changing facility. It also provides you with a written record of your purchases, and best of all, you often get delayed billing of up to four to six weeks after you have returned home. If you pay in cash, the money is gone immediately. With a credit card, the money stays in your bank account drawing interest until you need it to pay the final bill. The credit card company gives the rate of exchange on the day the receipt from the expenditure is submitted, and this can also work to your advantage if the dollar is rising. Emergency personal check cashing and access to ATM machines are benefits, as are free travel insurance and car rental collision insurance. Check with your issuing bank to determine the benefits you have . . . you may be pleasantly surprised. Finally, remember in Europe a MasterCard is Eurocard, and Visa is Carte Bleu. Every listing in *Cheap Sleeps in Paris* tells you whether or not plastic money is accepted. Thankfully, most two- and three-star hotels, and many more one-stars, accept at least one credit card. If, heaven forbid, your cards are lost or stolen, call one of these 24-hour hotlines in Paris, or call collect in the U.S. to report the loss as soon as possible.

In Paris:

American Express	47-77-72-00
Diners Club	47-62-75-75, 47-62-75-00
MasterCard (Eurocard)	45-67-84-84
Visa (Carte Bleu)	42-77-11-90, 42-71-11-90

From Paris, you can call the following U.S. numbers collect to report a theft or loss of your cards.

American Express	919-668-5271
American Express Optima	904-565-7875
MasterCard	314-275-6690
Visa	410-581-9994

Tipping

How much is too much, and what is enough? Here are a few guidelines.

In France, a service charge of 12 to 15 percent has already been added to hotel and restaurant bills. This service charge *is* the tip. While this eliminates the need for tips in general, there are certain times when an additional tip is appropriate.

Bars, cafés, restaurants	Leave a few extra francs in a bar or café, and up to 10 percent if the waiter in a restaurant has gone to extra lengths for you.
Hotels	Bellboy 6F per bag; chambermaid about 20F for a three-day stay; room service 10F.
Hairdressers	10–15 percent; shampoo girls 10–15F.
Taxi drivers	10–15 percent.
Theater usher	2–3F for seating two people.

NOTE: BEWARE OF THE TIPPING SCAM. There is an increasingly common practice in restaurants of putting the entire amount of the bill, to which a 12 to 15 percent service has *already* been added, in the top box of the charge slip, leaving the boxes marked "tip" and "total" empty. Do not be intimidated. Draw a line from the top figure to the total at the bottom and then write in the total figure yourself. If you are leaving a tip on top of this total (and remember you do not have to), leave it in cash. Often tips left on credit cards are not properly distributed.

The bottom line on tipping in Paris is the same as in anyplace else in the world: It is a matter of personal choice. If you liked the service, reward it; if not, do not feel guilty about not leaving an additional *sou.*

Safety and Security

In comparison to other cities, Paris is not a dangerous place. It is still important, however, to take the same sensible precautions you would in any major metropolitan city in the world. Be aware of your surroundings and do not go down dark streets at night, especially if alone. Wear a money belt or a neck pouch *inside* your clothing and carry in it *only* what you need with you: passport, some money, etc. Do not carry any valuables in your wallet, purse, or carry-bag. Thread a safety pin from the zipper on your backpack to pin it closed, and don't wear your fanny pack there . . . wear it in front of you. Keep a close eye on your possessions, and do not leave packages or suitcases unattended on the Métro or when making a phone call or hailing a taxi. Be careful of your camera and don't wear flashy jewelry. Lock up important papers, airline tickets, traveler's checks, extra money, etc., in the hotel safe. Even if there is a charge for this, it is nothing when you consider the cost, inconvenience, and hassle of a theft. Beware of pickpockets, especially on the Métro and in tourist areas. Watch out for the bands of gypsy children who will surround you and distract your attention by fluttering papers in your face, and then strip you of your valuables before you can think to say "Stop thief!" Thieves in Métro stations lurk around the turnstiles and try to grab your bag as you go through or reach for it as the train door closes. Always avoid Métro stations late at night, and when traveling, sit in the first car near the conductor. If you are alone, don't say so to a wide audience. Also, make sure someone at home knows your itinerary and that you have times to call to check in, just to let them know all is well. Always take a photocopy of your passport, airline tickets, list of credit card numbers (or the number of your credit card registry), and any other documents that are crucial to the successful completion of the trip. Also, take at least four passport-size color photos. These are handy if you have to replace a passport or purchase a weekly or monthly Métro pass.

The U.S. Department of State publishes a pamphlet called *A Safe Trip Abroad* ($1). For a copy call 202-783-3238, or write the Superintendent of Documents, U.S. Government Printing Office, Washington, D.C. 20402.

Telephones

It is not as simple as dropping a franc into the pay telephone, dialing 0, and requesting connection. Most public phones in Paris now require a prepaid phone card (*télécarte*), which you buy in increments: 40F for 50 *unités* and 96F for 120 *unités.* To make a call, insert the card into a slot on the phone. The amount of your call is automatically deducted from the remaining value. These cards offer several advantages: you do not need a pocketful of francs; calling from a public phone eliminates the surcharges in hotels, cafés, and restaurants; and the card has no expiration date, so you can use what is left on your card on your next trip. Where to buy the *télécarte?* Post offices, *tabacs,* and cafés.

Avoid going through your hotel switchboard when calling home. Even if you reverse the charges and use USA DIRECT, you will be charged a surcharge, sometimes up to 100 percent of the call. Check with the hotel operator about your hotel's policy, because they all differ. To avoid the surcharge, go to a pay telephone booth, use your *télécarte,* and dial USA DIRECT, which puts you in touch with an English-speaking AT&T operator. Tell the operator if you want to call collect or pay for the call using your AT&T calling card number. This is simple, painless, and definitely the least expensive way to stay in touch.

For further savings, call when the rates are low. Monday through Friday, 9:30 P.M.–8 A.M., Saturday, 2 P.M.–8 A.M., and Sunday all day you will save when calling any place in the European Community or Switzerland. To the U.S. and Canada, the lowest rates are Monday through Friday, noon–2 P.M. and 8 P.M.–2 A.M. and Sunday afternoon. Remember, Paris is six hours ahead of Eastern Standard Time and nine hours ahead of Pacific Standard Time.

Some Numbers You Might Need:

To call Paris from the U.S.	011-33-1 + number
To call the U.S. from Paris (you will reach an English-speaking AT&T operator)	19-00-11
To call directly from Paris to any international number	19 + code (listed in the phone book) + area or city code + number
To call any long-distance calls within France	16 + number
To call a number in Paris, if you are somewhere else in France	1 + number
Directory information	12
Operator	10
International information	19-33-12 + country code (1 for U.S.)
International operator	19-33-11
AT&T information (from the U.S.)	1-800-874-4000
AT&T from Paris and rest of Europe	1-412-553-7458 collect

Note: Every time a French person dials a call, they pay for it, even if it is just next door. You can be expected to be charged for every call you make from your hotel or apartment telephone.

Transportation

Getting into Paris from the Airports

Roissy-Charles de Gaulle Airport (General recorded information: 43-20-14-55; arrivals: 43-20-12-55; departures: 43-20-13-55)

A taxi is the easiest and most comfortable, but it is an expensive way to go. The ride into central Paris takes about 50 minutes on a good day; during rush hours add at least 30 minutes. Taxis will take no more than three people and charge a 5F surcharge for every piece of luggage. Fares range around 200–250F during the day and are more from 8 P.M.–7 A.M. A 15 percent tip is expected.

A more economical way is by the direct RER-B3 train to Paris. A free shuttle bus (look for the word *navette*) runs between Terminal 1 and 2 to take passengers to the Roissy train station where you board the Roissy Rail (RER B3) into the city, with stops at Gare du Nord, Châtelet-Les Halles, Luxembourg, Port Royal, and Denfert-Rochereau. The train leaves every 25 minutes between 5 A.M. and 11 P.M. and costs under $10. To go back to Roissy-Charles de Gaulle from Paris, take the RER B3 to Roissy and change to the shuttle bus. The train trip takes 30 minutes and the shuttle 15 minutes.

Air France Buses (to use them, you do not have to be a passenger on one of their flights) run to the Arc de Triomphe (Métro: Charles de Gaulle-Étoile) at avenue Carnot every 15 minutes from 5:30 A.M. to 11 P.M. It takes about 40 minutes and runs around 55F. The buses also stop at the place de la Porte de Maillot/Palais des Congrès, Métro Port de Maillot, and near the Gare Montparnasse at 113, boulevard Vaugirard. For recorded information call 43-23-82-20.

Orly Airport (49-75-15-15)

The easiest way to get into Paris is on the RER-C line, on the Métro. There is a free shuttle bus from the airport terminal to the station. Trains to Paris leave every 15 minutes and the fair is around 50F. The trip takes 30 minutes. Orlyval, a shuttle and a train combination service, runs between Orly and the Antony RER-B station every 7 minutes. The fare is around 50F during peak hours or 40F between 11 A.M. and 3 P.M., after 9 P.M., and Saturday noon–Sunday noon.

Buses run every 12 minutes between Orly Airport and the Air France air terminal at Les Invalides. The fare is around 40F, and the trip takes between 30 and 60 minutes, depending on traffic. Another bus option is the Orlybus, which leaves every 15 minutes going to and from the Denfert-Rochereau Métro station. Cost is 30F.

Taxis to and from Orly cost at least 150F during the day and up to 200F at night. Allow 45 minutes.

Le Bourget (48-62-12-12)

This is where Charles Lindbergh landed after his transatlantic flight. Now the airport is used mainly for charter flights within France. If you land here, take bus #350, which leaves every 15 minutes from 6 A.M. to 11:45 P.M. and costs two Métro tickets, to Gare du Nord or Gare de l'Est, where you can get the Métro to your Paris destination. You can also catch the #152 bus, which also makes these two stops and also goes to Porte de la Vilette, if this is better. Hours of operation and costs are the same.

Métro

The Paris Métro system is one of the most efficient in the world. It can take you within walking distance of almost everything you want to see and do in the city. Trains run from 5:30 A.M. until 12:15 A.M. You can buy individual tickets, but a *carnet* of ten is much more practical and cheaper by 40 percent. There is a special *Paris Visite* card which is *not* a good deal. If you are staying in Paris more than a few days, buy the weekly *Coupon Jaune* or the monthly *Carte Orange.* Both allow unlimited travel on the Métro and buses. To buy either, you must have a passport-size photo (there are photo booths in some larger Métro stations, but it is better to bring an extra photo from home). Always hold onto your ticket. If you are caught without it, you will be fined. You may buy Métro tickets at any Métro station, or from the Bureau de Tourisme RATP, place de la Madeleine (8th), Métro: Madeleine (open Monday through Saturday, 7:30 A.M.– 7 P.M.), Sunday and holidays, 6:30 A.M.–6 P.M. This office also has Métro maps. For the most detailed bus and Métro routes, consult the *Plan de Paris par Arrondissement* (see page 37). Métros are generally safe. Just use common sense and do not leave a wallet in a back pocket or your purse unzipped. Late at night, the following stations should be avoided: Barbes-Rochechouart, Pigalle, Châtelet, Les Halles, Trocadéro, and Anvers.

Bus

Because the Métro is so fast and efficient, visitors often overlook the buses in Paris. A free bus map, *Autobus Paris-Plan de Reseau,* is available at tourist offices and in some Métro stations. The routes of each bus line are generally posted at each stop. Buses no longer take the same tickets as the Métro. You can buy bus tickets in Métro stations, *tabacs,* and from the bus driver. If you have a weekly or monthly Métro pass, these *will* work on the bus; just show your pass to the driver . . . do not punch it. You should hold onto your ticket until you get off the bus. If caught without it, you will be fined. Most buses run from 7:30 A.M.–8:30 P.M. The *Noctambus* runs all night, but the routes are fewer. The pamphlet printed by the RATP—*Paris Bus, Métro, RER Routes*—lists several scenic bus routes and directions to major museums and monuments.

Taxis

The challenge of finding a taxi in Paris often rivals that of New York City on a busy Friday afternoon. Hailing a cab is difficult. You are better off to go to a taxi stand. Taxis are required by law to stop for you if the light on top is on (unless it is the driver's last half-hour on duty or the passenger is less than 50 meters from a taxi stand), take you anywhere you want to go in Paris or to either airport, follow a route of your choosing, accept all handicapped passengers, and give you a receipt. They are *not* required to take animals, take more than three persons, or accept an unreasonable amount of luggage. Taxi fares are based on area and time of day. Beneath the taxi light are three little lights—a, b, and c. One of these will light up according to what tariff applies. The tariff is also shown on the meter display inside the taxi. Additional charges include the base fee (11F), stationary time (waiting at traffic lights and traffic jams), luggage weighing over 5 kg, pets, and for the airport. A 15 percent tip is customary. If you want an early-morning taxi to take you to the airport, book it the night before. If you need a taxi at a specific time and don't want to chance not finding one, call ahead. If you do call a taxi, the fare starts when the driver gets the call, not when you get in.

Taxi Bleu	49-36-10-10
Taxi for Handicapped (24 hours)	48-37-85-85

Bicycles and Motor Scooters

I cannot imagine a worse fate than trying to negotiate Paris traffic while on a bicycle. To me it would be a suicide trip. However, there are those who are braver than I am and would consider a bicycle sightseeing trip actually fun. If you fall into that category, the best bike trip is **Mountain Bike Tours.** You will find them at the Three Ducks Hostel, 6, pl. Étienne Pernet (15th), Tel: 48-42-57-87, Métro: Felix-Faure. This guided, six-hour trip includes a lunch stop and is in English. Helmets are included in the price. Cost: 120F. You can rent a bike on your own for 100F per day, including the helmet and insurance. Open from March to October from 11 A.M.–7 P.M.

Two other places to rent bikes or scooters are: **Paris-Vélo,** 2, rue de Fer-a-Moulin (5th), Tel: 43-37-59-22, Métro: Censier Daubneton. Bicycles rent from 90–150F per day, or 1000–2000F per week, depending on the model. There is a 1000F deposit, which includes accident insurance. Open Monday through Saturday, 10 A.M.–12:30 P.M. and 2–7 P.M.

Motor Scooter: **Mondial Scooter,** 20 bis, avenue Charles De Gaulle, Tel: 46-24-63-64, Métro: Porte Maillot. 150F per day, 2500F deposit.

Car

What for? Parking is impossible, traffic is from hell, gasoline is expensive, and the one-way streets will drive you crazy. Is this a vacation? Behind the wheel, the Parisian driver is a kamikaze pilot taking no prisoners. They think nothing of driving and parking on the sidewalk, blocking traffic on narrow streets, cutting in and out with inches to spare, and flashing their lights to indicate displeasure (honking the horn is forbidden until the moment of impact). Then there is the *priorité à droite* to get used to: this gives the right-of-way to the car approaching from the right, regardless of the size of the street, the traffic on it, or the safety hazard of the moment. The best reason to drive a car in Paris is to get out of town and head for the provinces.

What to Wear

Naturally you will leave your heavy wool coat and long johns at home when you visit Paris in August. But what kind of coat makes sense in May or June? *USA Today* has a weather hotline (900-300-USAT) that gives you the time, temperature, and weather forecasts—as well as other travel information—for 490 cities around the world.

If you follow only one piece of advice given in *Cheap Sleeps in Paris,* let it be this: *travel light.* Porters are no longer roaming airports or train stations, and bellboys are almost relics of the past for most hotels in the Cheap Sleep category. Therefore, *you* are going to have to carry your own luggage, and believe me, after the first 10 minutes, less is definitely best. Take twice as much money as you think you will need and half as much clothing. Color coordinate your outfits, and remember, this is Paris, not Mars, so you can go out and buy something wonderful if you need to fill a gap in your travel wardrobe.

One of the favorite pastimes of Parisians and their expatriate friends is to sit in a café along a busy boulevard and pick out the tourists. You can spot them a mile away, in their summer tank tops and shorts, and bundled up in parkas in the winter, as if the ski slopes were just around the corner. Of course, they all wear jogging shoes and the men have baseball caps . . . often turned backwards.

Parisians are some of the most stylish people on earth. They are also some of the most conservative in their dress. Yes, you will see some off-the-wall outfits on bionic bodies, but you will never see short shorts on any Parisian man or woman. Big-city clothes are the call of the day, no matter what the weather may be. Jeans are universal and certainly acceptable for sightseeing and casual dining. However, they are not considered *in vogue* at more expensive restaurants or if you are invited to someone's home. Men will feel comfortable wearing slacks and a nice shirt or turtleneck, and a jacket if it is cool. Women will feel best in simple, well-tailored outfits. Gauzy, lime-green jumpsuits with sequined Eiffel Tower T-shirts, along with jogging shoes for every occasion, spell *tourist.*

Senior Citizen Discounts

Carte Vermeil If you have reached your 60th birthday, in France you are a member of the *troisième age* (third age) and eligible for a Carte Vermeil (CV).

This card entitles you to a number of significant discounts, including reductions on air and rail travel as well as on the bus and Métro in Paris.

The French domestic airline, Air Inter, honors "third agers" by giving 25–50 percent reductions on regular nonexcursion ticket prices. On French trains, you can save between 24 and 50 percent of the cost of a first- or second-class compartment and 10 percent of an excursion ticket. These air and rail reductions are not available during all times of the year, and restrictions do apply. However, if you can cash in on the savings, they can be significant. Other benefits include reduced entrance rates for theaters, museums, and cinemas. Wherever you go in France, ask if there are special rates for senior citizens; the answer will often be yes.

The Carte Vermeil is valid for one year from June 1 to May 31 of the following year. The card cannot be purchased in the United States, but it is available at any major railway station in France. Do not expect clerks to speak English, but you won't need much French to communicate your wishes, as most of them are used to dealing with foreigners who are privy to this super deal. When you go to purchase your card, you will have to show your passport as proof of age. For more information, contact the French National Railroads, 610 Fifth Avenue, New York, NY 10012, Tel: 212-582-2110.

Other Senior Citizen Discounts Members of the AARP are entitled to discounts on air tickets, hotel rooms, some train tickets, and car rentals. Always inquire when booking a reservation.

Elderhostel operates programs throughout Europe, and many are in France. Contact them at 75 Federal Street, Boston, MA 02110-1941, Tel: 617-426-7788.

Practical Information

Emergency Numbers

The American Hospital	63, bd, Victor Hugo, Neuilly; Métro: Pont de Neuilly, Tel: 46-41-25-25
The British Hospital	47-58-13-12
Search for hospitalized persons	40-27-30-81; 8:45 A.M.–5:30 P.M.
Burns (24 hours)	42-34-17-58
Fire	Dial 18
Homeopathic doctor	45-55-12-15
Poison (24 hours)	42-05-63-29, 40-37-04-04
Police	Dial 17
SAMU (Ambulance)	Dial 17 or 45-67-50-50
SOS Cardiac	45-45-41-00, 47-07-50-50
SOS Dentist	43-37-51-00

SOS Doctor (24 hours)	43-37-77-77, 47-07-77-77
SOS Drug Crisis	45-81-11-20
SOS Eye	40-92-93-94
SOS Handicap (medical assistance for the handicapped)	47-41-37-57, 47-41-32-33
SOS Help (Bilingual crisis hotline, 3–11 P.M.)	47-23-80-80, 47-20-89-98
SOS Lawyer	43-29-33-00; Mon.–Fri. 7–11 P.M.
SOS Nurse	48-87-77-77
SOS Pediatric Emergency pediatric doctors will make house calls Monday–Friday, Sunday and holidays, 7 A.M.–midnight; Saturday 2 P.M.–midnight.	42-93-19-99
24-hour pharmacy	Pharmacie Dhèry, 84, av. des Champs-Élysées (8th); Métro: Franklin D. Roosevelt; open 365 days a year; Tel: 45-62-02-41
American Pharmacy	Pharmacie Anglo-Américaine, 6, rue Castiglione (1st); Métro: Tuileries; open Monday–Saturday 9 A.M.–7:30 P.M.
To find the pharmacy open at night (on a rotating basis) nearest you	45-62-02-41

Useful Numbers

Alcoholics Anonymous	46-34-59-65
American Embassy	2, av. Gabriel (8th); Métro: Concorde; Tel: 42-96-12-02
American Express	11, rue Scribe (9th); Métro: Opera; open Monday–Friday 9 A.M.–5 P.M., Saturday 9 A.M.–noon; Tel: 45-75-62-16
Complaints about a hotel	Direction du Tourisme, 2, rue Linois (15th); Métro: Charles-Michels

Consumer complaints Write to this office in the ministry of Finance with any complaints you have as a consumer. Be sure to include an explanation, copies of your receipt, and any correspondence you have had with the seller.	Direction Départmentale de la Concurrence, de la Consommation, et la Répression des Fraudes, 8, rue Froissart, 75153 Paris Tel: 40-27-16-00
Emergency car repair	42-57-33-44
Lost and Found	Bureau des Objects Trouvés, 36, rue des Morrillons (15th); Métro: Convention; Tel: 45-31-14-18, ext. 4208; Monday–Friday 8:30 A.M.–5 P.M. No information given over the phone.
Lost object in street openings	44-66-49-25 A sewer worker will try to rescue that key or diamond earring that fell through the manhole grate.
Post Office (24 hours) This is where you go to pick up *Poste Restante* (General Delivery) mail. You must show your passport and pay a small fee for each letter you receive. You can also receive mail c/o American Express, 11, rue Scribe (9th); Métro: Opéra; Tel: 45-75-62-16; Monday–Friday 9 A.M.–5 P.M., Saturday 9 A.M.–noon	Hôtel des Postes, 52, rue du Louvre (1st); Métro: Louvre; Tel: 40-28-20-00
Time	44-63-84-00
Traffic	48-58-33-33
Weather	45-55-95-90
Tourist Information	Main office of French Government Tourist Office, 127, av. des Champs-Élysées (8th); Métro: Charles de Gaulle-Étoile; summer hours 9 A.M.–9 P.M. daily, winter hours 9 A.M.–6 P.M. daily; Tel: 47-23-61-72

French Government Tourist Offices in the U.S.	610 Fifth Avenue, New York, NY 10020; Tel: 212-757-1125; and 9454 Wilshire Blvd., Beverly Hills, CA 90212; Tel: 213-271-6665

Glossary of Hotel Terms

a room for one/two persons	*une chambre pour une/deux personnes*
a double bed	*un lit double*
twin beds	*deux lits*
a room with an extra bed	*une chambre avec un lit supplémentaire*
a room with running water and bidet	*une chambre avec cabinet de toilette*
a room with shower and toilet	*une chambre avec douche et WC*
a room with bath and toilet	*une chambre avec salle de bain et WC*
for one/two/three nights	*pour une/deux/troix nuits*
suite	*appartment*
two-level suite	*duplex*
a room on the courtyard	*une chambre sur la cour*
a room over the street	*une chambre sur la rue*
ground floor	*rez-de-chaussée*
first floor	*premier étage*
second floor	*deuxième étage*
sixth floor	*seizième étage*
with a view	*avec vue*
quiet	*calme*
noisy	*bruyant*
I would like breakfast	*Je voudrais prendre le petit déjeuner*
I do not want breakfast	*Je ne veux pas de petit déjeuner*
blankets	*couvertures*
to iron	*repasser*
key	*clef*
to do laundry	*faire la lessive*
pillow	*oreiller*
sheets	*draps*

A Few Last-Minute Tips

1. What's happening in Paris while you are there? The two best sources of events in Paris are the weekly magazines *Pariscope: Une Semaine de Paris* and *l'Officiel des Spectacles.* They come out on Wednesday, cost 3 to 4 francs, and are sold at every kiosk in the city. In these magazines you will find listings for the opera, theater, films, concerts, art exhibitions, special events, naughty nightlife, weekly TV programs, swimming pool hours, and interesting guided tours (in French). Although the magazines are

printed in French, a non-French speaker can quickly decipher the information given.

2. It is important to know that a *hôtel* is not always a hotel. The word *hôtel* has more than one meaning in French. Of course it means a lodging place for travelers. It also means a mansion or town house, like the Hôtel Lambert, or a large private home (a *hôtel particulier*). The city hall is the Hôtel de Ville; auctions are held at the Hôtel des Ventes; Hôtel des Postes refers to the general post office; and the Hôtel des Invalides, once a home for disabled war veterans, is now the most famous military museum in the world and the final resting place for Napoléon Bonaparte. Finally, if you are in the hospital, you are in a *Hôtel-Dieu.*

3. For avid museum-goers, there are now one-, three-, and five-day French passes that provide unlimited access to more than 60 museums, including the Louvre and Musée d'Orsay. The passes are on sale in the museums, major Métro stations, and tourism offices in Paris, including the one at 127, Champs-Élysées. *La Carte* passes can also be purchased before leaving the United States through Challenges International, Inc., 10 East 21st Street, Suite 600, New York, NY 10010, Tel: 212-529-8484. The passes start at $19 for one-day passes if bought here. The entrance fee for the Louvre is $6, so you can see, if many museums are on your list in Paris, this is a good investment. On Sundays all entry to government-run museums is free, but the crowds can be frightening.

How to Use
Cheap Sleeps in Paris

Abbreviations

The following abbreviations are used to denote which credit cards a hotel will accept.

American Express	AE
Diners Club	DC
MasterCard	MC
Visa	V

Stars

Hotels throughout France are controlled by a government rating system that ranks them from no stars to four-star deluxe. Every hotel must display prominently the number of stars it has.

A no-star hotel is mighty basic, with few, if any, private bathrooms and little in the way of English. Many of them, however, are spotlessly clean, well located, and excellent budget values. A one-star hotel has minimum facilities, but again, it may be well located and very clean. Two stars means a comfortable hotel with direct-dial phones in all rooms and an elevator in buildings of four or more stories. Three stars means a very comfortable hotel where all rooms have direct-dial phones, a majority have private plumbing, and there is an elevator. A four-star hotel is first-class all the way, usually with a restaurant, and a four-star deluxe is a virtual palace, with every service you could dream of.

Because the number of stars has nothing to do with the level of cleanliness, attitude of management or personnel, location, or value for money, you cannot always judge the quality of a hotel by its stars.

Accommodations: Checking In

The lobby is usually one of the most attractive parts of a hotel, both because first impressions are important and because it is where the owner and manager spend their day. When you arrive at your hotel, ask to see your room. This is a normal and expected practice in all hotels in France. If you are dissatisfied, ask to see another room. After approving the room, reconfirm the rate and whether or not you will be eating breakfast at the hotel. This advance work prevents any unpleasant surprises at checkout time.

In Paris, the hotel day begins and ends at noon. If you overstay, you can be charged the price of an extra day. If you are arriving before noon after a long international flight, the room might not be ready if the hotel is fully booked. If you *must* have your room at 8 or 9 A.M., you might have to book (and pay) for it the night before. If you think you might arrive after 6 P.M., be sure to notify the hotel; otherwise your room could be given away, even if you have a deposit.

In most hotels, you pay for the room, not for the number of persons occupying it. Thus, if you are alone and occupy a triple, you will pay the triple price, unless negotiated otherwise. Watch out! Most rooms are set up for two, and the few singles tend to be tiny and on a top floor without much view, or along the back side facing a blank wall. Most hotels have two kinds of double rooms: those with a double bed (*un grand lit*), and those with twin beds (*deux lits*). If you ask for a *double,* you will get a room with a double bed, so when reserving be sure to be specific about exactly what type of bed arrangements suit you.

Rates: Paying the Bill

Just like the French restaurant menus, hotel rates and their number of stars must be posted.

Starting January 1, 1994, the City of Paris now levies a visitors' tax on persons not liable for the resident tax (a tax raised on habitual residents of the City of Paris). This tax applies to all forms of paying accommodation: hotels and tourist residences, furnished flats, holiday camp sites, and RV parking. The tax is presently charged over and above the quoted rate. That may change, however, and the tax will be included in the total hotel rate. This is what hoteliers hope they can force the City of Paris's governing bodies to do. In any case, be sure to inquire at time of booking whether or not the city tax is included or extra. The following categories apply:

Type of accommodation	Price per person, per day
4-star hotels and other equivalent establishments	7 francs
3-star hotels and other equivalent establishments	6 francs
2-star hotels and other equivalent establishments	5 francs
1-star hotels and other equivalent establishments	3 francs
No-star hotels and other equivalent establishments	1 franc
Camping and RV areas	1 franc

The proceeds of the visitors' tax will be allocated for the development and the promotion of tourism in Paris.

The French government no longer tightly controls hotel prices, but they do give special authorization for hotels to increase prices by a certain percentage twice a year. Many hotels do this; others have held steady for two and three years at a time. It usually depends on the economy. Many hotels offer different rates at different times of the year, getting what they can when they can, based on the law of supply and demand.

All rates listed in *Cheap Sleeps in Paris* are for full price and do not reflect any special deals. The rates tell whether or not breakfast is extra or included and, if included, whether or not the hotel will allow you to deduct it if not taken. While I have made every effort to be accurate on the rates, I cannot control changes or fluctuations of the dollar against the franc, so please be fully prepared to have the prices vary (unfortunately upward). All listings state which credit cards are accepted. In most Cheap Sleeps, payment is required one night in advance. Very few low-priced hotels, youth hostels, or student accommodations accept credit cards or personal checks; it is cash up front in French francs *only.* I have yet to see one of these hotels bend on this important point, so be prepared.

Hotel exchange rates are terrible. If you plan to pay your bill in francs, convert your money at a bank before checkout time (see "Currency Exchange," page 18). Before leaving the hotel, go over your bill carefully, question anything you do not understand, and get a receipt marked *paid* before leaving.

Breakfast

Almost every Parisian hotel serves a Continental breakfast consisting of coffee, tea, hot chocolate, bread, croissants or other rolls, butter, and jam. Some throw in a glass of juice or a piece of cheese. Hotels stand to make as much as 200 percent profit on this meal, so they naturally encourage their guests to take it at the hotel. If you want anything extra, it will cost dearly and is usually not worth the extra expenditure. Many better hotels are now offering a buffet downstairs for the same price (or for a little more than the Continental they will serve in your room). An all-you-can-eat buffet with cereals, yogurt, hard-boiled eggs, and fruit added to the standard Continental fare can sometimes be worth the price, especially if you plan to skip lunch.

Unless otherwise noted, none of the hotels listed serve meals other than breakfast.

English Spoken

All the hotel listings in this book state whether or not English is spoken. If you can dust off a few French phrases, smile, and display good will, you will find that the hotel staff will prove to be friendly and go out of their way to help you. If you do not speak any French and want to avoid the stress of trying to communicate, it is important that you know whether someone at the hotel speaks English. While it is fun to practice your high-school French, it is not fun to try to deal with a problem while struggling to speak it.

Parking

Very few hotels have private parking. If a hotel does have it, it is stated in the Cheap Sleep listing, and so is the price per day. Public parking is well situated in Paris, and finding a facility close to your hotel should not be hard. The hotel will be able to advise you on the closest one. You should know that parking in Paris is not cheap.

Facilities and Services

A brief summary at the end of each hotel listing states which facilities and services are offered by the hotel. Of course, the better the hotel, the more offerings there will be.

Nearest Tourist Attractions

Each hotel listing tells you if the hotel is on the Right or Left Bank and gives you the nearest tourist attractions within a reasonable walking distance.

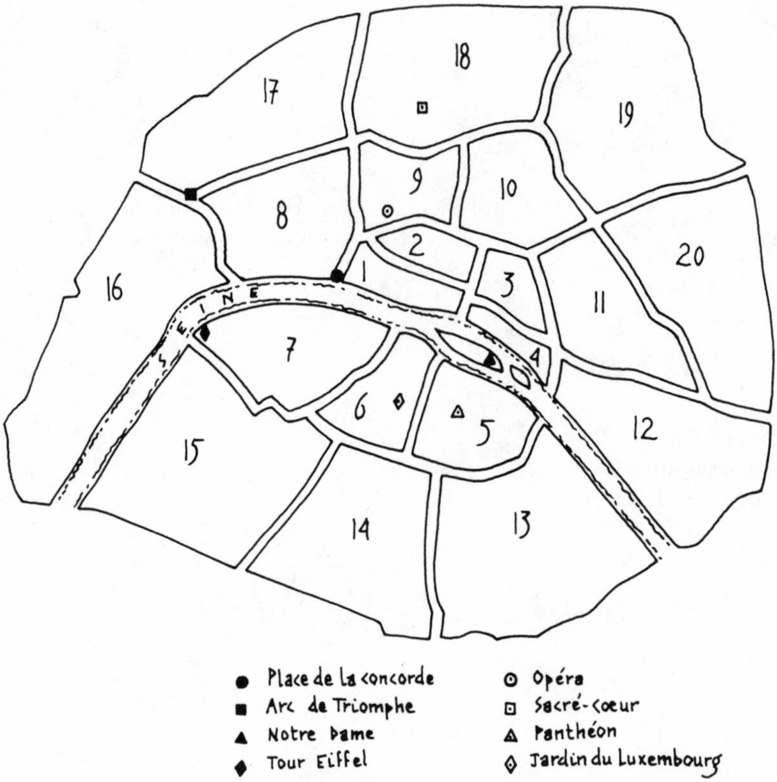

1
2
3
4
5
6
7
8
9
10
11
12
13
14
15
16
17
18
19
20
SEINE
Place de la concorde
Arc de Triomphe
Notre Dame
Tour Eiffel
Opéra
Sacré-coeur
Panthéon
Jardin du Luxembourg

Arrondissements

Paris has more than nine million inhabitants occupying 432 square miles. Despite these numbers, it is a very compact city, bound by a ring road known as the *périphérique* and divided into 20 districts called *arrondissements.* Anything outside the *périphérique* is the *banlieu,* and considered the suburbs. In the late 19th century, Paris was reorganized and modernized by Baron Haussmann, the farsighted planner who gave the city its wide boulevards, beautiful parks, and system of arrondissements that make up the city today. Each arrondissement has a character all its own, as well as its own mayor, city hall, police station, and central post office. Knowing which arrondissement is which is the key to understanding Paris and quickly finding your way around. Starting with the first arrondissement, which is the district around the Louvre, the numbering of the districts goes clockwise in a rough spiral. From a visitor's standpoint, the arrondissements of greatest interest are the first through the eighth, although there are interesting things to see and do in the others, too. For instance, the Eiffel Tower is in the fifteenth; Montmartre occupies most of the eighteenth; and to attend a performance at the new opera, you will journey to the eleventh. The river Seine divides Paris into the Right Bank (*Rive Droit*) and the Left Bank (*Rive Gauche*). Right Bank arrondissements are one, two, three, four, eight, nine, ten, eleven, twelve, sixteen, seventeen, eighteen, nineteen, and twenty. Left Bank arrondissements are five, six, seven, thirteen, fourteen, and fifteen. The arrondissement is given in every address in *Cheap Sleeps in Paris.* For example, (5th) indicates the fifth arrondissement. For mailing purposes, the Paris zip code is 750, followed by a two-digit number indicating the arrondissement. 75001 is the first, 75002 is the second, and so on.

The maps in this book are here to help you choose a hotel and also show major landmarks. They cover all but the 10th, 13th, 19th, and 20th arrondissements, because there are no hotels recommended in these neighborhoods.

However, if you plan to be in Paris for more than one day, a necessary investment, and one that will last forever, is a copy of the *Plan de Paris par Arrondissement.* This Parisian "bible" offers a detailed map of each arrondissement, with a completely keyed street index, Métro and bus routes, tourist sites, churches, and other valuable information. It is available at newsstands and bookstores. All Parisians have a copy, and so should you.

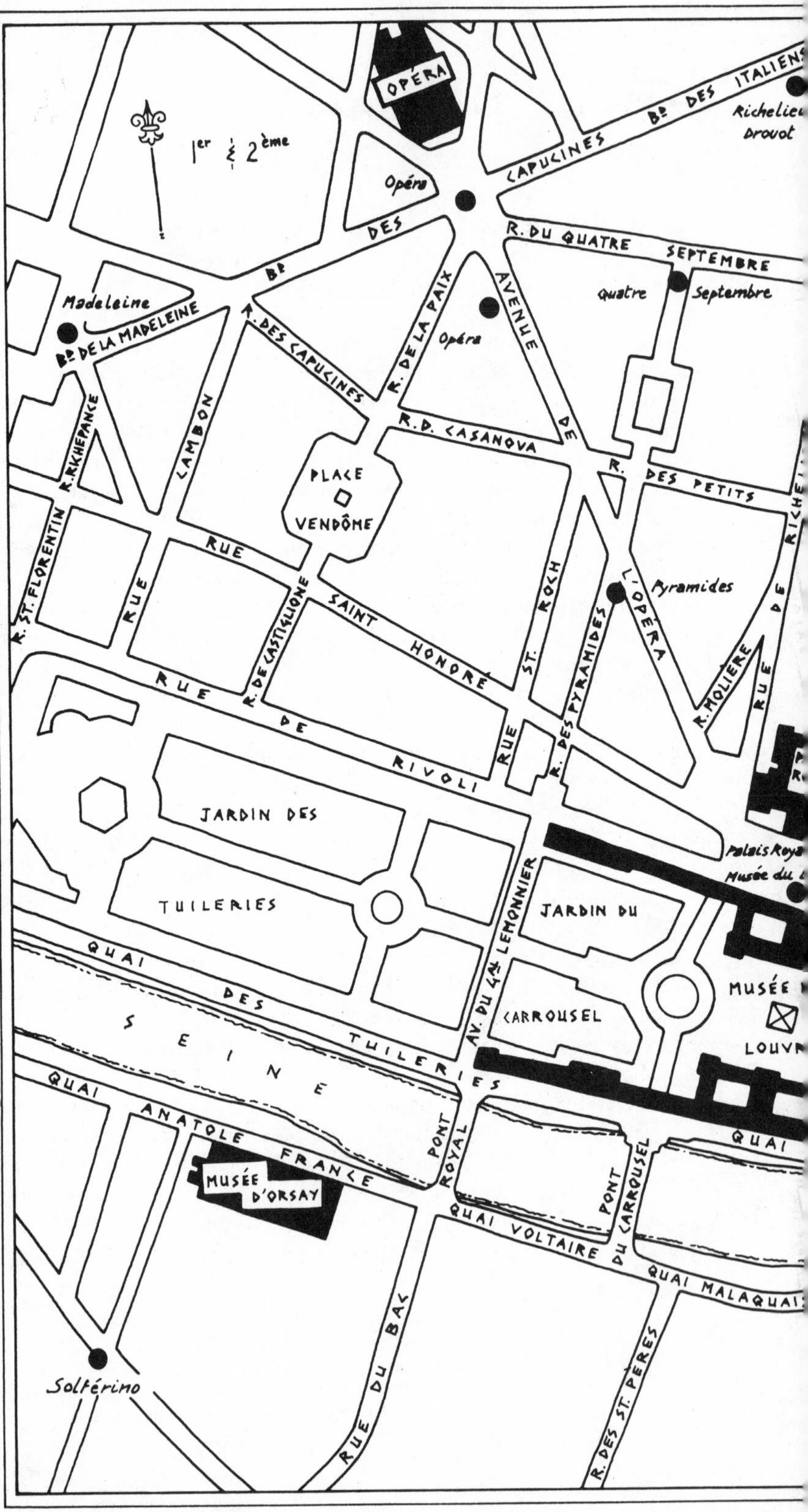
OPÉRA
1er & 2ème
Bd DES ITALIENS
Richelieu Drouot
CAPUCINES
Opéra
BD DES
R. DU QUATRE SEPTEMBRE
Quatre Septembre
Madeleine
Bd DE LA MADELEINE
R. DES CAPUCINES
R. DE LA PAIX
AVENUE DE L'OPÉRA
Opéra
R. D. CASANOVA
R. DES PETITS
CAMBON
PLACE VENDÔME
R. ST. FLORENTIN
RUE SAINT HONORÉ
RUE
R. DE CASTIGLIONE
RUE ST. ROCH
Pyramides
R. DES PYRAMIDES
R. MOLIÈRE
RUE DE RICHELIEU
RUE DE RIVOLI
JARDIN DES TUILERIES
Palais Royal
Musée du
JARDIN DU CARROUSEL
AV. DU 4 LEMONNIER
MUSÉE
LOUVRE
QUAI DES TUILERIES
SEINE
QUAI ANATOLE FRANCE
PONT ROYAL
MUSÉE D'ORSAY
QUAI VOLTAIRE
PONT DU CARROUSEL
QUAI
QUAI MALAQUAIS
RUE DU BAC
R. DES ST. PÈRES
Solférino

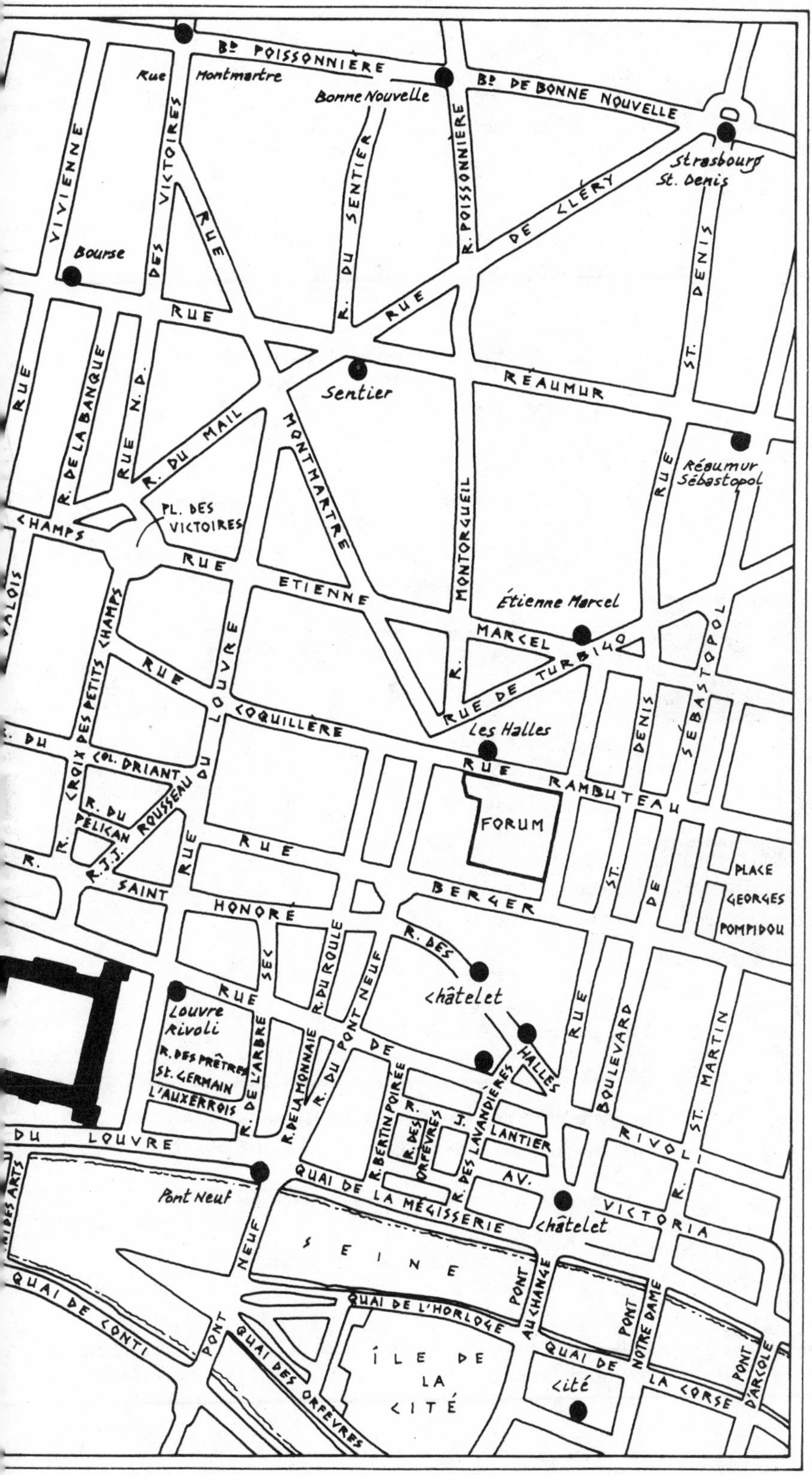
Bd POISSONNIÈRE
Rue Montmartre
Bonne Nouvelle
Bd DE BONNE NOUVELLE
Strasbourg St. Denis
VIVIENNE
RUE DES VICTOIRES
RUE DU SENTIER
R. POISSONNIÈRE
RUE DE CLÉRY
Bourse
RUE ST. DENIS
RUE RÉAUMUR
Sentier
RUE DE LA BANQUE
RUE N. D.
R. DU MAIL
MONTMARTRE
Réaumur Sébastopol
PL. DES VICTOIRES
CHAMPS
RUE MONTORGUEIL
RUE ETIENNE MARCEL
Étienne Marcel
VALOIS
CROIX DES PETITS CHAMPS
RUE DU LOUVRE
R. DE TURBIGO
BD DE SÉBASTOPOL
RUE COQUILLÈRE
Les Halles
R. DU
COL. DRIANT
RUE RAMBUTEAU
FORUM
R. DU PÉLICAN
R. J.J. ROUSSEAU
RUE SAINT HONORÉ
RUE BERGER
RUE ST. DENIS
PLACE GEORGES POMPIDOU
RUE SEC
R. DU ROULE
R. DES
R. DU PONT NEUF
châtelet
Louvre Rivoli
RUE DE
HALLES
R. DES PRÊTRES ST. GERMAIN L'AUXERROIS
R. DE L'ARBRE
R. DE LA MONNAIE
R. BERTIN POIRÉE
R. DES ORFÈVRES
R. J. LANTIER
R. DES LAVANDIÈRES
BOULEVARD
ST. MARTIN
RUE DE RIVOLI
DU LOUVRE
QUAI DE LA MÉGISSERIE
AV. VICTORIA
Pont Neuf
châtelet
DES ARTS
SEINE
PONT NEUF
PONT AU CHANGE
PONT NOTRE DAME
PONT D'ARCOLE
QUAI DE CONTI
QUAI DE L'HORLOGE
QUAI DES ORFÈVRES
QUAI DE LA CORSE
ÎLE DE LA CITÉ
cité

First Arrondissement

RIGHT BANK
Conciergerie, Île de la Cité, Pont Neuf, Les Halles, Louvre, Palais de Justice, Palais Royal, place Vendôme, Ste-Chapelle, St-Eustache, Notre Dame Cathedral

Paris began on the Île de la Cité, and Parisians still regard it not only as the center of their city, but of all France. The Tuileries Gardens and Louvre Museum are the cornerstone of this regal *quartier* and the center from which the arrondissement begins. Here you will find the rejuvenated Les Halles, with Forum des Halles housing 200 or more boutiques along with movie theaters, fast-food joints, several museums, and a Métro station, which has the reputation of being unsafe after dark. Ste-Chapelle, with its magnificent red-and-blue stained-glass windows, Notre Dame Cathedral—the geographical and spiritual heart of France—and St-Eustache, the largest Gothic Renaissance church in Paris, are all here. The palaces surrounding the moneyed place Vendôme include Cartier Jewelry, Ministry of Justice, and the world-renowned Ritz Hôtel, where room prices are within the budget of any average emir or Texas oil mogul.

HOTELS IN THE FIRST ARRONDISSEMENT

GRAND HÔTEL DE CHAMPAGNE ★★★

Angle 17, rue Jean-Lantier and 13, rue des Orfèvres, 75001 (1st)

43 rooms, all with showers or bath and toilet

TELEPHONE
42-36-60-00; toll-free from U.S. 1-800-44-UTELL

FAX
45-08-43-33

If you look carefully in the sitting area off the reception, you will see the date 1562 carved on one of the original wooden pillars. This tells you when the hotel was built, as a residence for the silversmiths who made the silver utensils used by the kings of France. Since that time the hotel has gone through several transformations before its present charmed life.

Hidden behind the sprawling Samaritaine department store, the family-owned hotel appeals to travelers who are looking for an A+ location for exploring the Louvre and Beaubourg. It is also within easy walking distance, across the Pont Neuf, to Île de la Cité, Île St-Louis, St-Michel, and St-Germain-des-Prés.

Different themes are carried out in each of the rooms and suites, with interiors running the gamut from masculine-modern to frankly feminine. Many of the rooms have hand-painted murals done by artists over the years (perhaps in lieu of a final payment?). Room no. 304 has a fanciful scene of Venice on the bathroom wall, and no. 302, one of my favorites, shows a pretty girl peeking through a cloud-filled sky. The viewless no. 308 reminds me of a chapel, with its stone walls, high-beamed ceilings, and extra quiet location. No. 301, in bright turquoise, yellow, and black, has a divided sitting area and a fantasy bathroom with double sinks. The unusual two-room suites are large. If you like sunken bathtubs, platform beds, conversation pits, and lots of open space splashed with color, these will undoubtedly please you.

Management is justifiably proud of the international breakfast served downstairs every morning. Designed to appeal to lumberjack appetites, it includes fresh fruit, juices, a variety of breads and rolls, several selections of meat, cheese and pâté, eggs, and cereals. After this meal, you won't need to eat until dinnertime.

English Spoken: Yes

Facilities and Services: Bar; direct-dial phone; elevator to fifth floor, stairs to three rooms on sixth floor; mini-bar in suites; TV with international reception; safe in office, no charge

Nearest Tourist Attractions (Right Bank): Forum des Halles, Beaubourg, Louvre, Île de la Cité, Île St-Louis, St-Michel, St-Germain-des-Prés, shopping at Samaritaine department store (which has the finest hardware department in France and is a do-it-yourselfer's heaven)

MÉTRO
Châtelet (exit rue de Rivoli, *nos impairs*—odd numbers), Pont Neuf

CREDIT CARDS
AE, DC, MC, V

RATES
Single 590–717F, double 640–800F, suites 1,100–1,1250F; children under 12 free

BREAKFAST
55F extra per person

HÔTEL BRITANNIQUE ★★★
20, avenue Victoria, 75001 (1st)
40 rooms, all with shower or bath and toilet

A sound choice between Châtelet and Hôtel de Ville is the Hôtel Britannique. In the refashioning of the hotel several years ago, original parts were kept and gracefully restored. The winding stairway with polished banister and the carved reception counter are beautiful examples of how the old can blend beautifully with the new.

TELEPHONE
42-33-74-59

FAX
42-33-82-65

MÉTRO
Châtelet

CREDIT CARDS
AE, DC, MC, V
RATES
Single 660F, double 800–900F; extra bed 100F
BREAKFAST
55F extra per person

Granite hallways lined with rose-print carpet lead guests to their rooms, which are behind eggplant purple doors. Best choices are on the top three floors, just high enough to escape the brunt of the street noise and to avoid blank-wall views on the back. The rooms, though small, are professionally decorated in soft colors with tone-on-tone wallpaper, faux marble accents, and coordinated print fabrics. Classical music soothes early morning diners in the pretty breakfast room that overlooks a small interior garden. A buffet is laid out here, or you can have a Continental breakfast sent to your room for the same price. The sunken lounge, with eye-level windows on the street, is accented with some lovely old heirlooms. Be sure to notice the birdcage, the early record player, and the intricately detailed model of an old sailing vessel.

English Spoken: Yes

Facilities and Services: Bar; direct-dial phone; hair dryer; elevator; mini-bar; TV with international reception; room safe, no charge

Nearest Tourist Attractions (Right Bank): Louvre, Tuileries, Beaubourg and Forum des Halles, Île de la Cité, Île St-Louis, St-Michel, Seine

HÔTEL DE LA PLACE DU LOUVRE ★★★

21, rue des Prêtres Satin Germain l'Auxerrois, 75001 (1st)

20 rooms, all with shower or bath and toilet

TELEPHONE
42-33-78-68
FAX
42-33-09-95
MÉTRO
Louvre, Pont Neuf
CREDIT CARDS
DC, MC, V
RATES
Single 500–700F, double 690–800F, suite 850F
BREAKFAST
45F extra per person

The name of the hotel gives you a hint. From the front door the Louvre is only a five-minute stroll, the quais along the Seine a block away, and all the Left Bank has to offer just a few minutes across the Pont Neuf to St-Michel. The hotel is imaginatively done from start to finish. Portions of the original stone walls are artistically exposed to the dramatically modern entry. Murals on curving walls lead to a tented sitting area with purple chamois wall covering highlighted by black-and-tangerine leather and chrome furniture. A multicolored curtain hangs above the front window, which faces the St-Germain l'Auxerrois Church across the street. All of the imaginatively done rooms are named for famous artists whose work hangs in the Louvre. The brilliant pink, third-floor Picasso suite has a view of the church, marble-topped bedside tables, a corner desk, mirrored wardrobes, and a wonderful upstairs bathroom with a skylight. If you check into the green-and-white

Kandinsky double, you will have good luggage space and a salmon-tiled bath with gray monogrammed towels and plenty of shelf space. Breakfast is served in the original stone-walled cave in the basement.

Note: Same management and owners as Hôtel Parc Saint-Séverin and Hôtel Mansart, in the fifth and first arrondissements (see pages 81 and 45).

English Spoken: Yes

Facilities and Services: Bar; direct-dial phone; hair dryer; elevator; mini-bar; radio; TV with international reception; room safe, no charge

Nearest Tourist Attractions (Right Bank): Louvre, Beaubourg, Seine, St-Michel, Île de la Cité, Île St-Louis

HÔTEL DE LILLE (no stars)
8, rue du Pelican, 75001 (1st)
14 rooms, none with shower or bath and toilet

TELEPHONE
42-33-33-42

FAX
None

MÉTRO
Palais-Royal, Louvre

CREDIT CARDS
None, cash only

RATES
Single 170F, double 200–270F; coin-operated shower 30F

BREAKFAST
None served

No private toilets, no closets—only hooks, no English spoken, and no breakfast served in a hotel housed in a 13th-century building with five floors and no elevator. Who needs this? Seekers of a very Cheap Sleep near the Louvre do, and believe me, they stay here in droves. If you do decide to stay here, don't expect thick towels, a particularly helpful staff, mini-bars (but there is a drink machine between the second and third floors), TVs, or other services or amenities. This is a Cheap Sleep thrill all right, but also a safe and clean one you can count on if all you need is a place to hang your hat and rest your weary head after a long day in Paris.

English Spoken: None

Facilities and Services: None

Nearest Tourist Attractions (Right Bank): Louvre, Palais-Royal, Les Halles, Tuileries, shopping on rue St-Honoré, Seine, Île de la Cité, Île St-Louis

HÔTEL DE LONDRES ET DE STOCKHOLM ★★
300, rue Saint-Honoré; entrance at 13, rue St-Roch, 75001 (1st)
30 rooms, all with shower, bath, and toilet

TELEPHONE
42-60-15-62

FAX
42-60-16-00

MÉTRO
Tuileries, Pyramides

CREDIT CARDS
AE, DC, MC, V

The Londres et de Stockholm is an old but well-patched-together budget choice in central Paris. Steep red-carpeted stairs lead off the street to the first-floor reception and lounge area, which is highlighted by a beautiful tropical fish tank. Next to this is a somber dining room, with red, green, and gold upholstered high-backed chairs placed around dark, wooden square

RATES
Single 390–480F, double 577F, triple 650F, quad 725F

BREAKFAST
35F extra per person

tables. All the rooms are in different colors and are outfitted in chenille, nondescript modern and reproduction furnishings. The only one to absolutely avoid is no. 8, with a dismal view. Some of the halls slope, the toilet paper is square, and there is noise, but at these prices and in this location, you can't have it all. Lots of restaurants in *Cheap Eats in Paris* are within an easy walk, and the area is pivotal for any visitor to Paris. Across the street is the Church of St-Roch, where Bonaparte fought the Royalists before he was Emperor Napoléon I. Within ten minutes you can be at the Louvre, admiring the place Vendôme and dreaming of staying at the famed Ritz Hôtel, jogging in the Jardin des Tuileries, or looking at the Chagall ceiling in the old Opéra.

English Spoken: Yes

Facilities and Services: Direct-dial phone; elevator to most floors; mini-bar; TV

Nearest Tourist Attractions (Right Bank): Louvre, Tuileries, old Opéra, place Vendôme, Seine, shopping on rue St-Honoré

HOTEL DU PALAIS ★
2, quai de la Mégisserie, 75001 (1st)
19 rooms, 14 with shower or bath and toilet

TELEPHONE
42-36-98-25

FAX
42-21-41-67

MÉTRO
Châtelet (exit Place du Châtelet)

CREDIT CARDS
MC, V

RATES
Single 200–275F, double 245-480F, triple 400–575F; extra bed 75F; 10 percent reduction between December 1 and March 31; free hall showers

BREAKFAST
35F extra per person

While the location is dynamite and the views from most rooms are spectacular, the hotel in general is a true fixer-upper. No elevator services to any of the floors; dim-watt bulbs sway from high-pitched ceilings; exposed pipes wrap themselves around the rooms; and the double beds roll to the middle. In addition, if you open the windows or forget your industrial-strength earplugs, it can be hopelessly noisy 24 hours a day. However, for the budgeteer who can sleep through anything, the Hôtel du Palais is priced to send you packing. If you land in one of the 14 rooms with their million-dollar views across the Seine to Nôtre Dame and the Left Bank, and you don't mind the attic school of decorating, this is a Cheap Sleep in Paris that won't disappoint.

Note: All the view rooms have their own bathrooms.

English Spoken: Yes

Facilities and Services: Direct-dial phone; no safe or elevator

Nearest Tourist Attractions (Right Bank): Louvre, Beaubourg and Forum des Halles, Île de la Cité, Île St-Louis, St-Michel

HÔTEL HENRI IV (no stars)
25, place Dauphine, 75001 (1st)
21 rooms, none with shower or bath and toilet

Four hundred years ago, King Henri IV's printing presses occupied this narrow town house on Île de la Cité's pretty place Dauphine. Today, it is a 21-room hotel that has been touted in every budget guide to Paris and has become a mecca for hardcore Cheap Sleepers and anyone else eager to experience a romantically threadbare hotel adventure in Paris. All guests *must* be philosophical about both the accommodations and the plumbing. The rooms, which passed their prime decades ago, could be a shock to some: the furniture looks like leftovers from a garage sale; the lighting is dim; the mattresses are spongy; the wallpaper has seen better days; and the exposed peeling pipes gurgle and sputter all day . . . and all night long. Only a bidet and basin come with each room, and the communal shower and toilets are reached via a steep, winding staircase in a dark and freezing-cold air shaft. On the other hand, it is *so* cheap, so perfectly located, so quiet, and the owners, M. and Mme. Balitrand and their son François, who now runs it, are so friendly, that thousands of young-at-heart guests continue to flock here from around the world and reserve many months in advance.

English Spoken: Yes

Facilities and Services: None

Nearest Tourist Attractions (Located on Île de la Cité): Île St-Louis, St. Michel, St-Germain-des-Prés, Latin Quarter, Left Bank, Louvre, Musée d'Orsay, place Dauphine

TELEPHONE
45-54-44-53

FAX
None

MÉTRO
Pont Neuf, St-Michel, Cité

CREDIT CARDS
None, cash only

RATES
Single 115–150F, double 175–225F; extra bed 30F; shower 15F

BREAKFAST
Included (bread and butter)

HÔTEL MANSART ★★★
5, rue des Capucines (place Vendôme, angle rue de la Paix), 75001 (1st)
57 rooms, all with shower or bath and toilet

To be close to the Ritz, except in price—because your budget does not allow spending upwards of $600 per night for a double (breakfast extra)—consider staying at Hôtel Mansart, named after the architect of Louis XIV, who designed the place Vendôme, Versailles, and the dome on the Invalides. The hotel used to be the Hôtel Calais, a rambling wreck totally devoid of style, with labyrinth halls, creaking floors, and turn-of-the-century plumbing. Not anymore! What a stunning transformation the owners of the Parc Saint Séverin (see page 81)

TELEPHONE
42-61-50-28

FAX
49-27-97-44

MÉTRO
Opéra, Madeleine, Tuileries

CREDIT CARDS
AE, DC, MC, V

RATES
1–2 persons 600–875F, suite 1,300–1,600F; extra bed 100F

BREAKFAST
50F extra per person

have achieved. It should be noted that during the two-year renovation project, the owners kept every staff member on full salary, thus creating a loyal and devoted group of employees, whose dedication to the hotel is reflected in the level of service offered to each guest.

By not making any structural changes other than adding spectacular new bathrooms, the owners have kept the spirit of the building intact. You will still find long hallways, high ceilings, marble fireplaces, stained-glass windows, well-worn period furnishings, and, in some cases, slightly sloping floors. No two rooms are alike, and all but the tiniest can be recommended. Some favorites include no. 603, a top-floor choice done in blue and gray with a mirrored armoire, marble bedside tables, and a tiled bathroom with double sinks. No. 505, a sunny back twin room, has a separate stall shower in addition to a stretch-out bathtub that is perfect for luxurious bubble baths. Rooms 506 and 508 have their own terraces. No. 502 is enormous, with a fireplace, built-in armoire, large round table with chairs, and a writing desk. No. 204 overlooks the place Vendôme. The room is done in royal blue with gold carpeting, and its high ceilings, collectable furniture, and lovely oil painting over the marble dresser are reminiscent of hotels on the Grand Tour of Europe that our grandmothers stayed in decades ago.

The stark simplicity of the lobby is created by an interesting mixture of geometric wall designs based on the gardens at Versailles. Antique chairs and love seats and tiny glowing ceiling lights complete the room. A Continental breakfast is served in a red-carpeted, formal room with arched stained-glass windows and suede-cloth-covered chairs placed around tables covered with yellow damask cloths. Everything works together throughout this impressive hotel and adds up to a smart address in a fine location.

English Spoken: Yes

Facilities and Services: Bar; direct-dial phone; hair dryer; elevator to fifth floor only; mini-bar; radio; TV with international reception; room safe, no charge

Nearest Tourist Attractions (Right Bank): Place Vendôme, place de la Concorde, old Opéra, Madeleine, Louvre, shopping on rue St-Honoré

HÔTEL MOLIÈRE ★★★
21, rue Molière, 75001 (1st)
32 rooms, all with shower or bath and toilet

TELEPHONE
42-96-22-01

FAX
42-60-48-68

MÉTRO
Palais-Royal

CREDIT CARDS
AE, DC, MC, V

RATES
Single 460–650F, double 575–750F, suite 1,550F; extra bed 100F

BREAKFAST
Buffet: 50F per person

You will have to look long and hard to top the overall comfort and services offered by the midcity Molière. The attractive yellow faux-finished lobby has azure blue velvet armchairs and a wonderful Art Nouveau beaded lamp gracing the reception desk. Unusual paintings by one of the hotel's employees are displayed in the bar and breakfast room that overlooks a small garden. The rooms, which are way above average in size and layout, are tastefully done in a rather formal French style. The amount of living space is exceptional; the views, even along the back, are pleasant; and the location puts guests within walking distance of many of the tourist "musts" in Paris.

I could check into no. 42 any day, with its rich brown-velvet easy chairs, two wide-view windows, and nostalgic black-and-turquoise tiled bathroom. No. 43, a mauve-and-pink single, is another favorite, and so is no. 46, with a large sitting room and a tango-sized bathroom. If you are looking for a twin-bedded room, no. 12, on the front, has an extra sofa bed and an old-fashioned bathroom with a roomy green tub.

English Spoken: Yes

Facilities and Services: Bar; collapsible clothes-drying rack; direct-dial phone; hair dryer; elevator to sixth floor; mini-bar; TV with international reception and videos; safe in office, no charge

Nearest Tourist Attractions (Right Bank): Old Opéra, Palais-Royal, Tuileries, Louvre, shopping on rue St-Honoré

HÔTEL RICHELIEU-MAZARIN ★
51, rue de Richelieu, 75001 (1st)
14 rooms, 12 with shower or bath and toilet

TELEPHONE
42-97-46-20

FAX
None

MÉTRO
Pyramides, Palais-Royal

CREDIT CARDS
MC, V

The tiny Richelieu-Mazarin can be recommended for budgeteers not in the market for anything fancy, but who are looking for good value. The entrance off the street is along a stone-walled, well-lighted hallway and up some steep steps to a reception area, which doubles as the breakfast room and lounge. Some of the simply done rooms are dark, most have open closets and only a stool or two for seating, but all have a bouquet of fake flowers to add a note of cheer. Those on the street are noisy, but all are clean enough to please your mother-in-law.

RATES
Single 210–325F, double 225–350F, triple 375–400F; extra bed 60F; shower 10F

BREAKFAST
25F extra per person downstairs; 30F extra per person served in room

No. 29 has a private flight of stairs, its own bath and toilet, and a ceiling window with a tip-toe view of neighboring rooftops. To some the hotel is cozy and cute; for others it is stuffy and claustrophobic. Definitely claustrophobic is no. 20, a closet-sized room with no window at all, only a ceiling vent. Long lines of regulars know this hotel and book it way in advance, so if you want a central Parisian address for not much money, please do the same.

English Spoken: Yes

Facilities and Services: Direct-dial phone; radio; safe in office, no charge; no elevator

Nearest Tourist Attractions (Right Bank): Palais-Royal, Louvre, Tuileries, shopping on rue St-Honoré, place Vendôme, old Opéra, place de la Concorde

LE RELAIS DU LOUVRE ★★★

19, rue des Prêtres Saint-Germain l'Auxerrois, 75001 (1st)

20 rooms, all with shower or bath and toilet

TELEPHONE
40-41-96-42

FAX
40-41-96-44

MÉTRO
Louvre, Pont Neuf

CREDIT CARDS
AE, DC, MC, V

RATES
Single 600–775F, double 800–900F, suite 1,300–1,500F

BREAKFAST
50F extra per person

Just down the street from the Hôtel de la Place du Louvre is Le Relais du Louvre, another top three-star pick hard by the Musée du Louvre. The small lobby, draped in dark red watermarked linen, offers comfortable seating on oversized sofas. A massive fresh floral spray sits atop an antique bureau. The rooms live up to the elegant promise of the lobby. All are attractively furnished with designer fabrics and have good closet space and marble bathrooms with fluffy towels. No. 35, a standard twin-bedded room, offers an armchair covered in quilted pink hydrangea pattern and a writing desk overlooking the church across the street. Appealing prints of Victorian ladies hang on the walls. If you need a little more space, consider no. 32, a quiet room on the back with a sitting area off the bedroom area. Even larger is no. 52, a suite with a direct view of the gargoyles on the St-Germain l'Auxerrois church across the street. An added bonus of this hotel is the charming, English-speaking staff, who succeed in making each guest feel welcome.

English Spoken: Yes

Facilities and Services: Direct-dial phone; hair dryer; elevator; mini-bar; TV with international reception; room safe, no charge

Nearest Tourist Attractions (Right Bank): Louvre, Beaubourg, Seine, St-Michel, Île de la Cité, Île St-Louis

TIMHÔTEL LOUVRE ★★

4, rue Croix des Petits Champs, 75001 (1st)

56 rooms, all with shower or bath and toilet

Thanks to the Timhôtel chain, modern, moderately priced two-star hotels are flourishing in Paris. Some of the locations appeal more to French business travelers than they do to tourists, and others are in Mars from a tourist's standpoint. Those listed here are in the general mainstream of things. This is the French version of Budget Inn, so old-world charm, individual attention, and fine furnishings are not part of the program. Clean rooms with private bathrooms and value for your money *are* part of the program. As an added bonus, the eleventh night is free in any of the chain's hotels throughout France, and the ten nights leading up to it do not have to be consecutive or spent in any one particular Timhôtel. Children under 12 are free if they occupy their parents' room. Some of the hotels have rooms for the handicapped, saunas, and conference rooms. For ease in booking a reservation at any Timhôtel, contact the central reservations center at 44-15-81-15 (telephone) or 44-15-95-26 (fax).

If you prefer, you may deal directly with each hotel. Check the index in the back of the book for other locations.

English Spoken: Yes

Facilities and Services: Bar; conference room; direct-dial phone; hair dryer; elevator; radio; TV with international reception; office safe, 20F per day

Nearest Tourist Attractions (Right Bank): Tuileries, Louvre, Palais-Royal, place de la Concorde, Forum des Halles, Beaubourg

TELEPHONE
42-60-34-86

FAX
42-60-10-39

MÉTRO
Palais-Royal

CREDIT CARDS
AE, DC, MC, V

RATES
Single 450F, double 550F, triple 695F

BREAKFAST
55F extra per person

TONIC HÔTEL LOUVRE ★★

12/14, rue de Roule, 75001 (1st)

34 rooms, all with shower or bath and toilet

A reader writes: "Christine at the desk was extremely helpful in giving assistance in English and just being an excellent hostess. I must say that the loft (in the new annex) was very quiet and cozy, and the Jacuzzi was an added bonus." This reader is not the only one who likes this budget address in central Paris. Physical fitness buffs who stay here can keep themselves in top shape. If you are a morning jogger or walker, it is only a hop, skip, and a jump to join fellow exercisers in the Tuileries or along the banks of the Seine. The hotel is also located

TELEPHONE
42-33-00-71

FAX
40-26-06-86

MÉTRO
Louvre, Châtelet

CREDIT CARDS
AE, DC, MC, V

RATES
Single 500–700F, double 600–900F

BREAKFAST
Included, but 30F per person can be deducted if you decline this service when you are reserving and stick to your plan of eating elsewhere during your stay.

well from a sightseeing standpoint, and there are many good restaurants within easy walking distance (see *Cheap Eats in Paris*).

The hotel consists of two parts: the main building and the new annex next door. In the main part, the simple, pastel rooms include luggage racks, mirrored wardrobes, and double-paned windows to keep out street noise. The bathrooms have either a built-in steam bath, a Jacuzzi in the bathtub, or a pulsating shower massager to ease away the aches and pains of daily tourist safaris through Paris.

I frankly found it hard to get excited about the newly done annex next door. Despite its bright yellow entry, old wood and stone stairway, and mirrored elevator, the views are unremarkable and so is the room space. Rooms do have the same great bathrooms as in the main building, and for the price, especially in the low season, they are worth considering if you plan to spend a minimum amount of time in your hotel room.

English Spoken: Yes

Facilities and Services: Bar; direct-dial phone; elevator; mini-bar; TV with international reception; hair dryer; shower massager or steam bath; some Jacuzzis; safe in office, no charge

Nearest Tourist Attractions (Right Bank): Louvre, Tuileries, Seine, Palais-Royal, Forum des Halles, Île de la Cité, Île St-Louis, St-Michel

Second Arrondissement

(See map, pages 38–39.)

RIGHT BANK
Bibliotèque Nationale, Bourse, Cognacq-Jay Museum, *passages,* place des Victoires

The second arrondissement is known as the area of finance (around the stock exchange, or Bourse), the press, and the rag trade (around place du Caire). It makes up for its small size with the beautiful Victorian shopping *passages* and the boutiques around Place des Victoires. The second is within walking distance to the Marais, Centre Pompidou (Beaubourg), and the Louvre Museum. The southern half around rue Montorgueil has some of the best food markets in Paris. The seedy northern half around rue d'Aboukir should definitely be avoided, and so should rue St-Denis, home of Paris hookers.

HOTELS IN THE SECOND ARRONDISSEMENT

HÔTEL VIVIENNE ★★
40, rue Vivienne, 75002 (2nd)
33 rooms, 31 with toilet, all with shower or bath

TELEPHONE
42-33-13-26

FAX
40-41-98-19

MÉTRO
Bourse, Richelieu Drouot

CREDIT CARDS
MC, V

RATES
1–2 persons 345–450F

BREAKFAST
40F extra per person

The picture on the reception desk was taken at the hotel in 1910. The little girl in the photo was born in this hotel, which her parents owned along with a restaurant next door. The present owner, Claudine Haycraft, bought the hotel from the family almost 20 years ago. Since then, she has slowly redone it, making it a popular budget destination in this part of Paris. The rooms are kept spotlessly clean by a team of career maids. Room decor falls into the typical two-star category: mix and match furniture, some chenille here and there, and industrial-strength carpeting. Bathrooms are adequate, if somewhat questionable in color schemes. Best room in the house? I think it is no. 14, which faces the street and is large enough to feel at home in for more than overnight.

English Spoken: Yes

Facilities and Services: Direct-dial phone; hair dryer; elevator to fifth floor only; TV; safe in office, no charge

Nearest Tourist Attractions (Right Bank): Bourse, old Opéra

TELEPHONE
42-61-53-90
FAX
42-60-05-39
MÉTRO
Bourse, Palais-Royal
CREDIT CARDS
AE, DC, MC, V
RATES
Single 460F, double 550F, triple 695F
BREAKFAST
55F extra per person

TIMHÔTEL BOURSE ★★

3, rue de la Banque, 75002 (2nd)

46 rooms, all with shower or bath and toilet

Next to Galerie Vivienne (see Cheap Chic, page 238). See page 49 for general information about Timhôtels.

English Spoken: Yes

Facilities and Services: Direct-dial phone; conference room; elevator; TV; office safe, no charge.

Nearest Tourist Attractions (Right Bank): Old Opéra, Louvre, Tuileries, Palais-Royal, place de la Concorde

Third Arrondissement

This area includes the northern parts of the revitalized Marais, which until rescued by Minister of Culture André Malraux in the 1960s was the worst slum in Paris. Today the magnificent 17th-century *hôtel particuliers* (private mansions) have been turned into museums, the most famous of which is the Picasso Museum in the Hôtel Salé.

RIGHT BANK
Carnavalet Museum (City of Paris Museum), French National Archives, Marais, Picasso Museum (Hôtel Salé)

HOTELS IN THE THIRD ARRONDISSEMENT

HÔTEL DES CHEVALIERS ★★★

30, rue de Turenne, 75003 (3rd)

24 rooms, all with shower or bath and toilet

The rooms are not large, but the great location near the Picasso Museum and on the edge of the vibrant Marais puts Hôtel des Chevaliers on the list of desirable Cheap Sleeps. The smartly done peach, blue, and pink pastel rooms have fabric-covered walls and are soundproofed by double-paned windows. I think those on the top floors are the most desirable. Guests will find a basket of fresh fruit upon arrival and a mint on the pillow each night. Bathrooms are *tiny* but modern. Sixteenth-century exposed supports line the stairway leading to the downstairs breakfast room, fashioned from an old *cave,* with the original water well still in one corner. Nicely upholstered chairs are placed around well-lighted tables, where breakfast is served on individual trays. Changing art exhibits line the reception area, and all the artwork is available for purchase. The management is very outgoing and friendly, and repeat guests are many.

English Spoken: Yes

Facilities and Services: Direct-dial phone; elevator to fourth floor; hair dryer; mini-bar; TV with international reception; room safe, no charge

Nearest Tourist Attractions (Right Bank): Marais, place des Vosges, Picasso Museum, Bastille Opéra

TELEPHONE
42-72-73-47

FAX
42-72-54-10

MÉTRO
Bastille, Chemin-Vert, St-Paul

CREDIT CARDS
AE, MC, V

RATES
1–2 persons 590–650F

BREAKFAST
45F extra per person

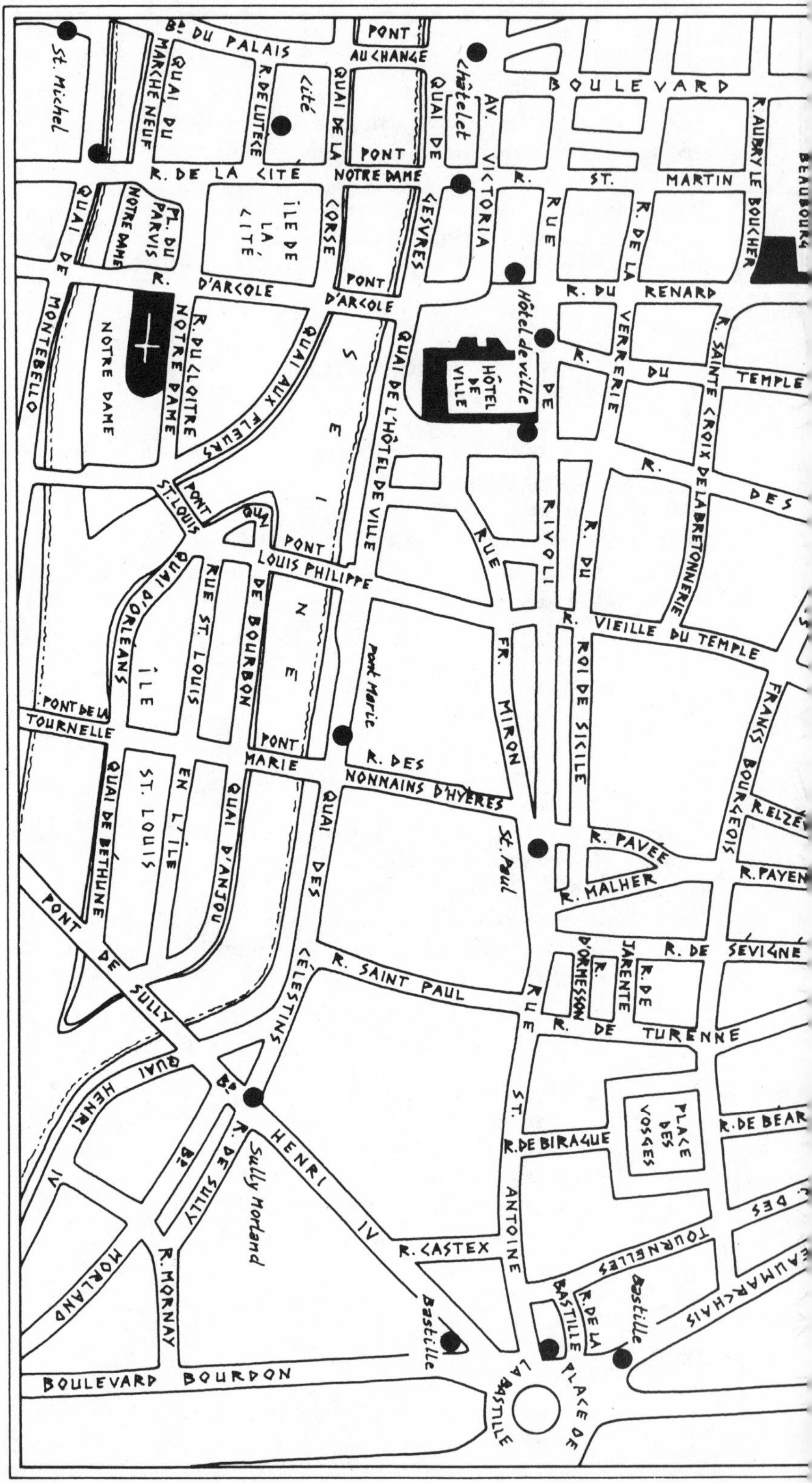

St. Michel
Bd. DU PALAIS
QUAI DU MARCHE NEUF
R. DE LUTECE
Cité
QUAI DE LA CORSE
PONT AU CHANGE
Châtelet
QUAI DE GESVRES
AV. VICTORIA
BOULEVARD
R. AUBRY LE BOUCHER
BEAUBOURG
R. DE LA CITE
PONT NOTRE DAME
R. ST. MARTIN
QUAI DE MONTEBELLO
PL. DU PARVIS NOTRE DAME
ÎLE DE LA CITE
R. D'ARCOLE
PONT D'ARCOLE
RUE R. DE LA VERRERIE
R. DU RENARD
NOTRE DAME
R. DU CLOITRE NOTRE DAME
QUAI AUX FLEURS
SEINE
QUAI DE L'HÔTEL DE VILLE
HÔTEL DE VILLE
Hôtel de ville
R. DE RIVOLI
R. DU TEMPLE
R. SAINTE CROIX DE LA BRETONNERIE
R. DES
PONT ST. LOUIS
QUAI
PONT LOUIS PHILIPPE
QUAI D'ORLEANS
RUE ST. LOUIS
QUAI DE BOURBON
ÎLE
RUE FR. MIRON
R. DU ROI DE SICILE
R. VIEILLE DU TEMPLE
FRANCS BOURGEOIS
Pont Marie
PONT DE LA TOURNELLE
PONT MARIE
R. DES NONNAINS D'HYERES
QUAI DE BETHUNE
ST. LOUIS EN L'ÎLE
QUAI D'ANJOU
QUAI DES CÉLESTINS
St. Paul
R. PAVEE
R. ELZÉ
R. PAYEN
R. MALHER
PONT DE SULLY
R. SAINT PAUL
R. D'ORMESSON
R. DE JARENTE
R. DE SEVIGNE
RUE ST. ANTOINE
R. DE TURENNE
QUAI HENRI IV
Bd. HENRI IV
Bd. R. DE SULLY
Sully Morland
PLACE DES VOSGES
R. DE BEAR
R. DE BIRAGUE
R. DES TOURNELLES
MORLAND
R. MORNAY
R. CASTEX
Bastille
R. DE LA BASTILLE
BEAUMARCHAIS
BOULEVARD BOURDON
PLACE DE LA BASTILLE

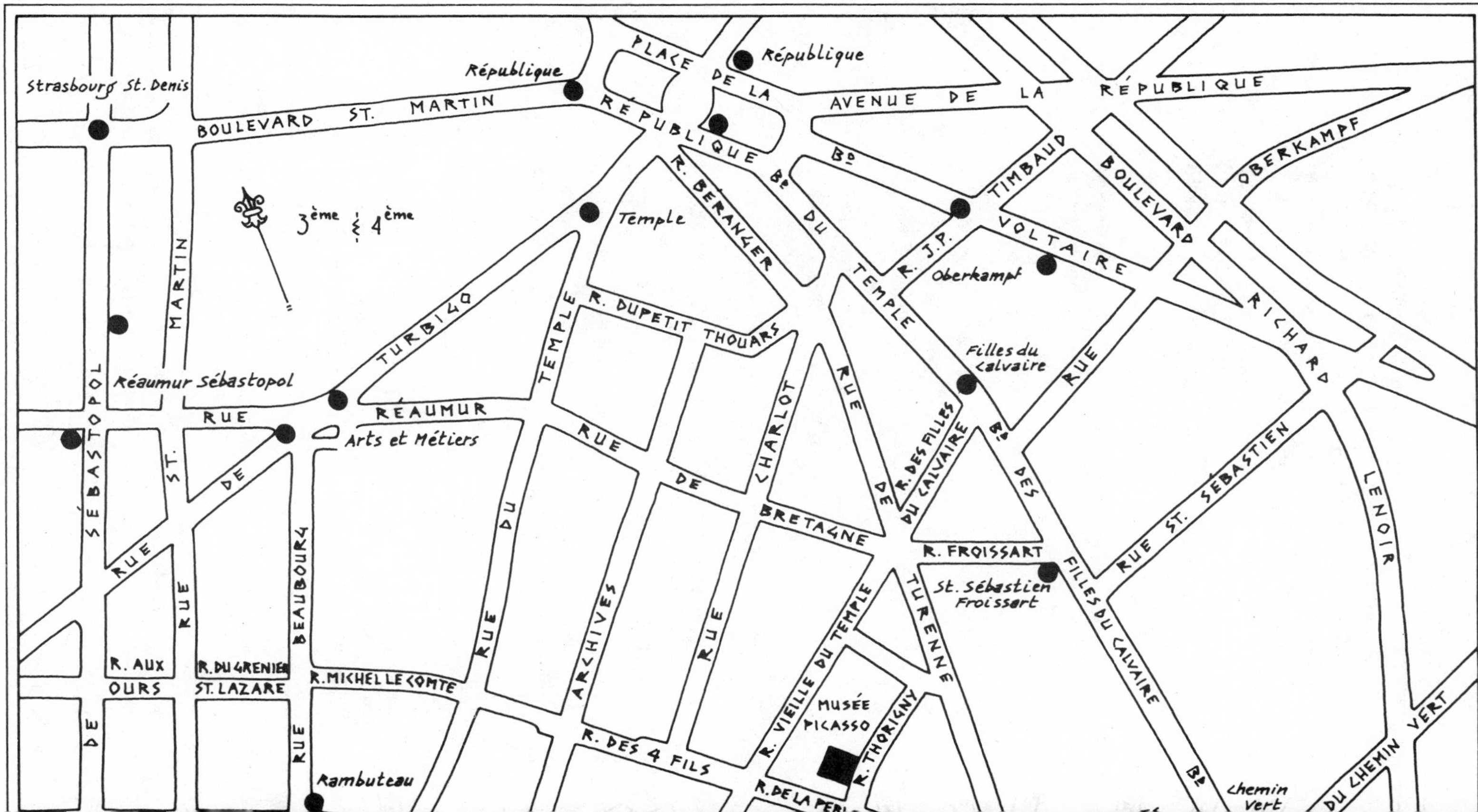
Strasbourg St. Denis
BOULEVARD ST. MARTIN
République
PLACE DE LA RÉPUBLIQUE
République
AVENUE DE LA RÉPUBLIQUE
OBERKAMPF
3ème & 4ème
Temple
R. BERANGER
Bd DU TEMPLE
Bd
TIMBAUD
R. J.P.
VOLTAIRE
BOULEVARD
Oberkampf
RICHARD
MARTIN
SÉBASTOPOL
Réaumur Sébastopol
TURBIGO
R. DUPETIT THOUARS
TEMPLE
Filles du Calvaire
RUE
RUE
RÉAUMUR
Arts et Métiers
RUE DE BRETAGNE
CHARLOT
RUE DE
R. DES FILLES DU CALVAIRE
Bd DES
RUE ST. SÉBASTIEN
LENOIR
RUE ST.
RUE DE
RUE DU
BEAUBOURG
R. FROISSART
St. Sébastien Froissart
FILLES DU CALVAIRE
RUE
ARCHIVES
RUE
TURENNE
R. VIEILLE DU TEMPLE
R. AUX OURS
R. DU GRENIER ST. LAZARE
R. MICHEL LE COMTE
MUSÉE PICASSO
R. THORIGNY
DE
RUE
R. DES 4 FILS
Rambuteau
R. DE LA PERL
Bd
chemin Vert
DU CHEMIN VERT

Fourth Arrondissement

RIGHT BANK
Centre Georges Pompidou (Beaubourg), Hôtel-de-Ville (City Hall), Île St-Louis, Jewish Quarter, Place des Vosges, Maison de Victor Hugo, continuation of the Marais

The fourth arrondissement stretches from the Marais through the ancient Jewish quarter on the rue des Rosiers to the Île St-Louis in the middle of the Seine. It is an area perfectly suited to exploring on foot, lending itself to discovery at almost every turn. Its immense charm comes from a wonderful mixture of past and present. Place des Vosges, with its historic pink-brick town houses set above wide arcade walkways, is the oldest square in Paris and one of the most beautiful. The Île St-Louis is one of the most desirable, and admittedly expensive, places to reside in Paris. The island is a capsule of all that is Paris, with interesting shops, art galleries, boutiques, baroque mansions, lines for the famous Berthillon ice cream, and lovely views along the romantic *quais.* Not to be missed is the controversial (from an architectural standpoint) Centre Georges Pompidou (Beaubourg), the modern art museum, which logs more visitors each year than the Eiffel Tower.

HOTELS IN THE FOURTH ARRONDISSEMENT

CASTEX HÔTEL ★★
5, rue Castex, 75004 (4th)
27 rooms, all with shower or bath and toilet

TELEPHONE
42-72-31-52
FAX
42-72-57-91

The friendly Bouchand family has been at the helm of the Castex since 1929. Virtually nothing changed at the hotel until a few years ago when a younger generation took over and modernized. In tossing out the old, the hotel lost some of its funky charm, as it became a neat-as-a-pin, very clean Cheap Sleep done in French Motel Moderne. The generic rooms have open closets, no drawers, and no televisions. The new bathrooms, however, with enclosed showers, rival some three-star numbers in the neighborhood. To watch television, guests must sit at one of the tables in the dining room. Also in this room is a life-size cutout of President Bill Clinton, obviously put there by a Republican prankster. The words on the cutout read: "Thanks for staying at the American administration's official hotel in Paris." While it may not quite live up to that statement, it does live up to being one of the best Cheap Sleeps in the arrondissement.

English Spoken: Yes

Facilities and Services: Direct-dial phone; no elevator; safe in office, no charge

Nearest Tourist Attractions (Right Bank): Bastille Opéra, Marais, Île de la Cité, Île St-Louis, St-Germain-des-Prés

MÉTRO
Bastille

CREDIT CARDS
MC, V

RATES
Single 220–275F, double 290–380F, triple 450F; extra bed for child 70F, for baby 30F

BREAKFAST
30F extra per person

GRAND HÔTEL JEANNE D'ARC ★★
3, rue de Jarente, 75004 (4th)
36 rooms, all with shower or bath and toilet

The Grand Hôtel Jeanne d'Arc sits on a quiet street leading into the Marais. Discovered long ago by astute Cheap Sleepers, the hotel offers spotless rooms with a minimum of snags and tears in the furnishings, and only a few rooms with two patterns of wallpaper and mismatched fabrics. Room 11 or 12 are good bets if there are two of you, and if there are four, no. 15 is a good choice. If you are alone, request no. 51, a small top-floor room with a desk, open closet, sunny rooftop view, and a compact bathroom with a stall shower (no curtain). Repeat customers comprise the bulk of the clientele, so book early if this one appeals to you.

English Spoken: Yes

Facilities and Services: Direct-dial phone; elevator; TV with international reception; safe in office, no charge

Nearest Tourist Attractions (Right Bank): Picasso Museum, Marais, place des Vosges, Bastille Opéra, rue des Rosiers (Jewish Quarter)

TELEPHONE
48-87-62-11

FAX
48-87-37-31

MÉTRO
St-Paul, Bastille

CREDIT CARDS
MC, V

RATES
1–2 persons 325–450F, triple 525F, quad 575F; extra bed 75F

BREAKFAST
40F extra per person

GRAND HÔTEL MALHER ★★
5, rue Malher, 75004 (4th)
31 rooms, all with shower or bath and toilet

Another one-star hotel bites the dust and comes back as a two-star winner. For more than fifty years, the

TELEPHONE
42-72-60-92

FAX
42-72-25-37
MÉTRO
St-Paul
CREDIT CARDS
MC, V
RATES
Single 595–650F, double 700–750F, junior suite 1,000F
BREAKFAST
45F extra per person

Fossiez family ran this hardcore Cheap Sleep hotel in the Marais. Staying here meant hiking up stairs to get to the faded and worn bedchambers, which featured nicks, dents, and orange chenille. When I visited the hotel this time . . . *quelle surprise!* In the last year, it has shed its frumpy image and is now a great two-star with many three-star features. The new lobby is dominated by a lovely gold mirror and blue-velvet chairs attractively arranged against a backdrop of centuries-old stone walls. Fresh flowers and bowls of potpourri soften the setting. Coordinated bedrooms with tiled bathrooms are welcome changes. Best choices are on the sunny top floors in rooms with balconies. Pamela and Didier Fossiez continue to be gracious hosts, and your stay with them should be delightful.

English Spoken: Yes

Facilities and Services: Conference room; direct-dial phone; hair dryer; elevator; mini-bar; TV with international reception; safe in office, no charge

Nearest Tourist Attractions (Right Bank): Marais, place des Vosges, Bastille Opéra, Picasso Museum, rue des Rosiers (Jewish Quarter), Île de la Cité, Île St-Louis, St-Germain-des-Prés

HOSPITEL: L'HÔTEL À L'HÔPITAL ★★★

1, place du Parvis Notre Dame de Paris, 75004 (4th)
The hotel is located on the sixth floor of Building 2 (*au 6ème étage du batiment B2*); see note below
14 rooms, all with shower or bath and toilet

TELEPHONE
44-32-01-00
FAX
44-32-01-16
MÉTRO
Cité
CREDIT CARDS
AE, DC, MC, V
RATES
Single 425F, double 495F
BREAKFAST
40F extra per person

Wanted: a quiet hotel room on the doorstep of Notre-Dame Cathedral, only seconds away from all the fun and frolic going on around place St-Michel and the Left Bank. Impossible? *Mais non!* Not if you check into Hospitel: l'Hôtel a l'Hôpital, located within the walls of Paris's most prominent hospital: L'Hôtel Dieu de Paris. Originally opened to serve relatives of patients, the 14 rooms are now open to anyone. Frankly I had my doubts when I first heard about it. I could just imagine depressing rooms with linoleum floors and institutional furnishings, all smelling like Lysol. How wrong I was. Actually, the hotel has a great deal going for it. In addition to the dynamite location, its contemporary rooms, done with Art Deco overtones and in vibrant primary colors, are blissfully quiet. The tiled baths are above average; it is, of course, absolutely spotless; and above all, the low prices are amazing for this expensive, touristy sector of Paris. The only downside to the hotel is its location on the sixth floor under a mansard roof. There are no real windows, only skylights—but they are ample and let in plenty of light and sunshine. The closet and drawer space is not geared to long stays, and you might see a few hospital patients in bathrobes *en route* to your elevator. If you can live with this, it is a Cheap Sleep find.

Note: To find the hotel within the hospital, enter directly through the door just beside the main door. The entrance is marked.

English Spoken: Yes

Facilities and Services: Direct-dial phone; elevator; TV; room service; office safe, no charge; rooms for the handicapped

Nearest Tourist Attractions (Right Bank): Notre-Dame, Île de la Cité, Île St-Louis, St-Michel, St-Germain-des-Prés

HÔTEL BASTILLE SPERIA ★★★
1, rue de la Bastille, 75004 (4th)
42 rooms, all with shower or bath and toilet

With the opening of the new Bastille Opéra, along with many galleries, new wave boutiques, trendy restaurants, and hot night spots throughout the *quartier,* the Bastille is one of the most popular places to be seen in Paris today. Visitors longing to be in the center of all this action can stay at the Bastille Speria, which is next to the famed brasserie Bofinger (see *Cheap Eats in Paris*) and only a few yards from the place de la Bastille. The interior of the hotel was renovated in the late 1980s and continues to be nicely maintained. The rooms have uncluttered lines and are decorated in soft grays and forest greens with contemporary furnishings. The modern breakfast area and lounge have the same trim lines.

English Spoken: Yes

Facilities and Services: Direct-dial phone; elevator; hair dryer; mini-bar; TV with international reception; room safe, 15F per day

Nearest Tourist Attractions (Right Bank): Bastille Opéra, Marais, place des Vosges, Picasso Museum. Typical outdoor market, Thursday and Sunday mornings, 8 A.M.–noon, on boulevard Richard Lenoir.

TELEPHONE
42-72-04-01

FAX
42-72-56-38

MÉTRO
Bastille

CREDIT CARDS
AE, DC, MC, V

RATES
Single 530–560F, double 560–630F, triple 765F

BREAKFAST
50F extra per person

HÔTEL CARON DE BEAUMARCHAIS ★★★

12, rue Vieille-du-Temple, 75004 (4th)

19 rooms, all with shower or bath and toilet

TELEPHONE
42-72-34-12

FAX
42-72-34-63

MÉTRO
Hôtel-de-Ville, St-Paul

CREDIT CARDS
AE, DC, MC, V

RATES
1–2 persons 630–700F; extra bed 100F

BREAKFAST
Continental 50F extra per person, brunch 70F extra per person

Named after the boisterous author of the *Marriage of Figaro,* the Caron de Beaumarchais is close to interesting shopping in the Marais, the Jewish Quarter, and the Bastille Opéra. The newly restored hotel opened for business in June 1993, run by father and son owners Etienne and Alain Bigeard. Between them they have all the credentials necessary to run a fine, small hotel. Service and attention to guests' needs is a dwindling commodity in today's hotel market, but not here. When I was at the hotel, guests could not say enough about the care and consideration extended to them during their stay.

The downstairs lobby features a Louis XVI fireplace, copies of 18th-century murals, and an atrium garden off to one side. A brunch with freshly squeezed orange juice, assorted pastries, fresh fruit, and yogurt is served here. If guests prefer, a Continental breakfast will be brought on a tray to their rooms.

The 19 bedrooms are small, but effective design and elegant 18th-century decor overcome this. No detail has been overlooked in providing a coordinated look. The Gustavian III style furniture was made especially for the hotel. Original pages from the *Marriage of Figaro* are framed and hang in each room. Handpainted and signed ceramic tiles highlight the bathrooms, where even the color of the soap in the soap dish was taken into consideration. In addition to being air-conditioned and soundproofed, each room has a fax hookup, and six have balconies with tables and chairs. In doing the hotel, the family wanted to re-create a typically French atmosphere where guests would feel at home and to which they would want to return. They have achieved their goal beautifully.

English Spoken: Yes

Facilities and Services: Air-conditioned and soundproofed rooms; direct-dial phone; hair dryer; elevator; mini-bar; TV with international reception; fax hookup; safe in office, no charge

Nearest Tourist Attractions (Right Bank): Place des Vosges, Marais, Jewish Quarter, Île St-Louis, Île de la Cité, Picasso Museum, Bastille Opéra

HÔTEL DE LA BRETONNERIE ★★★

22, rue Sainte-Croix-de-la-Bretonnerie, 75004 (4th)

31 rooms, all with shower or bath and toilet

A stay in this captivating hotel will make you feel like an inhabitant of old-world Paris. Set in a restored 17th-century town house in the heart of the picturesque Marais, it is just minutes from Beaubourg, place des Vosges, the Picasso Museum, the banks of the Seine, and Notre-Dame. Quality and taste are evident throughout the rooms, which are individually furnished in Louis XII style. For a special treat, request no. 7, 19, or 35. Set under medieval beams, no. 35 is magnificently done in soft mauve tones and has enviable antiques. It consists of a bedroom, a separate sitting room, and one of the most beautiful three-star marble baths in Paris. The only drawback of this recommended hotel lies in the halls, which are unfortunately draped in dismal brown. High praise goes to long-time owners M. and Mme. Sagot, who provide a warm welcome to their many returning guests. This is rightfully considered to be one of the best small hotels in Paris.

English Spoken: Yes

Facilities and Services: Bar; direct-dial phone; elevator; TV; room safe, no charge

Nearest Tourist Attractions (Right Bank): Place des Vosges, Bastille Opéra, Beaubourg, Marais, Picasso Museum, Seine, Île de la Cité, Île St-Louis, rue des Rosiers (Jewish Quarter)

TELEPHONE
48-87-77-63

FAX
42-77-26-78

MÉTRO
Hôtel-de-Ville

CREDIT CARDS
MC, V

RATES
1–2 persons 690–825F, suites 885F

BREAKFAST
50F extra per person

HÔTEL DE LA PLACE DES VOSGES ★★

12, rue de Birague, 75004 (4th)

16 rooms, all with shower or bath and toilet

A vigorous transformation project more than a decade ago turned this ancient little hotel into one of the top choices of many American visitors to Paris. It is located on the outside edge of the beautiful place des Vosges, the oldest square in Paris, and one that is steeped in the history of the city. Victor Hugo, Cardinal Richelieu, and Madame de Sévigné all lived on the square, and the present inhabitants of the area are no less influential, wealthy, or powerful. The setting puts you in the heart of the Marais and within easy walking distance to the Picasso Museum and the fashionable area around the new Bastille Opéra. It is also close to far-out nightspots and a host of Cheap Eats in Paris.

TELEPHONE
42-72-60-46

FAX
42-72-02-64

MÉTRO
St-Paul, Bastille

CREDIT CARDS
AE, DC, MC, V

RATES
Single 325–450F, double 450–475F

BREAKFAST
45F extra per person

In restoring the hotel, the owners displayed faithful attention to detail and maintained the architectural past of the building by keeping the original beamed ceilings, wood-paneled walls, large tapestries, and antique furnishings displayed in the lobby. Like the hotel, the prices are small, and so are most of the 16 rooms, which are unfortunately beginning to be a bit frayed around the edges. Miniscule bathrooms and closets complement the luggage space, which is almost nil. If you don't mind tiny and slightly tattered, this is a popular hotel in a fascinating part of Paris.

English Spoken: Yes

Facilities and Services: Direct-dial phone; elevator from the second floor; TV with international reception; safe in office, no charge

Nearest Tourist Attractions (Right Bank): Place des Vosges, Marais, Bastille Opéra, Picasso Museum, Seine, Île de la Cité, Île St-Louis

HÔTEL DE LUTÈCE ★★★
65, rue Saint-Louis-en-l'Île, 75004 (4th)
23 rooms, all with shower or bath and toilet

TELEPHONE
43-26-23-52
FAX
43-29-60-25
MÉTRO
Pont-Marie
CREDIT CARDS
None, cash only
RATES
Single 720F, double 825F, triple 1,000F
BREAKFAST
45F extra per person

The Île St-Louis is a small island in the middle of the Seine, six blocks long and two blocks wide. Every day and night, and especially on the weekends, crowds of tourists and Parisians surge down the main street, browsing through the boutiques and art galleries or stopping for an ice cream at the famed Berthillon. Lovers of this unique part of Paris check into either the Lutèce or the Deux Îles, both owned by husband-and-wife team Roland and Elisabeth Buffat. Stepping inside from the island's main street, you are welcomed by bouquets of fresh flowers and a large stone fireplace surrounded by soft couches and armchairs. The rooms at the Lutèce are not large by any standards, but they are nicely decorated and have the requisite exposed beams, provincial prints, and pretty rooftop views (if you are lucky and secure a top-floor room, particularly no. 62). Because the hotel exudes charm from top to bottom, it is booked months ahead, so you should reserve as far in advance as possible.

English Spoken: Yes

Facilities and Services: Direct-dial phone; elevator; hair dryer; TV with international reception; safe in office, no charge

Nearest Tourist Attractions (Right Bank): Île St-Louis, Île de la Cité, St-Germain-des-Prés, Latin

Quarter, St-Michel, Bastille, place des Vosges, Picasso Museum, Marais

HÔTEL DES DEUX-ÎLES ★★★
59, rue Saint-Louis-en-l'Île, 75004 (4th)
17 rooms, all with shower or bath and toilet

To capture the enchantment of Paris, stay on the Île St-Louis. But be forewarned—you may never want to leave!

Many people like being on the island because they are steps from the cluster of Notre-Dame Cathedral, Ste-Chapelle, and the Conciergerie; within walking distance to the Marais; and close to the Bastille Opéra and all the excitement the newly popular area generates. Only a few feel isolated and frustrated by its narrow streets, weekend crowds, and lack of easy parking. Personally, I love it, but I am biased because this is where I lived the first year I spent in Paris.

The Hôtel des Deux-Îles is a beautiful 17th-century mansion, owned by decorator Roland Buffat and his wife, Elisabeth (see Hôtel Lutèce). This hotel shows their touches at every turn, from the lobby with its atrium garden to the Louis XIV tiled bathrooms. The snug hotel breakfast area downstairs has a big fireplace and several secluded nooks with soft overstuffed sofas, making it a perfect place to start your Paris day. The rooms, where the very essence of Paris can be viewed from the top-floor windows, are very small, but they are well done with provincial prints, fabric wall covering, and bamboo furniture.

English Spoken: Yes

Facilities and Services: Direct-dial phone; elevator; hair dryer; TV with international reception; safe in office, no charge

Nearest Tourist Attractions (Right Bank): Île St-Louis, Île de la Cité, Latin Quarter, St-Michel, St-Germain-des-Prés, Marais, Picasso Museum, place des Vosges, Bastille Opéra

TELEPHONE
43-26-13-35

FAX
43-29-60-25

MÉTRO
Pont-Marie

CREDIT CARDS
None, cash only

RATES
Single 720F, double 835F

BREAKFAST
45F extra per person

HÔTEL DU GRAND TURENNE ★★★
6, rue de Turenne, 75004 (4th)
41 rooms, all with shower or bath and toilet

The Libertel hotel group has more than a dozen smart lodgings in Paris. All are beautifully done from top to bottom with coordinated colors and furnishings. L'Hôtel du Grand Turenne offers 41 charming rooms done in

TELEPHONE
42-78-43-25; central reservation number: 44-70-24-24

FAX
42-74-10-72; central reservation fax: 44-70-24-51
MÉTRO
Bastille
CREDIT CARDS
AE, DC, MC, V
RATES
Single 690F, double 750–850F, suite 950F
BREAKFAST
60F extra per person, buffet

blues, greens, or soft reds. The first floor is devoted entirely to nonsmokers. Full room service is available from the morning until 2 P.M., and again from 6–11 P.M. This is a lifesaver if you have children or are just arriving with a case of jet lag and need something to eat at an off-hour. The hotel location, only a five-minute walk from place des Vosges, offers visitors a solid base for exploring one of the most interesting *quartiers* in Paris. From here it is an easy walk to the Picasso Museum, Île de la Cité, Île St-Louis, the new Bastille Opéra, and all the wild and woolly nighttime fun in the burgeoning 11th arrondissement. In addition, many of the restaurants in *Cheap Eats in Paris* are close by.

English Spoken: Yes

Facilities and Services: Bar; direct-dial phone; hair dryer; elevator; mini-bar; TV with international reception; room service; safe in office, no charge

Nearest Tourist Attractions (Right Bank): Place des Vosges, Picasso Museum, Bastille Opéra, Île St-Louis, Île de la Cité

HÔTEL PRACTIC ★
9, rue d'Ormesson, 75004 (4th)
24 rooms, 15 with shower or bath and toilet

TELEPHONE
48-87-80-47
FAX
48-87-40-04
MÉTRO
St-Paul, Bastille
CREDIT CARDS
MC, V
RATES
Single 175–275F, double 250–375F
BREAKFAST
30F extra per person

A good choice for a thrifty stay in the Marais near place des Vosges is the Hôtel Practic. When making reservations, avoid room no. 15 unless you don't mind facing a blank wall. No. 25 is a better choice. Its sunny top-floor location affords a view over neighboring rooftops. Don't lament the lack of any style whatsoever in the rooms or the absence of ruffles and flourishes in the service department. Focus instead on the cleanliness of the hotel, its nice location on the pretty place Marché Sainte-Catherine, and the easy-on-the-wallet prices.

English Spoken: Yes

Facilities and Services: Direct-dial phone; no elevator or TV; safe in office, no charge

Nearest Tourist Attractions (Right Bank): Place des Vosges, Marais, Picasso Museum, Bastille Opéra, Île St-Louis, Île de la Cité

HÔTEL SAINT-MERRY ★★★
78, rue de la Verrerie, 75004 (4th)
11 rooms, 9 with shower or bath and toilet

TELEPHONE
42-78-14-15

The former presbytery of the 17th-century Gothic church of St-Merry is now the most unusual hotel in

Paris. It is the labor of love of owner M. Crabbe, who for more than 35 years has been working to create a true Gothic masterpiece. His immense pride in his achievement is well deserved, and the results are spectacular.

The entrance to the hotel is through a short hallway with exposed beams and stone steps leading up to the lobby and reception area. Each room in the hotel is different and showcases a wonderful collection of authentic Gothic church and castle memorabilia, mixed with custom-made pieces. All the back rooms share a common wall with the church, and wherever possible this stone wall has been kept visible. One room contains a carved-stone flying buttress, flowing from the floor to the ceiling over the bed. Others have rough red tiles from the Chateau de l'Angeres in the Loire Valley, hand-carved mahogany pews, converted confessionals serving as headboards, and impressive eight-lamp chandeliers. All of the windows in the hotel are stained glass, and the balcony rails still bear the St-Merry church crest. *Warning:* The hotel is located on a pedestrian walkway, making it accessible by car or taxi *only* to the determined.

English Spoken: Yes

Facilities and Services: Direct-dial phone; no elevator or TV; safe in office, no charge

Nearest Tourist Attractions (Right Bank): Beaubourg, Marais, Seine, Île de la Cité, Île St-Louis, St-Germain-des-Prés. Don't miss the St-Merry Church adjoining the hotel. It has a beautiful choir and the oldest church bell in Paris, cast in 1331.

FAX
40-29-06-82

MÉTRO
Châtelet, Hôtel-de-Ville

CREDIT CARDS
None, cash only

RATES
1–2 persons 425–1,100F (no two rooms alike; prices vary according to plumbing and how Gothic the room is)

BREAKFAST
45F extra per person

HÔTEL SANSONNET ★★

48, rue de la Verrerie, 75004 (4th)

25 rooms, 21 with shower or bath and toilet

The family-owned Sansonnet offers better two-star values than most of its competitors in the neighborhood. The hotel is clean, reasonably modern, and has been managed for 25 years by M. and Mme. Neau. A colorful aquarium sits at the lobby entrance, which is up an easy flight of stairs from the street. Several of the singles without facilities are miniscule, but if you have only a small suitcase and plan to just sleep in your room, these are buys. The doubles are good sized, with uniform color schemes and blended fabrics. The closets have shelves, and most of the showers have doors. From this address you won't find a better Paris location for exploring the area around Beaubourg and the Forum des Halles. For

TELEPHONE
48-87-96-14

FAX
48-87-30-46

MÉTRO
Hôtel-de-Ville, Châtelet

CREDIT CARDS
MC, V

RATES
Single 250–375F, double 350–400F; shower 20F

BREAKFAST
35F extra per person

sightseeing and shopping further afield, it is a ten-minute walk to the Islands, St-Michel, the big department stores on rue de Rivoli, and a number of good Cheap Eats in Paris.

English Spoken: Yes

Facilities and Services: Direct-dial phone; hair dryer in rooms with full facilities; no elevator; TV; safe in office, no charge

Nearest Tourist Attractions (Right Bank): Beaubourg, Forum des Halles, BHV and La Samaritaine department stores, Île de la Cité, Île St-Louis

Fifth Arrondissement

LEFT BANK
Cluny Museum, Jardin des Plantes, Latin Quarter, rue Mouffetard, Panthéon, Sorbonne, place de la Contrescarpe

The fifth is known as the Latin Quarter. *Latin* refers to the language heard here until 1798. The arrondissement stretches from the colorful street *marché* on rue Mouffetard to the dome of the Panthéon, through the botanical wonders of the Jardin des Plantes to the Sorbonne. This ancient, interesting, and exhilarating part of Paris is crisscrossed with networks of narrow, curved streets lined on both sides with bookshops, restaurants, and cafés that surge with action 24 hours a day. It is youthful, cosmopolitan, bohemian, and fun. Even though St-Michel has lost its penniless chic, it is still the soul of the Latin Quarter. Crowds of all ages and types gather daily around the St-Michel fountain to flirt, eat, drink, argue, and watch the sidewalk entertainment. The area around place de la Contrescarpe is where Hemingway lived when he was a starving writer first in Paris. You can see two of his addresses: 39, rue Descartes, a studio; and 74, rue de Cardinal Lemoine, where he lived with his wife Hadley.

HOTELS IN THE FIFTH ARRONDISSEMENT

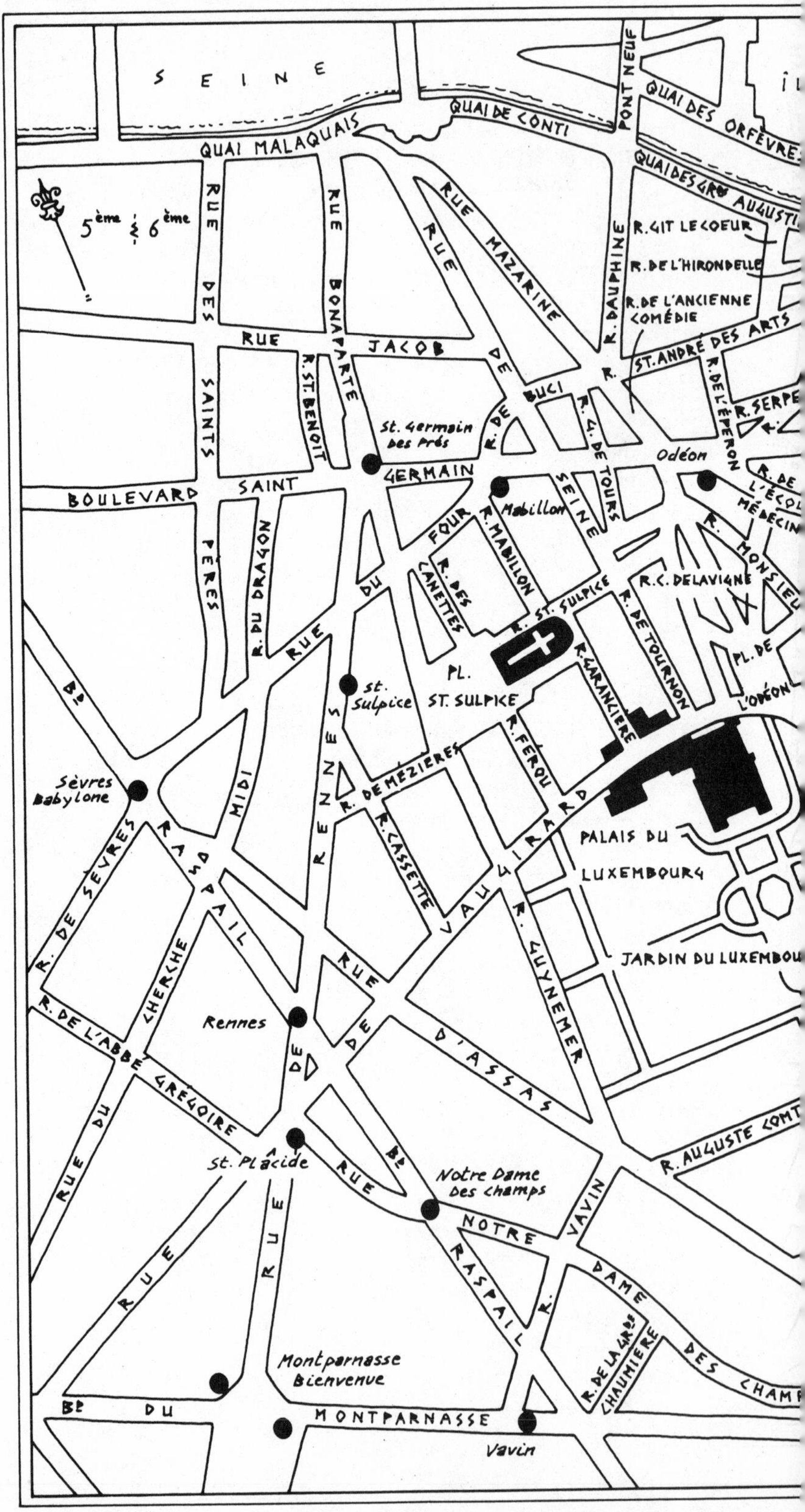
SEINE
QUAI MALAQUAIS
QUAI DE CONTI
PONT NEUF
QUAI DES ORFÈVRES
QUAI DES GDS AUGUSTINS
5ème & 6ème
RUE DES SAINTS PÈRES
RUE BONAPARTE
RUE MAZARINE
RUE DE SEINE
R. DAUPHINE
R. GIT LE COEUR
R. DE L'HIRONDELLE
R. DE L'ANCIENNE COMÉDIE
RUE JACOB
R. ST. ANDRÉ DES ARTS
R. ST. BENOIT
R. DE BUCI
R. DE L'ÉPERON
R. SERPENTE
St. Germain des Prés
BOULEVARD SAINT GERMAIN
R. DE L'ÉCOLE DE MÉDECINE
Mabillon
Odéon
R. 4 DE TOURS
R. DU FOUR
R. MABILLON
R. DES CANETTES
R. MONSIEUR
R. DU DRAGON
R. C. DELAVIGNE
R. ST. SULPICE
R. DE TOURNON
PL. DE L'ODÉON
RUE DU MIDI
St. Sulpice
PL. ST. SULPICE
R. GARANCIÈRE
Bd RASPAIL
R. FÉROU
RUE DE RENNES
Sèvres Babylone
R. DE MÉZIÈRES
RUE DE VAUGIRARD
PALAIS DU LUXEMBOURG
R. CASSETTE
R. DE SÈVRES
R. DU CHERCHE
R. GUYNEMER
JARDIN DU LUXEMBOURG
Rennes
R. DE L'ABBÉ GRÉGOIRE
RUE D'ASSAS
St. Placide
RUE DU
R. AUGUSTE COMTE
Notre Dame des champs
RUE NOTRE DAME DES CHAMPS
R. VAVIN
RUE
Montparnasse Bienvenue
R. DE LA GDE CHAUMIÈRE
Bd DU MONTPARNASSE
Vavin

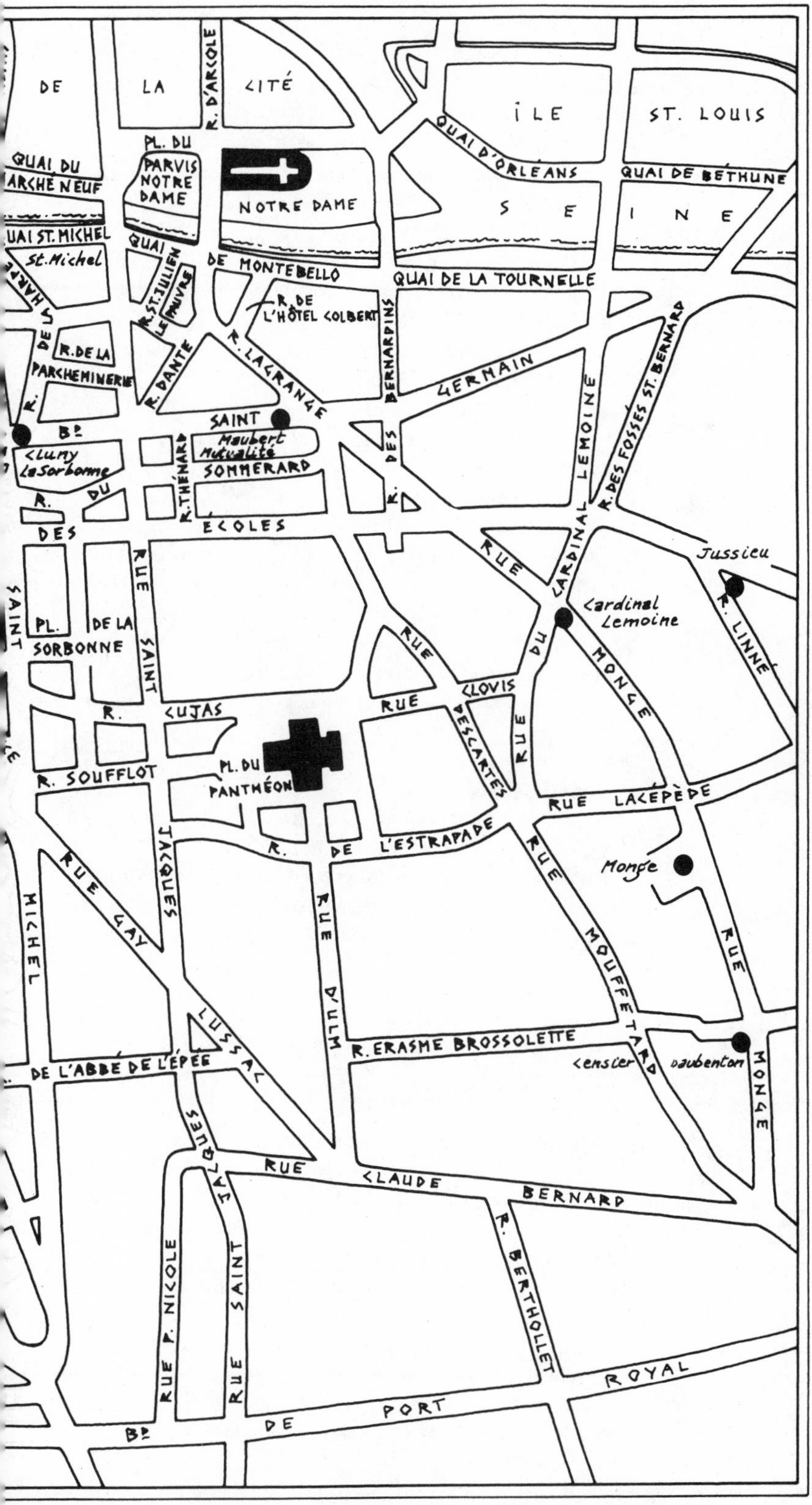

DE LA CITÉ
R. D'ARCOLE
ÎLE ST. LOUIS
PL. DU PARVIS NOTRE DAME
QUAI DU
ARCHÉ NEUF
NOTRE DAME
QUAI D'ORLÉANS
QUAI DE BÉTHUNE
S E I N E
QUAI ST. MICHEL
St. Michel
QUAI DE MONTEBELLO
QUAI DE LA TOURNELLE
R. ST. JULIEN LE PAUVRE
R. DE L'HÔTEL COLBERT
R. DE LA HARPE
R. DE LA PARCHEMINERIE
R. DANTE
R. LAGRANGE
R. DES BERNARDINS
SAINT GERMAIN
Bd.
Maubert Mutualité
Cluny La Sorbonne
R. THÉNARD
R. DU SOMMERARD
R. DES ECOLES
RUE DU CARDINAL LEMOINE
R. DES FOSSÉS ST. BERNARD
Jussieu
Cardinal Lemoine
R. LINNÉ
RUE MONGE
PL. DE LA SORBONNE
RUE SAINT
RUE CLOVIS
RUE DESCARTES
R. CUJAS
R. SOUFFLOT
PL. DU PANTHÉON
RUE LACÉPÈDE
R. DE L'ESTRAPADE
Monge
RUE MOUFFETARD
RUE GAY LUSSAC
JACQUES
SAINT MICHEL
RUE D'ULM
R. ERASME BROSSOLETTE
Censier Daubenton
DE L'ABBÉ DE L'ÉPÉE
MONGE
RUE CLAUDE BERNARD
R. BERTHOLLET
RUE P. NICOLE
RUE SAINT JACQUES
Bd. DE PORT ROYAL

DEGRÉS DE NOTRE-DAME HÔTEL (no stars)
10, rue des Grands-Degrés, 75005 (5th)
10 rooms, all with shower or bath and toilet

TELEPHONE
43-25-88-38
FAX
40-46-95-34
MÉTRO
Maubert-Mutualité
CREDIT CARDS
MC, V
RATES
1–2 persons 450–600F
BREAKFAST
35F extra per person

Ten rooms, all located up narrow, winding stairs; the required beams and views of the Left Bank from most rooms; a top-drawer location; quasi antiques here and there; portable heaters; and some odd closets. True, there is an upside as well as a downside to the Degrés de Notre-Dame Hôtel, but for the young in both body and spirit, its low prices, superior location within earshot of the chimes of Notre-Dame, and overall rustic charm, make it one to consider—if you know the pitfalls ahead of time. For instance, room no. 24, on the top floor, is huge and has a sunny view from its three windows, but the brick-floored bathroom with zero shelf space and the worn carpets make it one to avoid. On the other hand, the only room on the fifth floor under the eaves is enormous, with a new bathroom and a great skylight view of Notre-Dame Cathedral. No. 23 has a view, good drawer space, hardwood floors, a serviceable bathroom, and small closet. The hotel is above a restaurant of the same name that serves mundane French food you can find anyplace in Paris. Consult *Cheap Eats in Paris* for better alternatives.

English Spoken: Yes

Facilities and Services: Bar; direct-dial phone; no elevator; TV; safe in office, no charge

Nearest Tourist Attractions (Left Bank): Notre-Dame Cathedral, Île de la Cité, Île St-Louis, St-Michel, Latin Quarter

FAMILIA HÔTEL ★★
11, rue des Écoles, 75005 (5th)
30 rooms, all with shower or bath and toilet

TELEPHONE
43-54-55-27
FAX
43-29-61-77
MÉTRO
Jussieu, Cardinal-Lemoine, Maubert-Mutualité
CREDIT CARDS
MC, V
RATES
Single 370–440F, double 370–480F, triple 585F, quad 685F
BREAKFAST
35F extra per person

Many hotels on rue des Écoles are run by foreign managers for absentee owners in the Middle East. As a result, service, cleanliness, and upkeep are often drastically reduced, because no one at the hotel has any stake in it, or really cares. You will find none of this at the Familia Hôtel. The Gaucherons, who have owned the hotel for a decade, live on-site and take pride in being on top of things every minute. Theirs is a plain place, with no fancy airs, but they extend themselves so far beyond the others to accommodate their guests that the line of loyal Cheap Sleepers in Paris is long.

Recent improvements to the hotel include thick, double-glazed windows to ease the traffic noise along the front of the hotel; a new entry with an attractive mural painted by a friend of Eric Gaucheron; and white, beveled-glass doors leading from the entry and reception area into the peach dining room, which is set with black lacquered furniture.

Several years ago, the bedrooms were given an overhaul. Their size didn't change, and they are still a tight fit, with limited space for bulky luggage or shopping purchases. They do, however, provide more than just the basics, have good mattresses, and are always kept neat and tidy. The bird's-eye views of Notre-Dame Cathedral are best from the front rooms on the fifth and sixth floors. Staying at the Familia puts guests only a few minutes from St-Germain-des-Prés, the islands, and all the famous cafés in the Latin Quarter. Métro connections are good, and so is the bus transportation.

English Spoken: Yes, and Spanish

Facilities and Services: Direct-dial phone; hair dryer; elevator; mini-bar; TV with international reception; safe in office, no charge

Nearest Tourist Attractions (Left Bank): Latin Quarter, St-Germain-des-Prés, Île de la Cité, Île St-Louis

HÔTEL ABBATIAL SAINT-GERMAIN ★★★
46, boulevard St-Germain, 75005 (5th)
43 rooms, all with shower or bath and toilet

TELEPHONE
46-34-02-12

FAX
43-25-47-73

MÉTRO
Maubert-Mutualité

CREDIT CARDS
AE, DC, MC, V

RATES
Single 480–620F, double 580–750F, triple 850F; extra bed 160F

BREAKFAST
40F extra per person

Letters from readers told me that something had drastically changed at the Grand Hôtel de Lima. No longer was it a pleasant Cheap Sleep in Paris, due in large part to the attitude of the owners. Because I always personally recheck every entry at the time of revision, I returned to this old favorite expecting to be very disappointed. Instead I was delighted. Not only does the hotel now have astute new owners (see Hôtel Agora St-Germain, page 72, for their other hotel), but a new name, a new look, and an added star. I am happy to report that the hotel now offers atmosphere, service, and style at prices most guests can afford.

In totally redoing the hotel, the spirit of the Napoléon III building was kept with the exposure of original beams, tapestry-covered walls, and white antique furniture. Tiled bathrooms are well fitted with shower guards, large towels, and door hooks. The fifth- and sixth-floor rooms have balconies with views over Notre-Dame Cathedral and the Panthéon. The sunny streetside rooms are soundproofed with double-glazed windows. Connecting rooms, each with a private safe and air-conditioning, add to the appeal of this nice new Left Bank choice.

English Spoken: Yes

Facilities and Services: Air-conditioned rooms; direct-dial phone; hair dryer; elevator; mini-bar; TV; room safe, no charge

Nearest Tourist Attractions (Left Bank): Latin Quarter, St-Michel, Notre-Dame Cathedral, St-Germain-des-Prés, Panthéon, Sorbonne, Cluny Museum, Île de la Cité, Île St-Louis, shopping

HÔTEL AGORA ST-GERMAIN ★★★
42, rue des Bernardins, 75005 (5th)
39 rooms, all with shower or bath and toilet

TELEPHONE
46-34-13-00
FAX
46-34-75-05
MÉTRO
Maubert-Mutualité
CREDIT CARDS
AE, DC, MC, V
RATES
Single 540–590F, double 690F, triple 900F
BREAKFAST
45F extra per person

The Agora St-Germain continues to represent a success story for both owners and guests. It reopened in 1987 after undergoing a face-lift of remarkable proportions and has been popular ever since for its top-quality accommodations. The customized rooms with pretty silk wall coverings, ample space, and marble-tiled bathrooms are beautifully maintained. A Continental breakfast is served in a pleasing stone-walled dining room with baskets of fresh flowers and linen napkins on each table. The friendly owners, Pascale and Michèle Sahuc, and their staff see to the wishes of every guest. Firmly recommended by all who have stayed here, this haven for weary travelers is less than five minutes away from good restaurants (see *Cheap Eats in Paris*) and close to all the charm and excitement of this part of the Left Bank.

Note: The Sahucs have another hotel now, the Hôtel Abbatial Saint-Germain (see page 71).

English Spoken: Yes

Facilities and Services: Direct-dial phone; elevator; hair dryer; mini-bar; TV with international reception; room safe, no charge

Nearest Tourist Attractions (Left Bank): Latin Quarter, St-Michel, St-Germain-des-Prés, Île de la Cité, Île St-Louis

HÔTEL CLAUDE BERNARD ★★★
43, rue des Écoles, 75005 (5th)
30 rooms, all with shower or bath and toilet

The Claude Bernard continues to be a mixed bag: people either love it or leave it. After a remodeling project in 1986, things picked up considerably, but since then maintenance has been spotty and most of the pine furniture needs a big dose of TLC. Aside from the constant street noise, the other drawbacks for some might be the dim bedside lights, poorly fitted bedspreads, and dark maroon color scheme that pervades the halls. Upstairs, the rooms combine English country furniture with French provincial fabrics. During the remodeling, the intricately carved moldings and doors were kept, along with the double French windows overlooking the street. The tremendous triple rooms are good for families because the furniture is used to lots of wear and tear. These rooms do face the noisy street, so earplugs would be a must for light sleepers. Despite the list of pluses and minuses, the Claude Bernard is always a Latin Quarter favorite, thanks to its friendly atmosphere and key location as a base for exploring St-Michel, St-Germain-des-Prés, and the islands in the Seine.

English Spoken: Yes

Facilities and Services: Direct-dial phone; elevator; sauna (75F); mini-bar; TV with international reception; safe in office, 10F per day

Nearest Tourist Attractions (Left Bank): St-Michel, St-Germain-des-Prés, Île de la Cité, Île St-Louis, Latin Quarter

TELEPHONE
43-26-32-52

FAX
43-26-80-56

MÉTRO
Maubert-Mutualité

CREDIT CARDS
AE, DC, MC, V

RATES
Single 410F, double 580–700F, suite 825F

BREAKFAST
45F extra per person

HÔTEL D'ALBE ★★
1, rue de la Harpe, 75005 (5th)
45 rooms, all with shower or bath and toilet

This is the perfect site for Latin Quarter night owls and other urbanites who consider 11 P.M. to be the shank of the evening and bedtime to be somewhere around the crack of dawn. Rue de la Harpe is just off place St-Michel, the 24-hour, nonstop, pulsating hub of this *quartier.* The street itself is lined with restaurants and cafés geared to tourists out for a good time. So, I must warn you, while this hotel has a good location and is nice, it *is* going to be very noisy unless you use heavy-duty earplugs and sleep with the double-glazed windows tightly shut. Good closet space and new bathrooms complement renovated rooms with quilted bedspreads, salmon-colored walls, and green carpets. The bright modern breakfast room faces the street and has relaxing classical music playing while you are enjoying a morning croissant and *café au lait.*

English Spoken: Yes

Facilities and Services: Bar; direct-dial phone; hair dryer; elevator; TV; room safe, no charge

TELEPHONE
46-34-09-70

FAX
40-46-85-70

MÉTRO
St-Michel

CREDIT CARDS
MC, V

RATES
Single 525F, double 600F, triple 700F, quad 750F

BREAKFAST
40F extra per person

Nearest Tourist Attractions (Left Bank): Notre-Dame, Île de la Cité, Île St-Louis, St-Michel, Latin Quarter

HÔTEL DES ALLIES ★
20, rue Berthollet, 75005 (5th)
43 rooms, 10 with shower or bath and toilet

TELEPHONE
43-31-47-52
FAX
45-35-13-92
MÉTRO
Censier-Daubenton
CREDIT CARDS
MC, V
RATES
Single 150–160F, double 200–330F, triple 265–420F; shower 15F (bath towel, if using public shower, 4F)
BREAKFAST
35F extra per person

Three generations of contented clientele continue to reserve rooms in this pristine Cheap Sleep at the bottom of the fifth arrondissement. The location is not central by any means, but it is within walking distance to all the action and color around rue Mouffetard. It is obvious that money has not been spent on fancy decorating touches, but all the rooms are spotless, with no rips, tears, or dents in sight. The best part is that the rooms come with price tags no serious Cheap Sleeper in Paris can ignore. Room no. 22 is a steal, with a huge bathroom, twin beds, and nice wallpaper. No. 3 on the back, with only a basin and bidet, rents for under $60, and that is a price seldom seen in any acceptable hotel in Paris today. Another winner is no. 15, a large, streetside twin with a closet rivaling most found in better three-star hotels.

English Spoken: Yes

Facilities and Services: No elevator or TV; safe in office, no charge

Nearest Tourist Attractions (Left Bank): Rue Mouffetard

HÔTEL DES GRANDES ÉCOLES ★★
75, rue du Cardinal-Lemoine, 75005 (5th)
48 rooms, 39 with shower or bath and toilet

TELEPHONE
43-26-79-23
FAX
43-25-28-15
MÉTRO
Cardinal-Lemoine, Monge
CREDIT CARDS
MC, V
RATES
Single 300–450F, double 345–625F, triple (without toilet) 490F, quad 675F; extra bed 100F
BREAKFAST
45F extra per person

Once found, this hotel address is one that its loyal followers whisper only to a select few. Nestled in a beautiful garden and hidden from the world behind towering wooden doors opening off the street, it is definitely one of the most romantic havens of peace and quiet in Paris. The grandmotherly owner, Leonore LeFloch, and her receptionist, Marie, treat their guests like family members. As you can imagine, reservations for this very special hotel are essential months in advance.

Two facing houses make up the hotel: one is renovated and one is not. In both, the rooms are decorated with a feminine touch, sparing no ruffle or pretty flowered fabric from the Laura Ashley school of decorating. Unless you are on a bare-bones budget, reserve in the renovated building. The plumbing in the other is just too antique for most Americans. Almost all of the rooms in both buildings look out onto the large tree-shaded garden with trellised roses, singing birds, spring daffodils, and summer wildflowers. Tables and chairs are placed here, making it a lovely spot for reading and sipping a cool drink. When you look out of your window, you will imagine you are in a French country village, not in the middle of Paris.

The hotel is an uphill climb from the Métro, but once there you are close to the place de la Contrescarpe, which played such an important part in Hemingway's Paris. You can also walk to rue Mouffetard, famous for its colorful, daily street *marché,* some good places to eat (see *Cheap Eats in Paris*), and inexpensive clothing stores, geared to cute young things.

English Spoken: Yes

Facilities and Services: Direct-dial phone; hair dryer in renovated building; elevator in renovated building; office safe, no charge; no TV

Nearest Tourist Attractions (Left Bank): Rue Mouffetard, place de Contrescarpe, Panthéon, Latin Quarter

HÔTEL DES GRANDS HOMMES ★★★

17, place du Panthéon, 75005 (5th)

32 rooms, all with shower or bath and toilet

The Hôtel des Grands Hommes is one of the most stylish three-star hotels in Paris, thanks to the personal management of Corinne Brethous, who is young, energetic, and full of wonderful ideas. In restoring the 18th-century building, she spared no effort to create a personal and comfortable hotel, done with great taste and style. The engaging bedrooms heighten the feeling that one is a guest in a lovely Parisian home rather than in an anonymous hotel room. When reserving, request one of the front rooms with a balcony, where you can have breakfast and gaze onto the Panthéon across the street and see Sacré Coeur gleaming in the distance. Honeymooners will want to stay in no. 22, with a canopied brass bed and two view balconies, or in no. 32, with a white metal and brass bed, and a lovely marble bathroom filled with pink towels. The gracious formal lobby is decorated in peach colors with faux marble finishes and outfitted with plenty of soft seating, a small corner bar, and an atrium garden filled with blooming plants.

TELEPHONE
46-34-19-60

FAX
43-26-67-32

MÉTRO
St-Michel, RER Luxembourg

CREDIT CARDS
AE, DC, MC, V

RATES
Single 675–685F, double 725–775F, triple 875F; extra bed 100F

BREAKFAST
40F extra per person

English Spoken: Yes

Facilities and Services: Bar; direct-dial phone; hair dryer; elevator; mini-bar; TV with international reception; safe in office, no charge

Nearest Tourist Attractions (Left Bank): Panthéon, Sorbonne, St-Michel, Jardin du Luxembourg

HÔTEL DES 3 COLLÈGES ★★
16, rue Cujas, 75005 (5th)
44 rooms, all with shower or bath and toilet

TELEPHONE
43-54-67-30
FAX
46-34-02-99
MÉTRO
RER Luxembourg
CREDIT CARDS
AE, DC, MC, V
RATES
Single 375–625F, double 475–650F, triple 775F
BREAKFAST
45F extra per person

If you want a modern room with a reasonable price tag in a good Left Bank neighborhood between the Sorbonne and the Panthéon, this is the place to go. The operative word here is *simple.* the small, off-white lobby has a California look, with modern chairs, large green plants, and bleached wooden floors. The pocket-size rooms have all the necessities: luggage racks, desks and chairs, full-length mirrors, wall-mounted television sets, and fitted bathrooms. The glass-roof breakfast room off the lobby showcases a large green tree in the center, with white bistro tables and rattan chairs placed around it. Management and staff are pleasant and helpful in giving directions, making reservations, and confirming flights.

English Spoken: Yes

Facilities and Services: Direct-dial phone; elevator; hair dryer; TV; safe in office, no charge

Nearest Tourist Attractions (Left Bank): Panthéon, Sorbonne, St-Michel

HÔTEL DU COLLÈGE DE FRANCE ★★
7, rue Thénard, 75005 (5th)
29 rooms, all with shower or bath and toilet

TELEPHONE
43-26-78-36
FAX
46-34-58-29
MÉTRO
Maubert-Mutualité, St-Michel, Cluny-Sorbonne
CREDIT CARDS
AE
RATES
1–2 persons 500–550F; extra bed 100F
BREAKFAST
35F extra per person

Well placed in the heart of the Latin Quarter and across the street from the Collège de France, this is an outstanding value for a two-star hotel. The owner, M. Georges, is on hand daily to ensure that all runs smoothly. The rooms are plain, yet uniformly done in a dated beige-and-brown color scheme. The best ones are on the top floors and have wooden beams and paneling, glimpses of Notre-Dame Cathedral, and in summer are equipped with portable fans. All of the rooms are immaculate and soundproofed with double windows. The bathrooms are modern enough, with hair dryers, large towels, and space for more than just a toothbrush. The lobby and breakfast room repeat the upstairs color scheme, with the addition of green plants. The popularity of this little hotel is reflected in its guest register, which is almost filled months ahead, so plan accordingly.

English Spoken: Yes

Facilities and Services: Direct-dial phone; hair dryer; elevator; TV; safe in office, 30F per week

Nearest Tourist Attractions (Left Bank): Latin Quarter, St-Michel, St-Germain-des-Prés, Sorbonne, Panthéon, Luxembourg Gardens, Île de la Cité, Île St-Louis

HÔTEL DU PANTHÉON ★★★

19, place du Panthéon, 75005 (5th)

34 rooms, all with shower or bath and toilet

TELEPHONE
43-54-32-95

FAX
43-26-64-65

MÉTRO
St-Michel, RER Luxembourg

CREDIT CARDS
AE, DC, MC, V

RATES
Single 650–675F, double 775–790F; extra bed 100F

BREAKFAST
40F extra per person

The Hôtel du Panthéon, an elegantly converted town house, faces the imposing place du Panthéon in the fifth arrondissement. The Métro is about five blocks away, but if you love this part of Paris, you know that almost everything is within walking distance.

From the ground up, the hotel benefits from the impeccable taste and preservationist sensibilities of the gracious owner, Corinne Brethous, who also owns Hôtel des Grands Hommes next door (see page 75).

A dramatic entry leads to the attractive lounge, with a corner coffee bar and a small atrium garden to one side. The Continental breakfast is served under the stone arches in the house's original cellar, or in the privacy of your own room. Guests will feel at home immediately in any one of the 34 rooms, decorated with antique furniture, textile-covered walls, and floor-length curtains hanging from 14-foot ceilings. The front rooms facing the Panthéon are naturally in demand, but if you need absolute silence and calm, the viewless back rooms will guarantee this.

English Spoken: Yes

Facilities and Services: Conference room; direct-dial phone; elevator; hair dryer; TV with international reception; safe in office, no charge

Nearest Tourist Attractions (Left Bank): Panthéon, Sorbonne, Latin Quarter, Luxembourg Gardens

HÔTEL ESMERALDA ★

4, rue Saint-Julien-le-Pauvre, 75005 (5th)

19 rooms, 16 with shower or bath and toilet; 4 apartments next door, all with shower or bath and toilet

The Esmeralda is an unconventional hideaway directly across the Seine from Notre-Dame Cathedral. It is

TELEPHONE
43-54-19-20

FAX
40-51-00-68

MÉTRO
St-Michel

CREDIT CARDS
None, cash only

RATES
Very small single 175F, 1–2 persons 350–525F, triple 585F, quad 650F

BREAKFAST
45F extra per person

a hotel people either love or absolutely hate. Maybe it does not have the most modern accommodations in town, but it does have one of the best Left Bank locations and some of the most interesting guests. The lack of embellishments, which might disappoint some, is the lure that brings others back again and again. This is a hotel with character for people with character.

No two rooms are alike, and, just like the charming owner, they flaunt convention and are eccentric to the core. Some are the size of a walk-in closet; others have chandeliers, marble fireplaces, and picture-perfect postcard views of Notre-Dame Cathedral over the gardens of St-Julien-le-Pauvre, Paris's oldest church. All the rooms are reached by passing through a stone-walled lobby (complete with Mona, the house cat, occupying the most comfortable chair) and climbing up a winding flight of ancient stairs. Some of the floors slant, a few areas need more than just a paintbrush and others have only a nodding acquaintance with the housekeeper. It is also *noisy.* But its many cult followers do not care, because just being at the Esmeralda spells Paris for them. Be sure to bring earplugs and reserve way in advance.

Note: Insiders here for longer stays know to ask for one of the four apartments next door. These are, however, not for everyone. Reached via a dark, winding, wooden staircase right out of a Victor Hugo novel, the apartments offer Paris without apologies. Yes, they are *very* old and dusty, and not everything works all the time. But for some, this faded charm with a definite past has a great appeal, especially when sitting by one of the large windows and looking across the Seine to Notre-Dame bathed in moonlight.

English Spoken: Yes

Facilities and Services: Direct-dial phone; no elevator or TV; safe in office, no charge

Nearest Tourist Attractions (Left Bank): Notre-Dame, Île de la Cité, Île St-Louis, St-Michel, St-Germain-des-Prés, Latin Quarter

HÔTEL GAY-LUSSAC ★

29, rue Gay-Lussac, 75005 (5th)

35 rooms, none with private toilets, some with private showers

The sign posted in the reception area reads "Don't put bottles on the windowsill. Silence of one assures rest for us all." You get the idea. This is a no-nonsense Cheap Sleep that allows no funny business.

The 35 rooms vary from not-so-bad to my-goodness-this-*is*-basic. It is no wonder. Nothing much has been done to change the hotel, with the exception of adding an elevator, since the 1960s. But . . . you are on the Left Bank, close to the Luxembourg Gardens and the RER (the suburban transit express train) that will whisk you all over Paris in a wink. The owners and their German shepherd named Donna are nice, breakfast is good, the hall showers are free, and just think of all the money you will save by staying here. You can extend your Paris sojourn by at least a week, and that alone makes sleeping cheap at the Gay-Lussac worthwhile.

English Spoken: Limited

Facilities and Services: Direct-dial phone; elevator; no safe

Nearest Tourist Attractions (Left Bank): Luxembourg Gardens, Panthéon, Latin Quarter

TELEPHONE
43-54-23-96

FAX
None

MÉTRO
RER Luxembourg

CREDIT CARDS
None, cash only

RATES
Single 175F, double 240–475F, triple 345–525F, quad 550F; hall showers free

BREAKFAST
30F extra per person

HÔTEL LE COLBERT ★★★
7, rue de l'Hôtel-Colbert, 75005 (5th)
36 rooms, all with shower or bath and toilet

For a memorable stay in Paris, you simply cannot miss at this hotel. The location is fantastic. Built around a courtyard on a tranquil, almost traffic-free street, the centuries-old town house is one minute from the Seine and two from Notre-Dame. It is the perfect address for anyone who likes to wander through the winding streets around St-Michel and be within easy walking distance of many wonderful restaurants (see *Cheap Eats in Paris*).

Polished professionalism and good old-fashioned service underscore Le Colbert's many assets, making it one of the most sought-after small hotels in Paris. The rooms and suites are models of space and uncluttered decor, with slipper-style comfort and refined good taste. Windows in eight of the rooms frame Notre-Dame Cathedral; others look over the peaked rooftops of this ancient part of Paris; and some overlook the courtyard entrance. A favorite of mine is no. 17. Even though it is on the first floor and looks onto the courtyard, I like it for its space, beige and green colors, and wonderful corner marble bathroom with a huge tub and good shower. For more space and a Notre-Dame view, the suite or apartment makes an excellent choice. All of this does not come at bargain prices, but as anyone who has ever stayed at Le Colbert will tell you, it is well worth the extra francs for the Big Splurge.

TELEPHONE
43-25-85-65

FAX
43-25-80-19

MÉTRO
Maubert-Mutualité, St-Michel

CREDIT CARDS
AE, MC, V

RATES
Single 900F, double 1,000F, suite or apartment 1,700–2,000F

BREAKFAST
55F extra per person

English Spoken: Yes

Facilities and Services: Bar; direct-dial phone; hair dryer in most bathrooms; elevator; mini-bar; TV with international reception; safe in room, no charge

Nearest Tourist Attractions (Left Bank): St-Michel, St-Germain-des-Prés, Latin Quarter, Notre-Dame Cathedral, Île de la Cité, Île St-Louis

HÔTEL MARIGNAN ★

13, rue de Sommerard, 75005 (5th)

30 rooms, none with shower or bath and toilet

TELEPHONE
43-54-63-81

FAX
None

MÉTRO
Maubert-Mutualité

CREDIT CARDS
None, cash only

RATES
Single 190F, double 300F, triple 385F, quad 450F

BREAKFAST
Included, cannot be deducted

The Marignan lives up to the three Cs of all Cheap Sleepers: it is clean, convenient, and cheap, especially in November and December, when rooms for two, three, or four people are 15 percent less than the published prices. The hotel is usually jammed year-round with a frugal crowd of students, backpackers, and professors. A spirit of camaraderie prevails in this busy spot, making it impossible to feel lonely for long. To their credit, long-term owners/managers Paul and Linda Keniger have provided guests with a wealth of information on Paris, including a large detailed map of the *quartier* showing the Métro stops, banks, pharmacies, money-changing offices, bakeries, and tourist sites. The management also clearly states the rules of the hotel, and guests are expected to abide by them or move out. They are listed in plain sight at the check-in desk, so no one can claim "I didn't know" not to put my suitcase on the bed; leave empty bottles or cans in the room; turn off the light when leaving; and never go barefoot in public areas or on the stairs. Reservations are not taken for singles between March and September, and during this time are taken for two only for a stay of two nights or more. All reservations are payable in advance and no refunds are made if cancellation is less than one week before arrival. Last but not least in the rule department is the management's parsimonious breakfast philosophy. I quote Mr. Keniger: "If we give more, it encourages people to stay and eat, and then we won't have room to feed other guests." Since the breakfast (which is generous by one-star standards—it includes cheese along with bread and jam, but no croissant) is included in the rate and cannot be deducted, guests are stuck with an attitude that must reflect hard times for the owners.

English Spoken: Yes

Facilities and Services: Basement laundry and ironing area (no room laundry allowed); dining area where guests can eat food they bring in; no elevator or TV; safe in office, no charge

Nearest Tourist Attractions (Left Bank): Cluny Museum, Latin Quarter, St-Michel, St-Germain-des-Prés, Île de la Cité, Île St-Louis

HÔTEL PARC SAINT-SÉVERIN ★★★

22, rue de la Parcheminerie, 75005 (5th)

27 rooms, all with shower or bath and toilet

Dyed-in-the-wool aficionados of life around St-Michel, who also like elegantly understated surroundings, will love this hotel. The owners are to be applauded for turning a run-down building into an alluring, modern establishment that is serene, serious, and pleasing to the eye. Instead of the usual large bouquets of flowers in the lobby and reception area, there might be one perfect branch of orchids displayed against a cool gray wall. Abstract paintings complement the sleek, light charcoal breakfast furniture. For someone very, very special, reserve no. 70, the private penthouse suite with its own elevator entrance. The wraparound terrace provides unequaled views of Notre-Dame, St-Séverin Church (which is one of the most popular in Paris for weddings), the Panthéon, Collège de France, Tour Montparnasse, and, in the distance, the Eiffel Tower and the Sacré Coeur on Montmartre. The interior of this dream suite glows with a blend of antiques and contemporary furnishings. The other rooms in the hotel display the same standards of excellence, and many have impressive views. For those who want up-to-the-minute convenience and luxury in the heart of old Paris, the Parc Saint-Séverin is justifiably higher priced.

Note: For other hotels under the same ownership, see Hôtel de la Place du Louvre, page 42, and Hôtel Mansart, page 45.

English Spoken: Yes

Facilities and Services: Direct-dial phone; hair dryer; elevator; mini-bar; TV with international reception; room safe, no charge

Nearest Tourist Attractions (Left Bank): St-Michel, Latin Quarter, Cluny Museum, St-Germain-des-Prés, Île de la Cité, Île St-Louis

TELEPHONE
43-54-32-17

FAX
43-54-70-71

MÉTRO
St-Michel

CREDIT CARDS
AE, MC, V

RATES
Single 525–880F, double 610–1,100F, suite 1,100–1,700F

BREAKFAST
50F extra per person

HÔTEL RÉSIDENCE HENRI IV ★★★

50, rue des Bernardins, 75005 (5th)

14 rooms, all with shower or bath and toilet and fully fitted kitchenette

TELEPHONE 44-41-31-81
FAX 46-33-93-22
MÉTRO Maubert Mutualité
CREDIT CARDS AE, MC, V
RATES 1–2 persons 950–1,300F
BREAKFAST 45F extra per person

Twelve years ago, when I began writing *Cheap Sleeps in Paris,* this hotel had another name and an image of faded respectability. Recently it was taken over by Corinne Brethous, who owns Hôtel des Grands Hommes and Hôtel du Panthéon (see pages 75 and 77). Whatever Mme. Brethous touches speaks of style and distinction, and her latest renovated endeavor is certainly no exception. Quietly situated opposite the leafy square Paul l'Angevin, at the end of rue des Bernardins, the hotel offers 14 serenely beautiful rooms with the added plus of fully fitted kitchenettes, as well as all the hotel services and facilities a guest could want. I think the best buys are the beautiful two-room suites done in soft yellow, blue, green, or ochre. These offer separate sitting areas, marble fireplaces, and just enough extra space to make a long stay very comfortable. No. 22, in blue, has a magnificent gold-framed mirror over its fireplace. Hand-painted moldings and the original ceiling are carried through to the bedroom, which has a large armoire and a corner fireplace to add to its charm. The hotel is peaceful and calm, yet it is minutes away from almost everything on a visitor's A-list of things to see and do in the Latin Quarter and St-Germain-des-Prés.

English Spoken: Yes

Facilities and Services: Two air-conditioned rooms; direct-dial phone; hair dryer; elevator; TV with international reception; safe in room, no charge

Nearest Tourist Attractions (Left Bank): Latin Quarter, St-Michel, St-Germain-des-Prés, Île de la Cité, Île St-Louis, Cluny Museum

HÔTEL RÉSIDENCE SAINT-CHRISTOPHE ★★★

17, rue Lacépède, 75005 (5th)

31 rooms, all with shower or bath and toilet

TELEPHONE 43-31-81-54
FAX 43-31-12-54
MÉTRO Monge
CREDIT CARDS AE, DC, MC, V
RATES 1–2 persons 675F

At the Résidence Saint-Christophe, you can expect small, compact rooms, with orange tufted bedspreads, a desk, two upholstered chairs, and good luggage and closet space. The rooms also have nice bathrooms and no back views onto blank walls. Skillfully run by Michele Verrechia, the hotel is located near rue Mouffetard, famous for its animated outdoor market, and place Monge, where a jewel of a Sunday market is held. Lower rates in July and August and the friendliness of management and staff more than make up for the location, which is slightly south of Tourist Central.

English Spoken: Yes

Facilities and Services: Direct-dial phone; hair dryer; elevator; mini-bar; radio and TV with international reception; safe in office, no charge

Nearest Tourist Attractions (Left Bank): Rue Mouffetard, Jardin des Plantes

BREAKFAST
45F extra per person

LE JARDIN DE CLUNY ★★★
9, rue du Sommerard, 75005 (5th)
40 rooms, all with shower or bath and toilet

Occupying a key Left Bank location between boulevard St-Michel and boulevard St-Germain, the Jardin de Cluny is close to all the fun, glamour, and bright lights this animated *quartier* offers. The uniformly designed rooms, with black wicker furnishings and a soothing oriental theme, are larger than most others in the neighborhood. I like no. 601, a combination bedroom and sitting room with large closets and a view of the spires of Notre-Dame, or the large top-floor family suite that boasts a view of the cathedral from the bathroom. Breakfast is served on Villeroy and Bosch china in a stone-walled dining room. Nicely upholstered chairs arranged around large, lighted tables make this a pleasant place to start the day with a Continental breakfast or just a glass of orange juice.

English Spoken: Yes

Facilities and Services: Air-conditioning in some rooms; bar; direct-dial phone; hair dryer; elevator; mini-bar; TV with international reception; videos; safe in room, no charge

Nearest Tourist Attractions (Left Bank): Latin Quarter, St-Michel, St-Germain-des-Prés, Cluny Museum, Île de la Cité, Île St-Louis

TELEPHONE
40-54-22-66; toll-free from U.S. and Canada 1-800-528-1234

FAX
40-51-03-36

MÉTRO
Maubert-Mutualité

CREDIT CARDS
AE, DC, MC, V

RATES
Single 610–675F, double 675–775F, suite 1,100F

BREAKFAST
45F extra per person

LE NOTRE-DAME HÔTEL ★★★
1, quai St-Michel, 75005 (5th)
26 rooms, all with shower or bath and toilet

Refashioned with verve several years ago, this excellent hotel offers 26 beautiful rooms to lovers of Notre-Dame Cathedral's architectural beauty. Ask for a room facing the street and you will be able to look out across the *bouquinistes* (second-hand booksellers) lining the *quais* along the Seine and onto the great western facade of the famed cathedral. You will go to sleep and wake with the

TELEPHONE
43-54-20-43

FAX
43-26-61-75

MÉTRO
St-Michel

CREDIT CARDS
AE, DC, MC, V

RATES
Single 550F (no view), 760F (view); double 650F (no view), 870F (view); duplex 1,250F (view)

BREAKFAST
45F extra per person

sights and sounds of Paris, but the majestic view will be worth it.

Entrance to the hotel is through a mirrored ground-floor hall and up a short flight of steps. The inviting sitting room of the reception area has picture windows facing the cathedral and soft barrel armchairs. It is a relaxing place to be, especially on a cool day, sitting by the open fire, sipping a drink, and watching *toute* Paris surge by. The rooms display a smart mixture of antiques and reproductions, and they are comfortable if small. My favorites are nos. 22 and 32, corner rooms with two windows overlooking Notre-Dame. Another nice selection is the suite, but for some the ladder stairs to the sitting area could be difficult to maneuver. Management overlooks nothing, and quality service is provided for each guest.

English Spoken: Yes

Facilities and Services: Bar; direct-dial phone; elevator; hair dryer; mini-bar; TV; street parking is almost impossible, you must use a parking garage; safe in office, no charge

Nearest Tourist Attractions (Left Bank): Notre-Dame, Île de la Cité, Île St-Louis, Seine, St-Michel, St-Germain-des-Prés

PORT-ROYAL HÔTEL ★

8, boulevard Port-Royal, 75005 (5th)

48 rooms, 16 with shower or bath and toilet

TELEPHONE
43-31-70-06
Reservations accepted by phone 7 A.M.–7 P.M. only

FAX
None

MÉTRO
Gobelins

CREDIT CARDS
None, cash only

RATES
Single 145–275F, double 185–275F, triple 325F; shower 15F

BREAKFAST
25F extra per person

Cheap Sleepers looking for maximum value without sacrificing quality of surroundings or services will find the Port-Royal Hôtel impossible to beat. In fact, it is so far ahead of most other one-star hotels in Paris (and many two- and three-star hotels for that matter) that there simply is no contest. I will admit that I had my doubts at first, as I trudged along the long boulevard de Port-Royal in a driving rainstorm looking for the hotel. Once inside, however, I forgot all about feeling banished to the boonies by the location and found the hotel to be nothing short of amazing. It is obvious that the Giraud family, who has owned the hotel for more than 65 years, is paying close attention to every detail. On top of being an absolute steal for the money, it is spotless and exceptionally well decorated. The usual one-star dimestore taste displayed in dusty plastic floral arrangements, mismatched colors, and exhausted, sagging furniture is nowhere in sight. Instead, everything is in perfect order, from the red-carpeted stairs and hallways to the well-coordinated rooms, many with new wallpaper and carpeting. Those on the front have double-paned windows to let you sleep peacefully. Even the showers have doors, a rare find in Paris and almost a curiosity in one-star hotels. Those selecting the smallest rooms need not feel like Cinderella after midnight. These rooms have all the nice touches of their more expensive neighbors, including a piece of candy on the pillow at night. The inviting streetside sitting room, with its comfortable chairs, bubbling aquarium, and lacy curtains, belies the hotel's budget category. So does the breakfast room, overlooking a neatly manicured interior garden. Real flowers, caned chairs with upholstered seats, and an interesting collection of woodworking tools displayed on the walls add to the appeal.

The hotel is easily accessible to St-Michel, the Louvre, Musée d'Orsay, and the Champs-Elysées by bus. It connects to Orly by direct bus from the Métro stop. Close by is a huge shopping complex with 150 boutiques and a branch of Au Printemps department store. Also near are cinemas, a selection of restaurants and cafés (see *Cheap Eats in Paris*) and public parking. All in all it adds up to one of the best Cheap Sleeps in Paris.

English Spoken: Enough

Facilities and Services: No elevator; TV in sitting room; safe in office, no charge

Nearest Tourist Attractions (Left Bank): Gobelins Museum (tapestries), rue Mouffetard, Jardin des Plantes

SELECT HÔTEL ★★★
1, place de la Sorbonne, 75005 (5th)
69 rooms, all with shower or bath and toilet

In 1937 Eric Sevareid paid 50¢ a night at the Select. Things have changed . . . considerably.

Dramatically renovated in late 1987, the hotel now has one of the most spectacular interior garden courts in Paris, complete with blooming tropical plants, a waterfall, and singing birds. The lobby and newly redone reception area are studies in ultramodern design, with chrome and black leather furniture highlighted by posters of Paris. This sleek approach is carried into the intimate bar, breakfast room, and seating alcoves tucked around the skylit garden.

The rooms have as much appeal as the public areas, especially those overlooking the garden court or the

TELEPHONE
46-34-14-80

FAX
46-34-51-79

MÉTRO
St-Michel, RER Luxembourg

CREDIT CARDS
AE, DC, MC, V

RATES
Single 590F, double 700–800F, triple 980F, duplex 1,350F

BREAKFAST
Included, cannot be deducted. Larger than average Continental breakfast is served.

place de la Sorbonne in front. Those at the back have all the perks but are also dark and viewless. All the rooms skillfully combine the best of the old with the practicality and convenience of the new. Two of the nicest are nos. 33 and 53, which display the original stone wall of the hotel and centuries-old oak beams. Two large floor-to-ceiling windows open onto the *place* below. Comfortable armchairs, good reading lights, a large working desk, hidden storage space, and a split bathroom make these favorites for longer stays. An ideal Latin Quarter location and all these creature comforts make the Select Hôtel a front-runner in the *quartier.* Unfortunately, it will cost more than 50¢ a night.

English Spoken: Yes

Facilities and Services: Air-conditioning in some rooms; bar with light snacks; conference room; direct-dial phone; hair dryer; elevator; radio; TV with international reception; safe in office, no charge

Nearest Tourist Attractions (Left Bank): Latin Quarter, Sorbonne, St-Germain-des-Prés, Île de la Cité, Île St-Louis

Sixth Arrondissement

(See map, pages 68–69.)

Literary and artistic Paris *is* the sixth . . . a continuation of the Latin Quarter and one of the most stimulating parts of the city. Intellectual, elegant, and very appealing, it has tiny side streets, old buildings, antique shops, a thriving café life, and more atmosphere block-for-block than anyone could ever soak up. The square by the St-Germain Church is the main focus of the district. Aux Deux Magots and Café de Flore, the two most celebrated cafés in Paris, were the hangouts of Hemingway, Sartre, Simone de Beauvoir, and James Joyce. Today they are jammed with Parisians and tourists alike engaged in some of the best people-watching in the universe.

LEFT BANK
École des Beau-Arts, Luxembourg Gardens, Odéon National Theater, St-Germain-des-Prés Church, St-Sulpice Church

HOTELS IN THE SIXTH ARRONDISSEMENT

DHELY'S HÔTEL ★
22, rue de l'Hirondelle, 75006 (6th)
21 rooms, none with toilet or bathtub, 7 with shower

TELEPHONE 43-26-58-25
FAX None
MÉTRO St-Michel
CREDIT CARDS AE, DC, MC, V
RATES Single 150–370F, double 250–370F, triple 300–450F
BREAKFAST 35F extra per person

For the quintessential budget hotel, steps from the Seine and place St-Michel, look no farther than Dhely's. Many Left Bank hotels in this neighborhood are severely lacking in housekeeping, but not this one. Everything is shipshape, from the hall toilets and showers to the rooms, most of which have pretty floral wallpaper and window boxes with real flowers. The larger rooms have carpeting; the smaller ones have linoleum floors. Of course, the higher you climb, the better it gets in price and view. While the hotel *is* basic, it does have some redeeming architectural details such as the original 16th-century tiled entry way, open beams, and exposed stone walls. The hotel has been owned for 15 years by Mme. Kenneche, who also operates a seven day a week couscous restaurant in the fifth arrondissement that specializes in both take-out and delivery of this popular Middle Eastern food.

English Spoken: Some

Facilities and Services: Direct-dial phone; TV in the planning stage; safe in office, no charge; no elevator

Nearest Tourist Attractions (Left Bank): St-Michel, Île de la Cité, Île St-Louis, St-Germain-des-Prés

GRAND HÔTEL DES BALCONS ★★
3, rue Casimir-Delavigne, 75006 (6th)
55 rooms, all with shower or bath and toilet

TELEPHONE 46-34-78-50
FAX 46-34-06-27
MÉTRO Odéon
CREDIT CARDS MC, V

The Grand Hôtel des Balcons is one of the most dignified low-budget hotels in this part of the Left Bank and a perennial favorite with older, cost-conscious budgeteers.

The impressive lobby is a masterpiece of Art Nouveau design, with glorious stained-glass windows and masterfully turned wood. There are always beautiful fresh flower displays, arranged by the manager's wife, who is a recognized ikebana expert. Uniformed maids are relentless in keeping everything dust-free. Some of the rooms are beginning to unravel a bit and show their age, but to management's credit, most have recently been redecorated with nice wallpaper and good reading lights. Vintage baths tend to be small, but are spotless. The location is tops, close to loads of budget restaurants (see *Cheap Eats in Paris*) and near place de l'Odéon, boulevard St-Michel, St-Germain-des-Prés, and one of the city's most popular parks, the Jardin du Luxembourg.

English Spoken: Yes

Facilities and Services: Direct-dial phone; elevator; radio; TV; office safe, no charge

Nearest Tourist Attractions (Left Bank): St-Germain-dés-Pres, St-Michel, Luxembourg Gardens, Île de la Cité, Île St-Louis

RATES
1–2 persons 325–470F, triple 550F

BREAKFAST
45F extra per person

HÔTEL AVIATIC ★★★

105, rue de Vaugirard, 75006 (6th)

43 rooms, all with shower or bath and toilet

The hotel is named after the aviators who came here to have drinks around the turn of the century. Today the Art Deco glass and the black wrought-iron awning over the door—flanked by two brass and copper lamps—set the welcoming stage for this warm and inviting family-run hotel. The lobby has faux marble columns and small groupings of velvet chairs and antique marble chests topped with bouquets of fresh flowers. To one side is the breakfast room, papered with vintage Parisian art posters. A wide, winding stairway with overhead skylights leads guests up to forest green–carpeted hallways and the 43 rooms in two buildings. There is more than just a touch of class in these well-thought-out chambers, which all have built-in luggage racks, good space to spread out, armchair seating, and ample closets. The rooms in the front building are bright and airy, with pretty views of the surrounding Montparnasse neighborhood. Those in the back are sunny, but they don't have much of a view.

English Spoken: Yes

Facilities and Services: Bar; direct-dial phone; hair dryer; elevator; mini-bar; parking, 90F per day; TV with international reception; office safe, no charge

Nearest Tourist Attractions (Left Bank): Montparnasse

TELEPHONE
45-44-38-21; toll-free in the U.S. 1-800-845-6636

FAX
45-49-35-83

MÉTRO
Falguière, St-Placide, Montparnasse; also 10 bus lines at Montparnasse

CREDIT CARDS
AE, DC, MC, V

RATES
Single 650F, double 800F, triple 950F

BREAKFAST
Included, cannot be deducted

HÔTEL BUCI LATIN ★★★
34, rue de Buci, 75006 (6th)
27 rooms, all with shower or bath and toilet

TELEPHONE
43-29-07-20
FAX
43-29-67-44
MÉTRO
St-Germain-des-Prés
CREDIT CARDS
AE, DC, MC, V
RATES
1–2 persons 850–1,100F, duplex 1,500F, junior suite 1,600F
BREAKFAST
Included, cannot be deducted

Down the street from the picturesque Buci street *marché* is the new Hôtel Buci Latin. To say the hotel is different is the understatement of the year. Owners Ronald MacLeod and Laurence Raymond have mixed an aggressively imaginative interior with an old-period French building, and the results are nothing short of spectacular. The entrance immediately tells you that this is a hotel where creativity and pure whimsy have been raised to new levels. A wooden-planked walkway leads guests to the reception desk where three clocks display local time. To one side is a full-size race car, painted and polished within an inch of its life. Photos of all 27 guest-room doors, which were crafted and hand painted by nine local artists, hang in the lobby. You will have to see them . . . they defy description. If you take the elevator to your room, you will miss the graffiti-covered stairway, authentically done by a knowledgeable New York artist. The rooms are simple, yet extremely well planned. Orange walls offset crisp white duvet covers on electric beds with built-in headboards hiding closets. Long blond wall desks with halogen lights and a fabric-draped chair complement open-slat wooden armoires. What rooms are best? They are all recommendable, but no. 162, a top-floor junior suite with a circular Jacuzzi bath and a balcony with two chaise lounges wins by a nose. A close second is no. 140, a duplex with a huge upstairs bathroom housing skylight views of St-Germain Church, an old-fashioned bathtub on claw feet (and a modern stall shower for diehards), a beautiful antique sink, and an adobe-tiled floor with an Indian rug under a marvelous wicker *coiffeuse* (dressing table).

We are not through yet! The downstairs coffee shop is no less unusual, with its row of theater seats and chairs covered in pink, turquoise, and purple velvet. A collection of vegetable graters decorates a steamer trunk that doubles as a buffet displaying teatime pastries. A mirror made from beer caps set in cement, a collection of ceramic whiskey bottles, and a fish pond round out the experience.

Even if you do not stay here, please stop by for a look. The coffee shop is open for Sunday and holiday brunch and Tuesday through Sunday for afternoon tea and light meals. (Tuesday–Sunday from noon–6:30 P.M. with continuous service. Closed in August and on Mondays. All credit cards accepted.)

English Spoken: Yes

Facilities and Services: Air-conditioning in some rooms; bar; direct-dial phone; elevator; mini-bar; radio; TV with French cable; safe in office, no charge

Nearest Tourist Attractions (Left Bank): St-Germain-des-Prés, St-Michel, Île de la Cité, Île St-Louis

HÔTEL DANEMARK ★★★
21, rue Vavin, 75006 (6th)
15 rooms, all with shower or bath and toilet

TELEPHONE
43-26-93-78

FAX
46-34-66-06

MÉTRO
Vavin, Notre-Dame-des-Champs

CREDIT CARDS
AE, DC, MC, V

RATES
Single 625F, double 650–750F

BREAKFAST
45F extra per person

For the Nurit family, nothing seems to be too much trouble in pleasing their guests. They have a special fondness for Americans, many of whom have been repeat guests for years, even before the hotel was what it is today. The Nurits are proud of their 15-room hotel in Montparnasse, and they should be. It is an imaginative lesson in how to take an old student-style hotel and turn it into an eye-catching spot on the cutting edge of hotel chic.

Cool blues and grays dominate the downstairs color scheme, with artist-inspired furnishings that look like exhibits from the Museum of Modern Art in New York. The walls are dotted with a collection of dramatic posters of Parisian landmarks and famous race cars, along with a collection of bold paintings done by an architect friend of the family. The rooms, done in soft yellows, green, lavender, or cocoa brown, are constantly being upgraded. While compact, everything is provided for a comfortable stay. All rooms have their own Italian marble bathroom with heated towel racks, good make-up lighting, and, in a few, a Jacuzzi. The rooms from the third floor up have no interior views. Those on the front face a pretty, white-brick apartment building with terrace gardens, and those on the top floor are under sloping, beamed ceilings with skylights.

English Spoken: Yes

Facilities and Services: Direct-dial phone; hair dryer; elevator; some Jacuzzis; mini-bar; TV with international reception; office safe, no charge

Nearest Tourist Attractions (Left Bank): Montparnasse

HÔTEL D'ANGLETERRE ★★★

44, rue Jacob, 75006 (6th)

25 rooms, all with shower or bath and toilet

TELEPHONE
42-60-34-72

FAX
42-60-16-93

MÉTRO
St-Germain-des-Prés

CREDIT CARDS
AE, DC, MC, V

RATES
Single 650F, double 825–1,000F, suite 1,100–1,200F; extra person in suite 275F

BREAKFAST
50F extra per person

Benjamin Franklin refused to enter this building to sign the Treaty of Paris because it was the British Embassy and considered British soil. Ernest Hemingway had no qualms about it when he occupied room no. 14, describing it to his friends as "good and cheap." Today the Angleterre is no longer "cheap," but a declared national monument and a well-known classic hotel with a long list of guests clamoring to get in. Its only flaw continues to be the *very* frosty attitude of the desk staff. If they are not replaced soon, they could be a threat to the continued success of the hotel.

With the exception of no. 24, which needs redecorating, the traditional rooms and suites are all different and perfectly appointed, with high ceilings, exposed beams, large beds, exceptional closet space, and fabulous double-sink bathrooms. The lobby offers a bar and an intimate piano lounge. A plant-filled interior patio is a lovely spot to spend an hour or two in the afternoon, after a morning of browsing through all the interesting shops in the neighborhood. Breakfast is served in a sunny dining room with well-spaced tables and good lighting for reading the morning papers. The rates are on the high side, but the hotel is included for those seeking a distinguished location in one of the most popular tourist *quartiers* in Paris. When reserving, be sure to specify either a standard or a deluxe room or a suite (only two of which are serviced by an elevator), and get written confirmation. While the accommodations are all lovely, the standard rooms probably will be too small for two people with bulky luggage.

English Spoken: Yes

Facilities and Services: Bar; direct-dial phone; two rooms with Jacuzzi; elevator to most floors; TV with international reception; room safe, no charge

Nearest Tourist Attractions (Left Bank): Superb shopping and browsing, St-Germain-des-Prés, St-Michel, Île de la Cité, Île St-Louis

HÔTEL DE FLEURIE ★★★

32–34, rue Grégoire-de-Tours, 75006 (6th)

29 rooms, all with shower or bath and toilet

If you enjoy the colorful, round-the-clock atmosphere of St-Germain-des-Prés, then the dynamic Hôtel de

All the items are attractively packaged and make excellent gifts.

Hédiard
8th arr. - 21, pl. de la Madeleine
42 66 44 36
Hours vary from store to store. 5 other branches.

Only the finest, rarest foodstuffs are deemed worthy of entry into this shrine of epicureanism. Distinguished smoked salmon from the best "schools," sophisticated sugars and syrups, select vintage wines, ports and brandies, and over 4,500 carefully chosen grocery items attract virtually every cultivated palate in town. Even the ordinary is extraordinary here: mustard spiked with Cognac; vinegar flavored with seaweed; opulent fruits and vegetables, always prime, that hail from the ends of the Earth. Many of the items are as costly as they are exotic, but the wines consistently offer excellent value for the money.

Petit Quenault–Les Vieux Vins de France
1st arr. - 56, rue Jean-Jacques-Rousseau
42 33 46 85
Open 9 a.m.-12:30 p.m. & 2 p.m.-7 p.m. (Sat. 9 a.m.-noon & 3 p.m.-7 p.m.). Closed Sun. & Mon. morning.

Connoisseurs come here to store up on supplies of excellent canned and bottled vegetables, fruits, dried mushrooms (morels, girolles, cèpes) and other fine groceries. From ketchup to spices to baking needs (vanilla, chocolate, candied fruit), Petit Quenault has it, along with a fine range of quality kitchen staples, excellent Parma ham and, come Christmastime, smoked salmon. Prices tend to be well below standard retail; the wine department in particular offers some terrific bargains.

CAVIAR & SALMON

Caviar Kaspia
8th arr. - 17, pl. de la Madeleine
42 65 33 52
Open 9 a.m.-1 a.m. Closed Sun. Parking: Madeleine.

Caviar, it would seem, is best savored in a setting of serene austerity. Such is the impression made by the stark interior of Caviar Kaspia, where the choicest Russian and Iranian roes are sold (beluga for 6,900 francs per kilo), along with an assortment of superb smoked fish. The salmon is flawless, but we come for the fine smoked eel, trout or sturgeon, all of which are models of their kind. Should a hunger pang occur at the sight of these delights (how could it not?), just step upstairs to the first-floor restaurant, where all the house specialties may be ordered à la carte.

Le Coin du Caviar
4th arr. - 2, rue de la Bastille
48 04 82 93
Open 10 a.m.-midnight. Closed Sun. Parking: pl. de la Bastille.

No doubt about it, the neighborhood around the Bastille has become madly fashionable. The Coin du Caviar, right in the thick of things (across the street from the popular Bofinger brasserie), has made faithful customers out of the most finicky caviar and smoked-salmon fanciers. Prime Russian or Iranian caviars are featured (depending on the market); the pale, delicately smoky salmon hails from Denmark.

Comptoir du Saumon
15th arr. - 125, bd de Grenelle
40 56 97 96
Open 10:30 a.m.-1 p.m. & 3:30 p.m.-7:30 p.m. (Sun. 10:30 a.m.-1 p.m.). Closed Mon. & Aug. Parking: Métro La Motte-Picquet. Other branch: 60, rue François-Miron - 4th arr.

The French are crazy about smoked salmon. And it is this untempered enthusiasm that's behind the success of the Comptoir du Saumon, where Irish, Swedish, Norwegian and Scottish fish are sold at exceedingly attractive prices (from 350 to 450 francs for a one- to three-pound side). Also stocked are smoked or dill-marinated halibut, Dutch herring, Danish marinated herring and Iranian caviar.

Flora Danica
8th arr. - 142, av. des Champs-Elysées
43 59 20 41
Open 10 a.m.-10 p.m. (Sun. 11 a.m.-8 p.m.). Parking: Georges-V.

Does the phrase "Danish gastronomy" sound fishy to you? So it should, for salmon in myriad forms is its very foundation. Delicate pink specimens from the Baltic Sea are sold here, both smoked and marinated with dill. We stock a staggering assortment of Oriental food products. Throngs of Asian shoppers come here regularly to purchase their culinary supplies, but the crowds don't seem to faze the calm and amiable staff.

GOURMET SPECIALTIES

Augé

8th arr. - 116, bd Haussmann - 45 22 16 97
Open 8:30 a.m.-12:30 p.m. & 2:30 p.m.-7:30 p.m. (Mon. 2:30 p.m.-7:30 p.m.). Closed Sun.

Augé was one of the first shops in town (maybe the only?) where eccentric gourmets could purchase such rare delicacies as bear steaks, reindeer roasts and elephant trunks. Nowadays this rather luxurious little shop specializes in fine wines and brandies. There is still a small grocery section, which includes excellent canned foods (always handy to have in the cupboard) and an enticing assortment of boxed cookies.

Paul Corcellet

2nd arr. - 46, rue des Petits-Champs
42 96 51 82
Open 9:30 a.m.-7 p.m. (Mon. 11 a.m.-7 p.m.). Closed Sun.

Paul and Bernard Corcellet want to put a little spice in your life. Or, more accurately, they want to spice up your ordinary mustards and vinegars with pink peppercorns or coriander, with tropical fruit or unusual herbs. The tangy chutneys and other exotic condiments that Corcellet has been cooking up since 1760 have no peer in Paris. The firm is known, too, for its canned foods that incorporates wild animals; though that particular line of products seems doomed, given the ever-more-stringent importation regulations. Lion, bear and termite fanciers may have to find new suppliers.

Detou

2nd arr. - 58, rue de Tiquetonne
42 36 54 67
Open 8:30 a.m.-6 p.m. (Sat. until noon). Closed Sun.

Home-bakers browse happily among the pastry supplies that comprise Detou's principal stock-in-trade: baking chocolate, powdered almonds, candied fruit and the like. But there are also rare and delicious jams here, as well as unusual cookies and savory canned goods (the mushrooms are particularly fine), Champagnes and foie gras. Quality merchandise at surprisingly moderate prices.

Faguais

8th arr. - 30, rue La Trémoille
47 20 80 91
Open 9 a.m.-7:30 p.m. Closed Sun.

Yes, Grandmother would feel quite at home in this charming old grocery store. A dizzying variety of gourmet temptations is set out neatly on the shelves. Old-fashioned jams, oils, honeys, cookies, spices and condiments fairly cry out to be bought and sampled. As the shop's pervasive fragrance implies, fresh coffee beans are roasted on the premises daily.

Fauchon

8th arr. - 26, pl. de la Madeleine
47 42 60 11
Open 9:40 a.m.-7 p.m. Closed Sun.

In 1886, at the age of 30, Auguste Fauchon opened his *épicerie fine* on the place de la Madeleine, specializing in quality French foodstuffs. The rest is history. After more than a century, Fauchon is the uncontested paragon of what a gourmet grocery should be. The energetic and youthful president of Fauchon, Martine Premat, has brought a new luster and energy to the firm. All 300 employees are committed to the task of tasting, testing and selling the very finest, the rarest, the most unusual foods in the world. The number of spices alone—4,500—is enough to make your head spin. And you'll find such delicacies as black-fig or watermelon preserves, lavender or buckwheat honey, Mim tea from India or Keeyu tea from China, lavish displays of prime vegetables and fruits, and a world-renowned collection of vintage wines and brandies.

Fouquet

9th arr. - 36, rue Laffitte - 47 70 85 00
Open 9:30 a.m.-6:30 p.m. Closed Sat. & Sun.
Other branch: 22, rue François-Ier - 8th arr.

Christophe Fouquet is the most recent representative of the illustrious family of grocers who have been selling choice foodstuffs at this address since 1852. Fine chocolates are a longstanding specialty at this pretty, old-fashioned shop, but don't overlook the rare mustards (flavored with black currants, oranges or raspberries), appetizing bottled sauces, vinegars distilled according to a secret house recipe, liqueur-laced jams, fruity olive oils, imported cakes and cookies and excellent white brandies.

customers with magic fingers. Treatments are tariffed in the neighborhood of 400 francs.

EPILATION

Ella Bache

2nd arr. - 8, rue de la Paix - 42 61 67 14
Open 10 a.m.-6 p.m. (Sat. 9 a.m.-5 p.m.). Closed Sun. No cards.

Cold wax is Ella Bache's secret weapon against unwanted hair. The treatment starts with a mentholated disinfecting lotion, then waxing and the application of a soothing moisturizing cream. Prices? Legs, 108 francs; bikini line, 64 francs; underarms, 38 francs.

Institut Georges-V

8th arr. - 12, av. Georges-V - 47 23 49 77
Open 9 a.m.-7 p.m. Closed Sat. & Sun. No cards.

Nary an unwanted hair will survive once Antoinette gets through with you. For 23 years she has been removing unwanted hair from heavenly bodies. The salon is unprepossessing (just two rooms on the fifth floor), but the service and products are first-rate. Antoinette swears by a special pale-pink bees' wax, made just for her by an unnamed skilled artisan; and her far-famed technique leaves legs smooth and silky for at least three weeks. By appointment only, from 150 francs.

HAIR SALONS

Patrick Alès

8th arr. - 37, av. Franklin-Roosevelt
43 59 33 96
Open 9 a.m.-6 p.m. (Wed. 10 a.m.-6 p.m.). Closed Sun. & Mon. Parking: Rond-Point des Champs-Elysées. No cards.

Young Patrick Alès is the mind behind the excellent "Phyto" line of hair treatments. Formerly a stylist with Carita, Alès developed the products in his spare time (in his garage, no less) with the help of his friend and collaborator, Olga. She tried each formula on herself, and numbered them according to how many times each had been tested (shampoo S88: 88 trials). Today, Alès continues to come up with new products at his estate in Provence, while Olga runs the Paris salon.

Alexandre

8th arr. - 3, av. Matignon - 42 25 57 90
Open 9:30 a.m.-6:30 p.m. Closed Sun. & Mon. No cards.

Even if it's only once in your life, you really should visit this lovely old art deco salon, where socialites and celebrities have been elegantly coiffed for years and years. Alexandre is so passionate about hair that he has devoted a museum to it! Formal styles for weddings and gala evenings are a specialty.

Atelier Lyne Bertin

1st arr. - 78, rue Jean-Jacques-Rousseau
42 36 04 59
Open 10 a.m.-7 p.m. (Tues. 12:30 p.m.-9:30 p.m.). Closed Sun., Mon. & 3 wks. in Aug. No cards.

Svelte and elegant Lyne Bertin is a sculptor at heart, a hairdresser by avocation. She looks at each head of hair as she would a block of clay to be modeled: the results are beautifully precise hairstyles.

Bruno

6th arr. - 15, rue des Saints-Pères
42 61 45 15
Open 9:30 p.m.-7 p.m. Closed Sun. & Mon. No cards.

Ever since he opened his New York salon, Bruno (the hairstyling hero of many a fashion magazine) hasn't been seen much in Paris. His salon is now overseen by Régis, a charming young man to be sure, but he doesn't always realize that this season's pet cut and styling may not work with every customer's hair, or flatter her face. Some women may only feel secure if they know that their hair is coiffed in the latest fashion; but others among us prefer that the stylist ask our opinion before he starts to snip!

Camille Darmont

16th arr. - 61, rue de la Tour - 45 03 10 99
Open 10 a.m.-7 p.m. (Thurs. 6 p.m.-8 p.m., Sat. 10 a.m.-1 p.m. & 2 p.m.-7 p.m.). Closed Sun. Cards: V.

Camille Darmont, who holds diplomas in dermatology and pharmacy, for many years was the principal assistant of hair guru René Furterer. Now on her own, she is one of the most esteemed hair specialists in Paris. A two-hour treatment in her salon includes a thorough massage of head, neck and shoulders to improve circulation, followed by a mud pack and a hot-towel wrap. The client's individual hair problems are then treated with products formulated by Madame Darmont herself. A session of this serious hair care costs 300 francs for women, 200 francs for men.

Jean-Louis David International

8th arr. - 47, rue Pierre-Charron
43 59 82 08
Open 10 a.m.-7 p.m. (Wed. 11 a.m.-7 p.m.). Closed Sun. Parking: valet. No cards.

Businessman/coiffeur Jean-Louis David has done it again. His most recent venture, on the rue Pierre-Charron, is always swarming with heads eager to wear the latest JLD style. We must say, he is a first-rate manager, and he knows how to keep his customers satisfied, notably with innovative ideas like Quick Service for women in a hurry (dry cut, mousse and gel, you're out in twenty minutes), or the Mistershop (same principle, for men). Jean-Louis David International, the top-of-the-line division, charges 354 francs for a shampoo, cut and style, while the "diffusion" sector, less chic, charges 245 francs for the same services. Star stylists to ask for are Valérie (she specializes in show-biz types) or Maryse, Guy or Laurent for men.

TURKISH BATHS

The city's best-known hammam (and perhaps the best for an introduction to the luxury of the Turkish bath) is the Hammam Saint-Paul at 4, rue des Rosiers, 4th arr. (42 72 71 82); fee—85 francs. Exotic, but with minimal facilities, the Cleopatra Club is for women only and located at 53, boulevard de Belleville, 11th arr. (43 57 34 32); fee—50 francs. The oldest hammam in Paris also boasts a sauna, massage and beauty salon: Les Bains d'Odessa, 5, rue d'Odessa, 14th arr. (43 20 91 21); fee—73 francs. For all the pleasures of a hammam plus the services of a professional beautician, there's Plage 50, at 50, Faubourg-Saint-Denis, 10th arr. (47 70 06 64); fee—90 francs. And for authentic atmosphere, try the Hammam de la Mosquée, at the Paris Mosqué, 39, rue Geoffroy-Saint-Hilaire, 5th arr. (43 31 18 14); fee—56 francs. All (except the Cleopatra Club) are open to both men and women, but at different times. Call for information.

Jacques Dessange

8th arr. - 37, av. Franklin-Roosevelt
43 59 33 97, 43 59 50 08
Open 9:30 a.m.-6:30 p.m. Closed Sun. & Mon. No cards. 15 other branches.

With commendable concern for his customers' hygiene, Jacques Dessange has decreed that a brand-new brush be used for each client. Efforts have also been made to warm up what was once a pretty uppity, stiff reception. But best of all, the stylists no longer systematically impose Master Dessange's latest creation on every head that passes through the salon's front doors. Women are charged 280 to 330 francs for a shampoo, cut and style; men's tariffs range from 200 to 240 francs.

René Furterer

8th arr. - 15, pl. de la Madeleine
42 65 30 60
Open 9 a.m.-6 p.m. Closed Sun., holidays & Sat. in Aug. Parking: Madeleine. Cards: V.

Back when permanents meant frizz, and hairstyles were inevitably the product of rollers and pincurls, René Furterer virtually invented, singlehandedly, the science of hair care. Now retired, he leaves an impressive legacy: an institute that bears his name, where scientific hair treatments continue to be formulated by the Pierre Fabre laboratory. Simone Vasconi, who heads up the institute, is a respected expert in her field. If you are lucky enough to get an appointment with her, you won't regret it. She offers clear explanations, technical advice and a treatment program that may include massage or plant-based rinses. Sessions last from 25 to 45 minutes, at a cost of 250 francs. One is never urged to buy more than two or three products, which are always reasonably priced. For our money, René Furterer is the best hair-care institute in Paris.

Marianne Gray

6th arr. - 52, rue Saint-André-des-Arts
43 26 58 21
Open 9:30 a.m.-7 p.m. (Sat. until 6 p.m., Fri. 11 a.m.-9 p.m.). Closed Sun. Cards: V, MC.

Marianne Gray is a cheerful, unpretentious salon where natural-looking styles are the order of the day. The massage that precedes the shampoo is sheer heaven, and reason enough to make an appointment with Marianne, Sendera or (for men) Claude.

Léonor Grey

9th arr. - 57, rue de Châteaudun
45 26 57 63
Open 9:30 a.m.-6:30 p.m. (Thurs. until 8:30 p.m.). Closed Sun. & Mon. No cards.

With the help of her husband, a chemist who formulates her products, Léonor Greyl works wonders on dull, lifeless hair with her various powders, freeze-dried roots, wheat-germ oil and sundry other secret ingredients. But make no mistake: there's nothing hocus-pocus about her hair-care treatments (shampoo, manual and electric massage, scalp packs and the list goes on), and they yield excellent results. Women pay 280 to 310 francs; men 180 to 200 francs.

Harlow

16th arr. - 70, rue du Ranelagh
45 24 04 54
Open 9:30 a.m.-6:30 p.m. Closed Sun. & Mon. No cards. 2 other branches.

Many women want a good haircut that doesn't require elaborate upkeep. For them, Harlow and company have come up with wash-and-wear hair. The salon's atmosphere is relaxed, and service is fast. A shampoo and styling is 110 francs; with a cut, the price is 260 francs.

Jean-François Lazartigue

8th arr. - 5, rue du Faubourg-Saint-Honoré
45 65 29 24
Open 9 a.m.-6:30 p.m. Closed Sun. Cards: V, AE, DC.

Decorated in tonic tones of green and white, the Lazartigue salon presents the highest standard of creature comforts. Each private booth boasts a telephone and an individual closet (including, of course, a lock for your fur). The staff is perfectly charming, too. There's just one hitch: for an examination and an assessment of your hair problems, treatments and a "prescription" for Lazartigue products, the bill will come to something over 1,000 francs! Now for that kind of money, wouldn't you think that the ingredients would be listed on the label of the hair-care products you've been strong-armed into buying? We suppose that Monsieur Lazartigue wants to keep his "miracle" formulas secret.

Jean-Marc Maniatis

8th arr. - 18, rue Marbeuf - 47 43 30 14
Open 9:30 a.m.-6:30 p.m. Closed Sat. & Sun. Parking: François-Ier. No cards.. 2 other branches.

His first clients were photo stylists from the fashion press; they raved about the Maniatis technique of precision scissoring one tiny section of hair at a time for chic, superbly shaped cuts. His reputation grew, and now Maniatis is one of the city's best-known coiffeurs. The stylists who work with him are well trained and fast; they do a lot of work for celebrities, models, journalists and so on. The salon is friendly, noisy and always busy. Be prepared to wait. A shampoo, cut and styling cost 435 francs for a woman, 243 francs for a man.

Mod's Hair

11th arr. - 9, rue Saint-Sabin - 43 38 90 78
Open 10 a.m.-7 p.m. Closed Sun. & Mon. No cards. 2 other branches.

At its salon near the Bastille, Mod's Hair caters to the younger crowd, with saucy, fashionable styles. The walls of the salon are decorated with the work of talented artists, giving you something to contemplate besides your face in the mirror. "Training Day" provides a special value: a cut by an aspiring coiffeur for only 30 francs; normally, a shampoo, cut and style go for 278 francs.

Alexandre Zouari

16th arr. - 1, av. du Président-Wilson
47 23 79 00
Open 9:30 a.m.-6:30 p.m. Closed Sun. Parking: valet. No cards.

Celebrities seem to appear wherever you look in this luxurious (but ever-so-slightly gaudy) salon: their PR people insist that Alexandre Zouari is the very last word in hairstyling for the rich and famous . . . well, now we know! Figure on spending 225 francs for a shampoo and blow-dry styling, and throw in another 200 francs for a cut.

MANICURE & PEDICURE

Carita

8th arr. - 11, rue du Faubourg-Saint-Honoré - 42 65 79 00
Open 9 a.m.-7 p.m. Closed Sat. & Sun. Parking: Madeleine. Cards: V, AE, DC, MC.

Entrust your feet to Monsieur Ho, and he will work his brand of Oriental magic to make your tired tootsies new again (288 francs). Ask for Sophie or Kekko if you want an expert "French manicure": white polish is applied to the very end of the nail, resulting in an impeccably groomed finish (but don't even contemplate it unless your hands are in perfect condition).

Institut Laugier

17th arr. - 39 bis, rue Laugier
42 27 25 03
Open 10 a.m.-7 p.m. Closed Sun. & Aug. Cards: V.

The best manicures and pedicures in Paris are performed at the Institut Laugier. Hands are cared for on the ground floor, where the exclusive Supernail treatment is yours for the asking, as are vitamin baths and artificial nails for both sexes (just 38 francs per nail). Downstairs, feet are pampered with massage, vibrating baths, pumice stones and a skin-sloughing treatment (120 francs). Before they leave, clients are strongly encouraged to purchase a whole slew of (effective, but costly) products to prolong the benefits of the salon's treatments.

Institut Yung

9th arr. - 22, rue Caumartin - 47 42 20 63
Open 9 a.m.-7 p.m. Closed Sun. No cards.

No mere cutters or scissors are used here: Monsieur Yung's pedicure equipment is limited to a simple series of steel blades of varying lengths with more or less sharp points. In just 30 minutes, his fancy footwork will rid you of calluses, bumps, corns and dead skin. Treatment and polish cost just 100 francs.

L'Onglerie

9th arr. - 26, rue Godot-de-Mauroy
42 65 49 13
Open 10 a.m.-8 p.m. (Mon. & Sat. until 7 p.m.). Closed Sun. Cards: V, DC, MC.

The house specialty is American-style artificial nails, made of the same tough resins used in dentistry. These nails are absolutely "unchewable," besides being revolting tasting (280 francs for ten). Complete manicure and pedicure services are also offered.

Revlon

8th arr. - 95, ave. des Champs-Elysées - 47 23 71 44
Open 9:45 a.m.-7 p.m. Closed Sat. & Sun. Parking: Georges-V. No cards.

Revlon's reputation for nail care is worldwide and well deserved. The institute on the Champs-Elysées employs four medically certified pedicurists, as well as seven manicurists who will take your hands in hand and make them as lovely as they possibly can be. The house products are excellent and most effective. Manicures are tariffed at 145 francs (165 francs with a hot-cream treatment), pedicures at 210 francs.

PERFUME

L'Artisan Parfumeur

7th arr. - 84 bis, rue de Grenelle
45 44 61 57
Open 10 a.m.-7 p.m. Closed Sun. Cards: V, AE, DC. 2 other branches.

Jean Laporte's shops look like stage sets, rich with gilt and velvet drapery. The fragrances he devises are equally voluptuous, based on musk, gardenia, rose iris . . . not, we emphasize, the sort of scents worn by shrinking violets. His two best-sellers are L'Eau du Grand Siècle (280 francs) and L'Eau du Navigateur. Quite popular as well are the aromatic pomanders that diffuse Laporte's heady perfumes (180 to 350 francs and 595 francs) and an exquisite selection of gift items: jewelry, fans, combs and other decorative trifles.

Fleurie is for you. This exceptional hotel is owned and managed by the Marolleau family, who for two generations owned Brasserie Balzar (see *Cheap Eats in Paris*). When they sold the brasserie they bought this down-and-out hotel, and with a year of hard work, completely transformed it into what it is today.

The facade of the hotel has been restored to its former glory and is embellished with statues that are illuminated at night. The inside is no less inspiring. The lobby and sitting rooms are models of gracious comfort and charm, showcasing Mme. Marolleau's stunning collection of Art Nouveau plant and flower containers. A spiral staircase leads from the reception desk down to a stone-walled *cave,* where a full buffet is served. Continental breakfasts, which include fresh orange juice, pound cake, and cheese in addition to the usual croissants and fresh bread, are served only in the rooms. Almost all of the rooms have modern marble bathrooms and a good layout of space. All are air-conditioned . . . a welcome relief during the dog days of summer in Paris, and all come equipped with a mini-bar, remote-controlled television with CNN reception, and terry robes for after showering. Room no. 60, on the top floor with no elevator access, overlooks a beautiful mosaic-covered building across the street. Other deluxe choices include nos. 11, 14, 24, and 34.

English Spoken: Yes

Facilities and Services: Air-conditioning; bar; direct-dial phone; hair dryer; elevator to all but top floor; mini-bar; TV with international reception; room safe, no charge

Nearest Tourist Attractions (Left Bank): St-Germain-des-Prés, St-Michel, Île de la Cité, Île St-Louis

TELEPHONE
43-29-59-81

FAX
43-29-68-44

MÉTRO
St-Germain-des-Prés, Odéon

CREDIT CARDS
AE, DC, MC, V

RATES
Single 650–810F, double 890F, deluxe room 1,400F; extra bed (available only in deluxe rooms) 150F; children under 12 free

BREAKFAST
55F extra for either buffet or Continental (served only in rooms)

HÔTEL DE L'ABBAYE ★★★
10, rue Cassette, 75006 (6th)
46 rooms, all with shower or bath and toilet

In the 16th and 17th centuries, the Abbaye Saint Germain was a Catholic convent. Today it is the favorite hotel of many who love its quiet location near Saint-Sulpice, discreet staff, and commendable service. The entrance is off the street through 15-foot-high green doors that open onto a plant-filled, cobblestone courtyard, where the nuns once gathered before going to chapel for daily prayers. The central reception room is handsomely furnished with magnificent antiques and

TELEPHONE
45-44-38-11

FAX
45-48-07-86

MÉTRO
St-Sulpice

CREDIT CARDS
AE, MC, V

RATES
1–2 persons 950–1,500F, suite 1,950F
BREAKFAST
Included, cannot be deducted

comfortable sofas centered around a marble fireplace. Behind this is an exquisite garden salon with intimate seating, a profusion of flowers, and a nice bar with big wicker armchairs.

Returnees clamor for the top-floor suites, with their arched ceilings and rooftop views, or the two ground-floor rooms with private gardens. I like no. 303, a two-level oriental suite with a wonderful terrace and huge marble bath with plenty of shelf space. Another favorite is no. 4, a twin with brass beds and a private patio. No. 2, one of the smallest rooms, is smartly done in salmon colors with matching fabrics and coordinated striped wallpaper. It overlooks the garden.

Because the l'Abbaye is so special, it is higher in price and included for those whose budgets allow for more flexibility.

English Spoken: Yes

Facilities and Services: Air-conditioning in some rooms and suites; bar; direct-dial phone; hair dryer; elevator; mini-bar; TV; room service for light snacks; safe in office, no charge

Nearest Tourist Attractions (Left Bank): Latin Quarter, Luxembourg Gardens, St-Germain-des-Prés, St-Sulpice, good shopping

HÔTEL DE L'ODÉON ★★★
13, rue Saint-Sulpice, 75006 (6th)
29 rooms, all with shower or bath and toilet

TELEPHONE
43-25-70-11
FAX
43-29-97-34
MÉTRO
Odéon
CREDIT CARDS
AE, DC, MC, V
RATES
Single 650–775F, double 890–950F, triple 1,100F
BREAKFAST
50F extra per person

Hôtel de l'Odéon has become a popular Paris destination for many travelers who want luxury and impeccable service in a distinguished hotel that is still small enough to maintain a personal touch.

The interior is in the style of a 17th-century inn, beautifully blending antique charm and atmosphere with all the modern conveniences one expects in a top three-star hotel. In the charm department, the Odéon has it all: high beamed ceilings, stunning furniture, massive tapestries, intricately scrolled brass-and-metal beds with hand-crocheted coverlets, skylights, blooming flower boxes under the windows, lovely oil and watercolor paintings hanging throughout, and a manicured atrium garden sitting to one side of the breakfast area. On the convenience side, the baths are large and the bedside lighting is good. Double-paned windows keep street noise to a minimum, and the closets are large enough for more than the contents of an overnight bag.

English Spoken: Yes

Facilities and Services: Air-conditioning in some rooms; bar; direct-dial phone; hair dryer; elevator; TV with international reception; room safe, no charge

Nearest Tourist Attractions (Left Bank): St-Germain-des-Prés, Latin Quarter, St-Sulpice, St-Michel, Île de la Cité, Île St-Louis, Luxembourg Gardens

HÔTEL DE SEINE ★★★
52, rue de Seine, 75006 (6th)
30 rooms, all with shower or bath and toilet

For years this frumpy dowager hotel plugged along in its sensible beiges and browns, never thinking about brightening its image. Finally it has shed its old skin and, thanks to new ownership (which is the same for the Hôtel des Deux Continents and Welcome Hôtel; see pages 96 and 111), the Hôtel de Seine now has a contemporary, coordinated look to it. Bright orange faux finishing with turquoise highlights, orange tapestry upholstery, and colorful flowers have helped to upgrade the overall appearance. The best furniture was kept and so was the pretty wood and brick fireplace in the breakfast room. The bedrooms are done in sunny provincial prints and have mirrored closets, good mattresses, luggage space, functional bathrooms, and decorator fabrics. Rooms on the back are still dark and viewless, and there is the occasional ugly floor lamp or odd chair, but by and large the hotel is nice and recommendable. The location is great . . . just a heartbeat away from the best shops, restaurants, and local color on the Left Bank.

TELEPHONE
46-34-22-80

FAX
46-34-04-74

MÉTRO
Odéon, Mabillon, St-Germain-des-Prés

CREDIT CARDS
None, cash only

RATES
1–2 persons 700–925F

BREAKFAST
45F extra per person

English Spoken: Yes

Facilities and Services: Direct-dial phone; hair dryer, elevator; TV with French cable; safe in office, no charge

Nearest Tourist Attractions (Left Bank): St-Germain-des-Prés, Île de la Cité, Île St-Louis, St-Michel

HÔTEL DES ACADÉMIES ★
15, rue de la Grande Chaumiére, 75006 (6th)
21 rooms, 17 with shower or bath and toilet

When planning your trip to Paris, you may begin to wonder where all the nonmillionaires sleep. Many of them have been sleeping at Hôtel des Académies for years, because they do not have to dig too deeply into their pockets to pay the final bill. The owner, Mme. Charles, who was born in the hotel more than 80 years

TELEPHONE
43-26-66-44

FAX
None

MÉTRO
Vavin

CREDIT CARDS
None, cash only

RATES
Single 185F, double 245–300F

BREAKFAST
30F extra per person (no croissants, only bread, butter, and jam), served in rooms only

ago and still lives there, runs it with a firm hand, not standing for a *soupçon* of hanky-panky. Her plain, little upstairs Montparnasse location delivers small but spotless rooms at unheard-of rates to a band of devoted regulars, who keep in touch by sending her postcards and souvenirs that she proudly displays in her tiny reception room. There are no extras here, and the rooms mix 1950s chrome and plastic with varying color and pattern schemes. But with these breathtakingly low prices, who cares? Certainly not the generations of families who return year after year making it their home base in Paris.

English Spoken: None

Facilities and Services: None

Nearest Tourist Attractions (Left Bank): Montparnasse, Luxembourg Gardens

HÔTEL DES DEUX CONTINENTS ★★★
25, rue Jacob, 75006 (6th)
41 rooms, all with shower or bath and toilet

TELEPHONE
43-26-72-46

FAX
43-25-67-80

MÉTRO
St-Germin-des-Prés

CREDIT CARDS
MC, V

RATES
1–2 persons 700–775F, triple 975F; extra bed 275F

BREAKFAST
45F extra per person

The Hôtel des Deux Continents has changed. Lifelong owner Mme. Chresteil sold the hotel in 1994, and the new owner, M. Henneveux, who also has the Welcome Hôtel and Hôtel de Seine (see pages 111 and 95) has dramatically turned it into a study in good taste. In an all-out pursuit of elegance, the hotel displays rich decorating touches throughout. The beautiful breakfast room, done in shades of deep green and gold, overlooks a small garden. Lush paintings of Florence, Venice, and Paris hang on the walls. In the adjoining sitting room, beautiful red, blue, and gold-striped wall fabric is accentuated by exposed beams lining a deep red ceiling.

If you are traveling alone, no. 1 is a quiet choice. It has matching fabrics on the headboard, bedspread, and curtains, in addition to a garden view. No. 301 is now a pretty twin also on the garden. Lovely blue walls with ceiling trim form the backdrop for coordinated swag curtains, quilted bedspreads, and red carpeting. Soft upholstered chairs, a large armoire, and a marble bath with separate toilet make it very comfortable for longer stays. Pinks and yellows harmonize to make the double-windowed no. 6 one of the prettiest choices.

Long-time guests of the hotel will be glad to know that Gilles Rouault, the competent manager of the hotel, is still in command, and that Mme. Chresteil's staff of devoted maids diligently continues to uphold her high standards. The hotel has an enviable Left Bank location, surrounded by avant-garde art galleries and shops where you can browse among Art Deco treasures, amusing antiques, and fabulous period furniture. The hotel is less than five minutes from boulevard St-Germain and its famous cafés, and just around the corner from place Furstenburg and the atelier where Delacroix painted.

English Spoken: Yes

Facilities and Services: Air-conditioning in some rooms; direct-dial phone; hair dryer; elevator to most floors; TV with international reception; office safe, no charge

Nearest Tourist Attractions (Left Bank): Latin Quarter, St-Germain-des-Prés, St-Sulpice, St-Michel, Île de la Cité, Île St-Louis

HÔTEL DU DRAGON (no stars)
36, rue du Dragon, 75006 (6th)
28 rooms, 19 with shower and toilet, all with shower

TELEPHONE
45-48-51-05

FAX
42-22-51-62

MÉTRO
St-Germain-des-Prés, Sevres-Babylone

CREDIT CARDS
MC, V

RATES
Single 275–325F, double 390–450F, triple 450F; extra bed 30 percent

BREAKFAST
28F extra per person, served in room

Despite its no-star status and typical industrial carpeting, plastic plants, and calendar art, the Hôtel du Dragon is one of the last outposts for decent budget anchorage in the heart of the Left Bank. This genuine cheapie displays untouched, prewar furnishings—some of which belonged to the owner's grandparents—in spotless rooms bedecked in flowered or striped wallpaper. Of course there is no elevator, and the air-conditioning consists of opening the window. However, you do get orange juice with your morning baguette and jam, a television in your room, and a warm welcome from the Rabier-Roy family, who have owned the hotel since the 1960s. The bottom line for Cheap Sleepers is this: you get a good deal for your money, and in this day and age, that is not always easy to do.

Important Note: The hotel is closed in August and often for 2 weeks at Christmas.

English Spoken: Yes

Facilities and Services: Direct-dial phone; TV; safe in office, no charge; no elevator

Nearest Tourist Attractions (Left Bank): St-Germain-des-Prés, St-Michel

HÔTEL DU LYS ★★

23, rue Serpente, 75006 (6th)

22 rooms, all with shower or bath and toilet

TELEPHONE
43-26-97-57

FAX
44-07-34-90

MÉTRO
St-Michel, Odéon

CREDIT CARDS
None, cash only

RATES
Single 375F, double 460F, triple 560F

BREAKFAST
Included, cannot be deducted

The Hôtel du Lys has more French charm and romantic appeal than many three-star hotels in the area, which charge almost twice as much. The owner, Marie-Hélène Ducharne, who took over when her father retired after running the hotel for 50 years, has made some welcome improvements that have earned the hotel an additional star. Apart from redecorating some of the rooms and restoring the staircase to its original luster, the most significant change has been the addition of bathrooms to all the rooms that were without.

The rooms are done in a cozy *vielle* French style with beams, a stone wall here and there, and matching bedspreads and curtains. If you are reserving by telephone, please bear in mind that Mme. Ducharne is usually at the hotel only on weekday mornings from 9 A.M.–noon. Otherwise, you will probably be dealing with a desk clerk with limited English and authority. When reserving, I would request no. 11, a beautiful twin-bedded room with a beamed ceiling and stone wall. Two windows opening onto flower boxes let in plenty of light in a room with an orange-and-blue color scheme carried out in the wall covering, bedspreads, and curtains. A blue-tiled bath with a nice tub, two chairs, and a large armoire complete the picture. No. 6 is a brightly done double with cabbage rose print dominating. I would avoid no. 14 because of its strange WC perched on a platform. Other than that, all the rooms are very acceptable.

English Spoken: Yes, if Mme. Ducharne is there; otherwise, limited

Facilities and Services: Direct-dial phone; hair dryer; no elevator; TV; safe in office, no charge

Nearest Tourist Attractions (Left Bank): St-Michel, St-Germain-des-Prés, Île de la Cité, Île St-Louis, Latin Quarter

HÔTEL EUGÉNIE ★★

31, St-André-des-Arts, 75006 (6th)

30 rooms, all with shower or bath and toilet

TELEPHONE
43-26-29-03

FAX
43-29-75-60

Situated on one of the busiest pedestrian streets in the very core of old Paris, the Eugénie offers good value for your hotel franc, while giving you pulsating, round-the-clock atmosphere in the bargain. The upbeat little rooms in blues, grays, and maroon have double-paned windows and remote-controlled TVs, and they are big enough to turn around in. They are, however, short on luggage, closet, and seating space. The baths have the extras that tend to make a difference: hair dryers, absorbent towels, and the latest fixtures. As you can see, there will be few surprises, but it is a useful Cheap Sleep in a popular location within easy walking distance to good shopping, good sightseeing, and good eating (see *Cheap Eats in Paris*).

English Spoken: Yes

Facilities and Services: Direct-dial phone; elevator; hair dryer; mini-bar; mini-safe in room, 20F per day; TV with international reception

Nearest Tourist Attractions (Left Bank): St-Germain-des-Prés, St-Michel, Île de la Cité, Île St-Louis, shopping

MÉTRO
St-Michel, Odéon

CREDIT CARDS
AE, DC, MC, V

RATES
Single 500–550F, double 600–675F, triple 725F

BREAKFAST
40F extra per person

HÔTEL FERRANDI ★★★
92, rue de Cherche-Midi, 75006 (6th)
42 rooms, all with shower or bath and toilet

The Hôtel Ferrandi continues to be on everyone's top-ten list of wonderful small hotels on the Left Bank. Thoroughly dignified in every way, the hotel is unusually successful in combining the best in old-world style with modern comforts and expectations. The attractive owner, Mme. La Fond, is on top of details that make a difference in a guest's stay.

The downstairs sitting area is dominated by an ornate marble fireplace and a crystal chandelier. Loads of comfortable chairs, fresh flowers, attractive art, and daily papers in French and English create a pleasing place to relax. The hallways, lined with ocher fabric, are gracefully joined by a winding staircase painted in a faux marble finish. The large rooms are furnished with period antiques and coordinated in soft shades of blues, browns, and pinks. They have all the comforts of home. Most have extra closet and luggage space and are just the ticket for those of us who do not travel lightly. For longer stays, I like room no. 50, a ground-floor, two-room apartment with a roomy pink-marble bathroom. Another favorite is no. 23, with a blue-and-white half-canopy bed, marble fireplace, and massive armoire. No. 27, with a brass bed, double closet, and single chair, is the least expensive room, and perfect for one. Some of the bathrooms, especially in the smaller rooms, tend to be cramped, but most are equipped with heated towel

TELEPHONE
42-22-97-40

FAX
45-44-89-97

MÉTRO
Sèvres-Babylone

CREDIT CARDS
AE, DC, MC, V

RATES
Single 480F, double 610–1,000F, triple 1,000F, apartment 1,100F; private hotel parking 125F per day, must reserve ahead

BREAKFAST
60F extra per person

racks, and all have an assortment of soaps and toiletries. Motorists will appreciate the hotel garage, and shoppers will love all the discount shopping stores within easy reach.

English Spoken: Yes

Facilities and Services: Bar; direct-dial phone; hair dryer; elevator to four floors; some mini-bars; private parking; radio; TV with local cable; safe in office, no charge

Nearest Tourist Attractions (Left Bank): Montparnasse, Luxembourg Gardens, Bon Marché department store (all quite a walk); good discount shopping (close)

HÔTEL LE RÉGENT ★★★
61, rue Dauphine, 75006 (6th)
25 rooms, all with shower or bath and toilet

TELEPHONE
46-34-59-80

FAX
40-51-05-07

MÉTRO
Odéon

CREDIT CARDS
AE, DC, MC, V

RATES
1–2 persons 775–975F; extra bed 150F; children under 12 free

BREAKFAST
60F extra per person

For Parisian atmosphere in a setting of nonstop activity, it is hard to beat Le Régent, which offers guests traditional charm in a renovated 18th-century building. Fresh flowers and green plants add soft touches to the stone entry and reception areas, which are decorated with antiques and tapestry-covered chairs. A selection of Deux Magots teas, jams, champagne, and dishes is for sale in a display case. The downstairs breakfast room has pink linen cloths and a fresh bouquet on each table. It is a nice place to read the International Herald Tribune or Le Figaro while enjoying a Continental breakfast. All the rooms are well maintained and have the creature comforts most deem necessary, with the added bonus of terry robes (which are available upon request) and trouser presses. The bathrooms are modern, but the real showstoppers are in the rooms on the highest floors. For one of the prettiest pink-tiled bathrooms in Paris, request room no. 52. No. 41 has another outstanding bathroom with loads of space, monogrammed towels, a lighted magnifying mirror, and a deep tub. Room no. 43 is a nice twin in greens, with bed quilts matching the beautiful fabric-covered walls. If I had to pick a favorite room, I would select no. 62, nestled under the eaves on the sixth floor. Gingham bed coverlets complement the blue and white colors in the room and in the bathroom. From the room, you can look out and see Notre-Dame Cathedral. Sitting on the balcony, you will be looking over the rooftops to La Tour Montparnasse.

English Spoken: Yes

Facilities and Services: Air-conditioning; direct-dial phone; hair dryer; elevator from first floor; mini-bar; radio; TV with French cable; terry robes upon request; trouser press; safe in office, no charge

Nearest Tourist Attractions (Left Bank): St-Germain-des-Prés, St-Michel, Île de la Cité, Île St-Louis

HÔTEL LE SAINT-GRÉGOIRE ★★★
43, rue de l'Abbé Grégoire, 75006 (6th)
20 rooms, all with shower or bath and toilet

TELEPHONE
45-48-23-23

FAX
45-48-33-95

MÉTRO
St-Placide, Rennes

CREDIT CARDS
AE, DC, MC, V

RATES
1–2 persons 775–900F, suite 1,300F

BREAKFAST
60F extra per person

Everyone raves about it because on all counts the Hôtel le Saint-Grégoire is a stunning hotel. Although it is on the high side for a Cheap Sleep, I can assure you it is worth every *sou,* not only for the comfort and surroundings, but for the welcome and assistance extended by the staff, skillfully headed by M. François de Béné.

The color scheme is purple, yellow, orange, red, and beige . . . and it works. Decorator David Hicks has created an elegantly intimate atmosphere in this 20-room hotel by mixing period antiques with handsome modern pieces and sprinkling interesting fabrics and rich silks throughout a garden setting. As a result, the hotel has a feeling of well-being, from the fireplace in the rose-filled lobby to the linen-clad tables in the *cave* dining room, where yogurt and freshly squeezed orange juice are served with the Continental breakfast.

Please forward all mail to me care of room no. 100, a bright yellow, ground-floor double opening onto a small garden. It has a marble-topped coffee table, a bureau large enough to hold the contents of my suitcase, and two comfortable chairs for lazy late-night reading. The bath has heated towel racks and enough towels to last almost forever. If this room is not available, I would be supremely happy in no. 102, a junior suite, also on a garden, with its own entryway leading to a large room with a sofa, two easy chairs, and a table at one end. No. 14 is a pink double with its own terrace, and just perfect if you are alone.

After one or two nights at this hotel, there will be a problem; you will wish you *never* had to leave Paris.

Note: Also under the same ownership, and no less impressive, is the Hôtel le Tourville in the seventh arrondissement (see page 125).

English Spoken: Yes

Facilities and Services: Some rooms air-conditioned; bar; direct-dial phone; hair dryer; TV with international reception; room service from La Marlotte Restaurant (owned by the hotel, see *Cheap Eats in Paris*); safe in office, no charge

Nearest Tourist Attractions (Left Bank): Luxembourg Gardens, discount shopping, Montparnasse, Bon Marché department store

HÔTEL LOUIS II ★★★
2, rue Saint-Sulpice, 75006 (6th)
22 rooms, all with shower or bath and toilet

TELEPHONE 46-33-13-80
FAX 46-33-17-29
MÉTRO Odéon
CREDIT CARDS AE, DC, MC, V
RATES 1–2 persons 520–600F, triple 900F
BREAKFAST 45F extra per person

Restored in the style of Louis II, with beams, brocade and damask, red-tiled floors, and graceful, hand-rubbed antiques, this hotel is one of the best examples of what a little imagination, taste, and money can do to revive an exhausted Left Bank site. All the old wood alcoves and rooms under the eaves were saved. Flowered wallpaper, lacy bed covers, and period furnishings have been combined to create the small bedchambers. If space is a priority, request room no. 5, a double with a small bathroom and separate toilet, crocheted bed and pillow covers, and a hand-painted mural that extends from one corner to the door. An elegant salon off the main entrance doubles as the breakfast room and is a place where you can sit in the afternoon with a luscious pastry from the corner *pâtisserie* and order a cup of tea or coffee to go with it. This would truly be the perfect hotel if more of the rooms were just a bit bigger, if any luggage space existed, and if the closets held more. However, if you are traveling by yourself or without piles of suitcases, and you love the charm of this part of Paris, then this hotel will please you.

English Spoken: Yes

Facilities and Services: Air-conditioning in two rooms; direct-dial phone; hair dryer; elevator; mini-bar; TV; safe in office, no charge

Nearest Tourist Attractions (Left Bank): St-Germain-des-Prés, Luxembourg Gardens, St-Michel, Île de la Cité, Île St-Louis, shopping

HÔTEL RÉCAMIER ★★
3, bis place Saint-Sulpice, 75006 (6th)
30 rooms, 22 with shower or bath and toilet

TELEPHONE 43-26-04-89
FAX None

The same owner has been here for years, and there are no plans afoot to change anything, even to bring the office up to speed by adding a fax. Never mind, it is all part of the folksy charm the faithful Cheap Sleepers who stay here love. For Paris, the location overlooking the church on place St-Sulpice is calm. A peaceful night's rest is further assured because the hotel does not appeal to a *branché* crowd of late-night revelers. Breakfast is served in a room papered in a loud burgundy print, with a brass chandelier, an old bistro coatrack and umbrella stand with hooks, and dining chairs covered in a provincial print. You will see egg-yolk yellow chenille set against pink floral wallpaper in the neat and clean, style-free rooms. You will not, however, find much that is run down or worn to a nub anywhere in this hotel.

English Spoken: Yes

Facilities and Services: Direct-dial phone; elevator; safe in office, no charge; no TV

Nearest Tourist Attractions (Left Bank): St-Germain-des-Prés

MÉTRO
St-Sulpice, Mabillon

CREDIT CARDS
MC, V

RATES
1–2 persons 385–600F, large room 700–900F; shower 20F

BREAKFAST
35F extra per person

HÔTEL SAINT-ANDRÉ-DES-ARTS ★

66, rue Saint-André-des-Arts, 75006 (6th)
34 rooms, 31 with shower or toilet

Warning: This hotel is not for everyone!

The location is strategic; the prices low; and the unconventional crowd of fashion groupies, hip musicians, budding actors, and starving backpackers is party-loving and carefree. For some, the rooms are so small that cabin fever sets in immediately. Others may object to the unpleasant symphony of noises drifting through the walls at all hours or to the dim bulbs dangling from the ceilings. For its devoted regulars, this wrinkled old hotel has a tattered charm they love to romanticize and a laissez-faire attitude by the management they eagerly applaud. Now that you know both sides of the coin, it is up to you which camp you are in.

English Spoken: Yes

Facilities and Services: Direct-dial phone; no elevator, TV, or safe

Nearest Tourist Attractions (Left Bank): St-Germain-des-Prés, St-Michel, Île de la Cité, Île St-Louis

TELEPHONE
43-26-96-16

FAX
43-29-73-34

MÉTRO
Odéon

CREDIT CARDS
MC, V

RATES
Single 310–345F, double 450–475F, triple 550F, quad 570F

BREAKFAST
Included, cannot be deducted

HÔTEL SAINT-GERMAIN-DES-PRÉS ★★★

36, rue Bonaparte, 75006 (6th)
30 rooms, all with shower or bath and toilet

The Saint-Germain-des-Prés is the kind of small hotel everyone hopes to find in Paris. Superbly located in the very *coeur* of St-Germain, only a minute or two from two of the most famous cafés—Deux Magots and Café

TELEPHONE
42-26-00-19

FAX
40-46-83-63

MÉTRO
St-Germain-des-Prés
CREDIT CARDS
MC, V
RATES
1–2 persons 800–1,050F, suite 1,350–1,650F; extra bed 225F
BREAKFAST
Included, cannot be deducted

Flore—it has a long history of famous guests. It began in 1778 as a Masonic lodge to which Voltaire, Benjamin Franklin, and U.S. Navy Captain John Paul Jones belonged. After it became a hotel, it housed philosopher Auguste Comte, American playwright Elmer Rice, and authors Henry Miller and Janet Flanner. Ms. Flanner lived here for years and wrote her "Letters from Paris" column for the *New Yorker* from her top-floor suite.

The hotel is known for its lovely displays of fresh flowers, which are massed everywhere from the entryway, with its Venetian glass chandelier and hand-painted celestial ceiling, to the antique and tapestry-filled salon overlooking a walled garden filled with blooming hydrangeas and azaleas. The rooms, which are all different, are done in dark woods, with fabric-covered walls, brass beds, and good lighting. The suites, with their separate sitting rooms, are captivating, especially no. 26, which has Oriental rugs tossed on polished wooden floors, a canopy bed, leaded-glass windows, flower boxes, and a marble bath with Art Nouveau lights and fixtures. Air-conditioning in 15 rooms is an added bonus on hot days in this noisy part of Paris.

The hotel's deserved popularity today is due in no small measure to the thoughtfulness of the staff members, who go to great length to cater to the needs of their guests. Everyone who stays here agrees that it is definitely worth the Big Splurge.

English Spoken: Yes

Facilities and Services: Air-conditioning in 15 rooms, 100F extra; bar; direct-dial phone; elevator; hair dryer; mini-bar; radio; room service for light meals; TV; room safe, no charge

Nearest Tourist Attractions (Left Bank): St-Germain-des-Prés, Latin Quarter, Île de la Cité, Île St-Louis

HÔTEL SAINT-MICHEL ★
17, rue Git-le-Coeur, 75006 (6th)
25 rooms, none with toilet or bath, 3 with shower

TELEPHONE
43-26-98-70
FAX
None
MÉTRO
St-Michel
CREDIT CARDS
None, cash only

This little down-and-out hotel is a great stop for those with slim budgets and romantic notions about bohemian accommodations in Paris. The reception room is textbook one-star: a red love seat with fringe, assorted fake plants, and floral bouquets; a knickknack collection of varying quality, and a display behind the desk of soft drinks and bottled water available for sale. The hotel is included here because the modest prices and super location help to offset the basic rooms—none have a toilet, and only a few boast a shower. A fresh coat of white paint has enhanced some of the rooms, while others are beginning to show their age. A few have only hooks for closets, but all are clean. My advice is to inspect the room before accepting it. Night owls take note: The front door is closed and locked at 1 A.M., and front door keys are *not* provided to guests.

English Spoken: Not much, but Italian, Spanish, and Portuguese are

Facilities and Services: No elevator (steep stairs); TV; office safe, no charge

Nearest Tourist Attractions (Left Bank): St-Michel, St-Germain-des-Prés, Latin Quarter, Île de la Cité, Île St-Louis

RATES
Single 215–370F, double 250–400F, triple 500–540F; shower 12F

BREAKFAST
Included, cannot be deducted; includes a croissant

HÔTEL SAINT-PAUL ★★★
43, rue Monsieur-le-Prince, 75006 (6th)
31 rooms, all with shower or bath and toilet

In the 17th century, this building served as a hostel for Franciscan monks. For the last 35 years, it has been a hotel owned by the Hawkins family and is now competently run by their daughter Marianne, who is ably assisted by an accommodating staff and the house cat, Perkin. The family's collection of antiques, Oriental rugs, and watercolors has been used in the hotel with elegant results. The seasonal fresh flower bouquets that grace the public areas are grown and arranged by one of the housekeepers, who has been with the hotel for two decades. Custom-made curtains, fabric-covered walls, and interesting brass and four-poster beds combine with modern baths to create the pleasing rooms. There are four rooms similar to no. 31, a single overlooking the garden and done in beige grass cloth with a white and brass metal bed. No. 14 has a high ceiling that accommodates a four-poster bed with a tapestry-covered headboard and matching canopy. One of my favorites is no. 51: Situated under the eaves, it has a cozy bedroom with a small sitting room and a bird's-eye view of École de Médecine. For those insisting on total calm, no. 36 on the back is a pretty choice, with its adorable brass bed, big bath, lovely old beams, and open window framing a big tree and rooftop garden across the way.

English Spoken: Yes

Facilities and Services: Direct-dial phone; hair dryer; elevator; mini-bar; TV with international reception; room safe, no charge

TELEPHONE
43-26-98-64

FAX
46-34-58-60

MÉTRO
Odéon

CREDIT CARDS
AE, DC, MC, V

RATES
Single 575F, double 675–875F, triple 975F, duplex 1,180F

BREAKFAST
Continental 50F extra; American with two eggs and ham 70F extra

Nearest Tourist Attractions (Left Bank): Luxembourg Gardens, St-Germain-des-Prés, St-Michel, Panthéon

HÔTEL SAINT-PIERRE ★★
4, rue de l'École de Médecine, 75006 (6th)
50 rooms, 25 with shower or bath and toilet, all with shower and sink

TELEPHONE
46-34-78-80
FAX
40-51-05-17
MÉTRO
Odéon
CREDIT CARDS
AE, DC, MC, V
RATES
Single 325–425F, double 350–475F, triple 425–550F
BREAKFAST
35F extra per person

If you want a central Latin Quarter location without spending big bucks to get it, the Saint-Pierre, next to the École de Médecine, is a smart Cheap Sleep. Fortunately, the hotel has had a modest face-lift. Gone are the sagging mattresses, dull halls, and garage-sale-reject furniture in the lobby. Twin beds have been added, and so have stall showers *with* doors, double-glazed windows where necessary, and black leather couches on a marble-tiled floor in the sitting area. The unexceptional bedrooms will continue to inspire you to leave early and return late, spending your time discovering Paris, not snoozing in your room. The rooms pay homage to plain plastics and oddly matched colors, but they are always neat and well maintained and have decent closet and luggage space. Management keeps a tight lid on loud voices, carry-in food, and nonpaying guests in the rooms.

English Spoken: Yes

Facilities and Services: Direct-dial phone; elevator; TV with international reception; safe in office, no charge

Nearest Tourist Attractions (Left Bank): Latin Quarter, St-Michel, St-Germain-des-Prés, Île de la Cité, Île St-Louis, Luxembourg Gardens

L'ATELIER MONTPARNASSE HÔTEL ★★★
49, rue Vavin, 75006 (6th)
17 rooms, all with shower or bath and toilet

TELEPHONE
46-33-60-00
FAX
40-51-04-21
MÉTRO
Vavin
CREDIT CARDS
AE, DC, MC, V
RATES
Single 650F, double 775F, triple 1,050F; extra bed 100F
BREAKFAST
45F extra per person

The present Montparnasse landscape of fast-food stops, blockbuster movie theaters, and urban renewal projects almost makes one forget that this was once the artistic heart of Paris. The Atelier Montparnasse reminds guests of these past times by dedicating each floor of the hotel to the work of a famous Montparnasse artist, including Modigliani, Matisse, Erté, and Picasso. Each of the plain, concise rooms has noise-proof double-paned windows, a mini-bar, a television, and a modern bathroom with a mosaic work of the artist represented on that floor. The 1920s-inspired lobby has curved gray-and-blue walls, Art Deco furniture, and an impressive display of contemporary original paintings selected by young artists who Marie-José Tible, the hotel owner, has discovered. A floor mosaic—based on a cartoon drawing from the Musée des Arts Decoratifs—as well as the mosaics in the bathrooms were done by Martine Lionel du Pont, the mother of the former owners of the hotel. In addition to being one of the more interesting places to sleep in this area, the hotel is within an easy walk to the Métro and the famous cafés, brasseries, and restaurants of Montparnasse (see *Cheap Eats in Paris*).

English Spoken: Yes

Facilities and Services: Direct-dial phone; elevator; mini-bar; TV; safe in office, 6F per day

Nearest Tourist Attractions (Left Bank): Montparnasse, Luxembourg Gardens, discount shopping

LATITUDES ★★★
7–11, rue Saint-Benoît, 75006 (6th)
117 rooms, all with shower or bath and toilet

There is no question about it—Latitudes is one of the most sought after three-star hotels on the Left Bank. Yes, it is part of a French hotel chain (the only link of this chain in Paris), and, yes, it costs more, but sometimes comfort, unsurpassed service, and convenience cost a bit more and are *worth* it.

On the main floor, the marble-and-glass-lined lobby is as sophisticated as any in Paris. A subterranean jazz bar features a different musician Tuesday through Saturday nights. Complimentary newspapers are offered to guests enjoying a buffet breakfast in the sleek dining room, which looks onto a painted wall where the original door to St-Germain still stands and is visible. The extremely comfortable and attractive rooms are decorated in a different muted color on each floor: salmon pink, blue, green, and rose. The premier rooms are the large, corner doubles or those that join. The location is one of the best in the *quartier* for quality shopping, memorable strolling, and tempting restaurants in every price range (see *Cheap Eats in Paris*).

English Spoken: Yes

Facilities and Services: Air-conditioning; jazz bar with live entertainment Tuesday–Saturday nights; bellhops; concierge; direct-dial phone; elevator; hair dryer; rooms for handicapped; room service; mini-bar; TV with international reception; safe in office, no charge

Nearest Tourist Attractions (Left Bank): St-Germain-des-Prés, Île de la Cité, Île St-Louis, St-Michel, shopping

TELEPHONE
Reservations 42-60-25-54; reception 42-61-53-53

FAX
49-27-09-33

MÉTRO
St-Germain-des-Prés, Mabillon

CREDIT CARDS
AE, DC, MC, V

RATES
1–2 persons 650–975F, triple 850–1,275F; rates depend on season and whether or not it is a business or tourist rate. Always ask for the lowest rate. Children under 12 free

BREAKFAST
65F extra per person in room (Continental) or for buffet downstairs

LEFT BANK HÔTEL ★★★

9, rue de l'Ancienne Comédie, 75006 (6th)

31 rooms, all with shower or bath and toilet

TELEPHONE
43-54-01-70; toll-free in the U.S. and Canada 1-800-528-1234

FAX
43-26-17-14

MÉTRO
Odéon

CREDIT CARDS
AE, DC, MC, V

RATES
Single 910F, double 1,100F, suite 1,425F; extra bed 100F

BREAKFAST
35F extra per person

It is hard to imagine a small hotel in Paris more appealing than the Left Bank Hôtel. Quite frankly it is just the sort of hotel that will make anyone fall in love with Paris forever.

Located in the ever-popular St-Germain *quartier* and convenient to everything, it is run beautifully by the same owners who operate the Hôtel Lido in the eighth arrondissement (see page 138), so it is no surprise to find the Left Bank Hôtel just as beautiful, from the entrance with a whimsical antique baby carriage filled with beautifully dressed vintage dolls, to the large top-floor suite with dormer window views onto Notre-Dame, Beaubourg, and Sainte-Chapelle. To add to the overall allure, there are fresh flowers everywhere, museum-quality tapestries, polished antiques, open oak beams, stone walls, and a very helpful, English-speaking staff. The standard-size rooms are done in paisley prints with built-in mini-bars and room safes. The bathrooms are excellent. For my hotel franc, the suites and larger doubles are the best choices because they have alcove seating with soft armchairs, larger baths, and loads of out-of-sight storage space. As you can see, I am sold on this hotel as a wonderful choice for those with more flexible budgets.

English Spoken: Yes

Facilities and Services: Air-conditioning; direct-dial phone; elevator; hair dryer; mini-bar; radio; TV with international reception; same-day laundry service; room safe, 50F per day

Nearest Tourist Attractions (Left Bank): St-Germain-des-Prés, St-Michel, Île de la Cité, Île St-Louis

LE RELAIS-HÔTEL DU VIEUX PARIS ★★★

9, rue Gît-le-Coeur, 75006 (6th)

13 rooms, all with shower or bath and toilet

In its heyday in the 1950s and early 1960s, this hotel had no proper name, just a street number: 9, rue Gît-le-Coeur. It was the haunt of the movers and shakers of the beat generation: Allen Ginsberg, Harold Norse, William S. Burroughs, Harold Chapman, Thelma Shumsky, and many others. Things were happening in each room. People were painting, writing, talking, and planning, and the inflexible owner, Mme. Rachou, presided over it all while standing on a box behind the little zinc bar by the entrance. There were no carpets, no telephones, and the antiquated 19th-century electrical system provided a hit-or-miss service to the rooms. Toilet facilities consisted of a hole in the floor on each stair landing, and advance notice was necessary for a shower. Suddenly, in the mid-1960s, Mme. Rachou sold the hotel. The new owners named it, carpeted and painted the rooms, installed phones, and, of all things, even installed private bathrooms in some rooms. The hole-in-the-floor toilets went the way of the zinc bar. Canvases, manuscripts, and sketches that may have been worth millions of dollars were burned in the battle to disinfect the hotel. Art dealers came in later offering to buy any walls with murals, but they had been covered with wild wallpaper or painted, rendering the original artwork underneath worthless. Currently under its third owner, Mme. Claude Odillard, the hotel has been completely redone and bears no resemblance to its earlier days as a fleabag shrine to the beat generation in Paris. That famous clientele has long since moved on, replaced today by chic, well-traveled guests, many of whom are not aware of the nostalgic history of the hotel. All that remains now are photos, hung in the lobby, of some of the people who lived here in its early days and a piece of the hideous old wallpaper preserved on an outside beam.

On all counts, Mme. Odillard must be praised for her beautiful transformation of this now outstanding three-star hotel, which includes her own collection of French antiques, judiciously placed throughout, creating a feeling of warmth and comfort seldom seen today. All of the rooms are coordinated in Pierre Frey fabrics and top-of-the-line furnishings. They include absorbent terry cloth robes, ample closet and drawer space, recessed lighting, piped-in music, oversize towels, and, of course, all the other facilities discriminating guests have come to expect in fine three-star hotels. The suites have Jacuzzis, roof-top gardens, or views of Ste-Chapelle or the Palais du Justice. Fresh flowers and candy are welcoming touches everyone enjoys. The hotel is now recommended as the perfect stopover for those who want romance on their doorstep and the best of Paris at their feet.

English Spoken: Yes

Facilities and Services: Direct-dial phone; fax outlet in rooms; hair dryer; elevator; mini-bar; radio; TV with international reception; room safe, no charge

Nearest Tourist Attractions (Left Bank): St-Michel, St-Germain-des-Prés, Île de la Cité, Île-St-Louis

TELEPHONE
43-54-41-66

FAX
43-26-00-15

MÉTRO
St-Michel

CREDIT CARDS
AE, DC, MC, V

RATES
1-2 persons 990–1,500F

BREAKFAST
50F extra per person, includes fresh orange juice and cheese

PENSION JACQUELINE POIRIER (no stars)
120, boulevard Raspail, 3rd floor, 75006 (6th)
11 rooms, 4 with shower and toilet, 5 with sink and shower only, 2 with sink only

TELEPHONE
45-48-24-15
FAX
42-22-33-41
MÉTRO
Notre-Dame-des-Champs
CREDIT CARDS
None, cash only
RATES
Room and board—single: daily 250–350F, monthly 6,000–7,100F; double: daily 350–450F, monthly 7,750–9,750F. If you don't eat dinner, deduct 30F per person, but you must stay with this choice; don't expect dinner one night, and not the next.
BREAKFAST
Included, cannot be deducted

Close to the Alliance Française and geared to students or those in Paris for the long haul, this family-run pension provides accommodations along with breakfast and a hot dinner Monday through Friday, a Saturday lunch, and a cold plate on Sunday. The homey decor in this second-floor lodging runs from tasteful to tacky in the pretty lounge with a television on the marble fireplace to the basically functional rooms with an occasional antique. It is all presided over by sweet Jacqueline and her dour husband, who wears slippers and a frown most of the time. The house rules are just like those at home, one of the students told me. For example, there will be no surprise parties, no cooking in the rooms, no overnight guests of either sex, no visitors after 9:00 P.M., and you must keep your feet off the tables. The rooms are cleaned every other day, the sheets changed every ten days, and clean towels are passed out once a week. For between-meal munch-outs, there is a refrigerator and microwave, and for sprucing up before a date or some other special event, an iron and ironing board are available. Between December 24 and January 2, no food or services are provided.

English Spoken: Not by Jacqueline or her husband, but there is usually a bilingual student around

Facilities and Services: Elevator; room and board for 2 meals a day

Nearest Tourist Attractions (Left Bank): Montparnasse, Luxembourg Gardens

PENSION LE MARRONNIERS (no stars)
78, rue des Assas, 75006 (6th)
12 rooms, 1 with shower and toilet

TELEPHONE
43-26-37-71
FAX
43-26-07-72
MÉTRO
Vavin, Notre-Dame-des-Champs
CREDIT CARDS
None, cash only

For one of the most *incroyable* Cheap Sleeps in Paris, check into Pension les Marronniers. The philanthropically low prices include not only a Continental breakfast but a three-course dinner with cheese as well. With advance notice, special dietary needs can be catered for. Students, Frenchmen from the provinces doing a work-study program, and smart budgeteers fill this third-floor walk-up home, which has the Laura Ashley decorating seal of approval in the dining and living rooms, complete with the house cat asleep in the most comfortable chair or on the sunniest window ledge. The bedrooms might seem primitive to many, but all are cleaned on a regular basis, and the linens changed weekly. Reservations are absolutely essential months in advance, and guests who stay for a long time are preferred. Meals are part of the program and cannot be deducted for any reason.

English Spoken: Some, but many guests speak English

Facilities and Services: Room and board

Nearest Tourist Attractions (Left Bank): Montparnasse, Luxembourg Gardens

RATES
Room and board—single: 160–390F per day, 6,800–9,700F per month; double: 490F per day, 12,400F per month

BREAKFAST
Included, as is dinner

WELCOME HÔTEL ★★
66, rue de Seine at corner of boulevard St-Germain, 75006 (6th)
30 rooms, all with shower or bath and toilet

Unpretentious rooms in a fun-filled location combine with moderate prices to make a stay here more than welcome. Composed of 30 rooms on six floors, this friendly spot on the corner of rue de Seine and boulevard St-Germain is directly across from the picturesque rue de Buci street *marché.* Because many of the rooms are on the small side, it is an especially suitable stopover for singles. Those wanting more spacious accommodations should ask for no. 52, a corner twin-bedded room, or no. 62, an attic nest with beams and a peaked ceiling. Despite double windows, QUIET is *not* the buzzword here. For the least noisy bunks, request rooms on rue de Seine, not on boulevard St-Germain. Top-floor rooms can get hot and stuffy in warm weather, but they are very desirable otherwise. These drawbacks are overcome for the most part by the super location. The hotel is within walking distance of more things to see and do than you will finish in a week. The *quartier* has scores of inexpensive eating places (see *Cheap Eats in Paris*), and shoppers will never finish browsing and wishing.

English Spoken: Yes

Facilities and Services: Direct-dial phone; elevator; TV; safe in office, no charge

Nearest Tourist Attractions (Left Bank): St-Germain-des-Prés, Île de la Cité, Île St-Louis, St-Michel, Luxembourg Gardens, shopping

TELEPHONE
46-34-24-80, 43-26-98-97

FAX
40-46-81-59

MÉTRO
Odéon, Mabillon, St-Germain-des-Prés

CREDIT CARDS
None, cash only

RATES
Single 370–540F, double 540–565F

BREAKFAST
45F extra per person

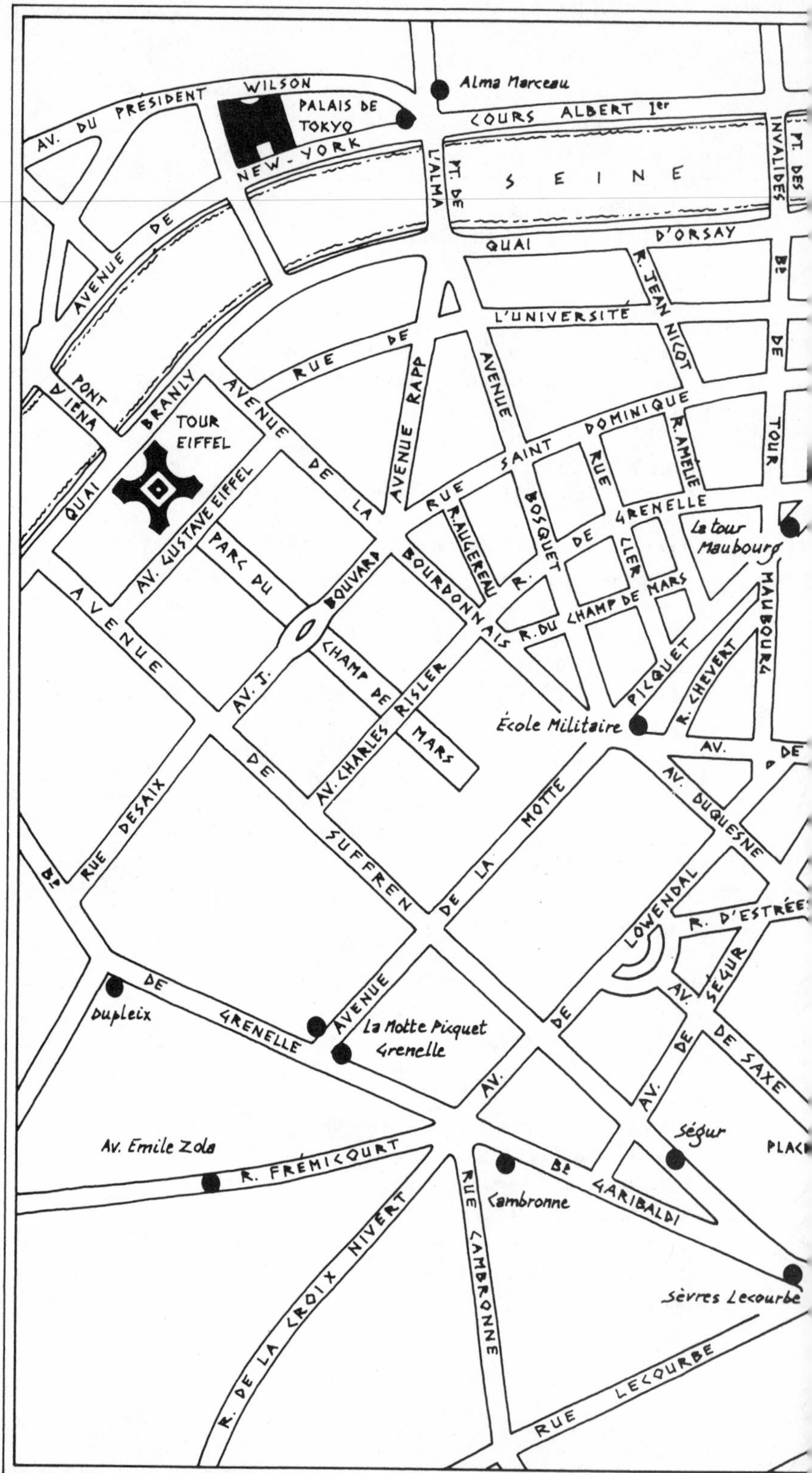

Alma Marceau
AV. DU PRÉSIDENT WILSON
PALAIS DE TOKYO
COURS ALBERT 1er
NEW-YORK
PT. DE L'ALMA
SEINE
PT. DES INVALIDES
AVENUE DE
QUAI D'ORSAY
R. JEAN NICOT
L'UNIVERSITÉ
RUE DE
AVENUE RAPP
AVENUE
PONT D'IÉNA
BRANLY
TOUR EIFFEL
AVENUE DE LA
DOMINIQUE
RUE SAINT
R. AMÉLIE
TOUR
QUAI
AV. GUSTAVE EIFFEL
RUE
R. AUGEREAU
BOSQUET
RUE
GRENELLE
DE
R.
LLER
La tour Maubourg
PARC DU
BOUVARD
BOURDONNAIS
R. DU CHAMP DE MARS
MAUBOURG
AVENUE
AV. J.
CHAMP DE
RISLER
PICQUET
R. CHEVERT
École Militaire
MARS
AV. CHARLES
AV.
DE
DE
AV. DUQUESNE
RUE DESAIX
MOTTE
SUFFREN
DE LA
LOWENDAL
R. D'ESTRÉES
Bd
SÉGUR
DE
Dupleix
GRENELLE
AVENUE
La Motte Picquet Grenelle
DE
AV. DE
DE SAXE
AV.
AV.
Ségur
PLACE
Av. Emile Zola
R. FRÉMICOURT
Bd
GARIBALDI
Cambronne
RUE
CAMBRONNE
R. DE LA CROIX NIVERT
Sèvres Lecourbe
RUE LECOURBE

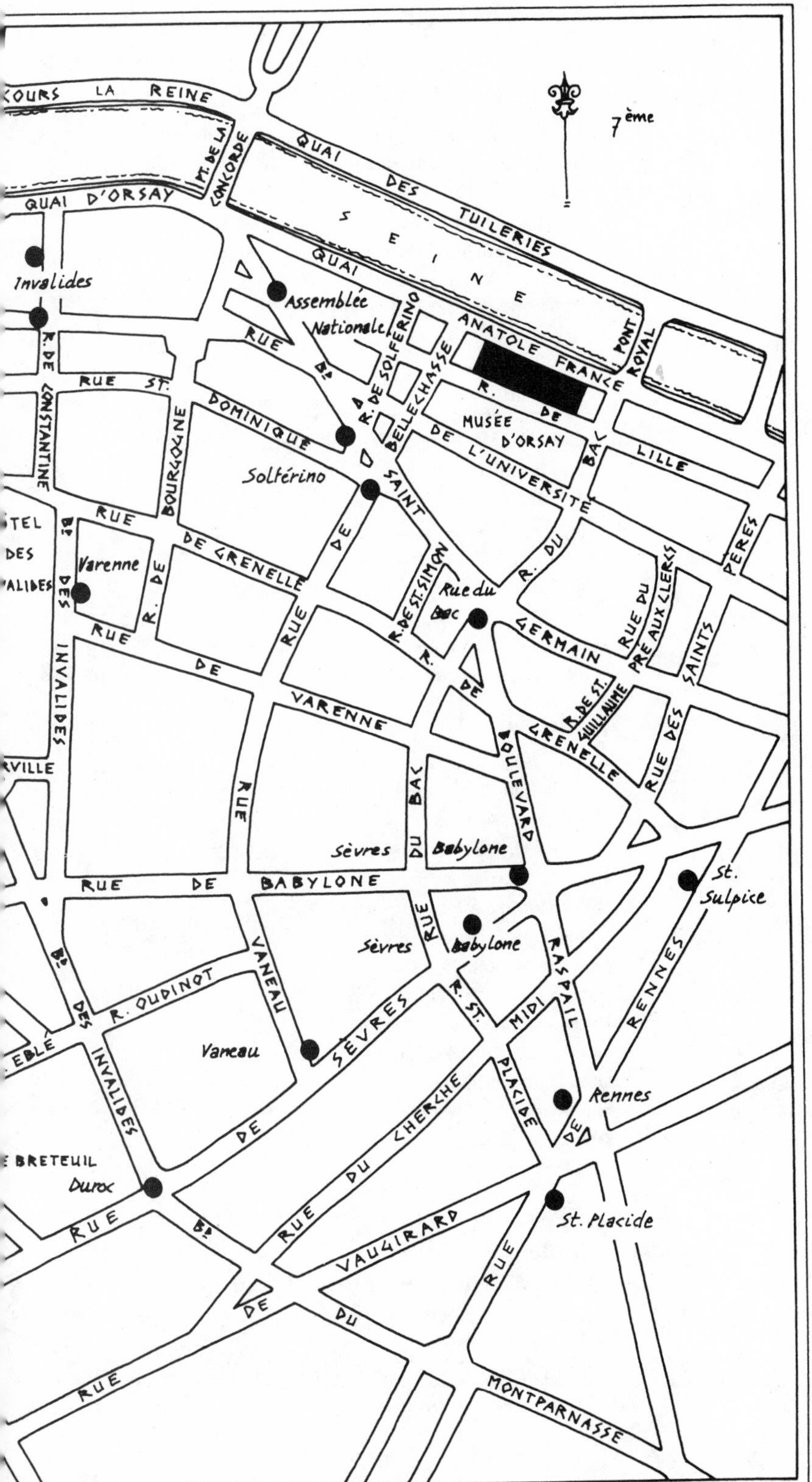
COURS LA REINE
7ème
PT. DE LA CONCORDE
QUAI DES TUILERIES
QUAI D'ORSAY
SEINE
Invalides
QUAI ANATOLE FRANCE
Assemblée Nationale
PONT ROYAL
RUE DE SOLFERINO
R. DE BELLECHASSE
R. DE CONSTANTINE
R. DE LILLE
MUSÉE D'ORSAY
RUE ST. DOMINIQUE
BOURGOGNE
DE L'UNIVERSITÉ
Solférino
BD SAINT GERMAIN
R. DU BAC
RUE DE GRENELLE
HÔTEL DES INVALIDES
BD DES INVALIDES
Varenne
R. DE ST. SIMON
Rue du Bac
RUE DU PRÉ AUX CLERCS
SAINTS PÈRES
RUE DE VARENNE
R. DE ST. GUILLAUME
RUE DE GRENELLE
RUE DES SAINTS
BOULEVARD RASPAIL
RUE DU BAC
Sèvres Babylone
RUE DE BABYLONE
St. Sulpice
RUE VANEAU
Sèvres Babylone
RENNES
R. OUDINOT
R. ST. PLACIDE
MIDI
EBLÉ
Vaneau
RUE DE SÈVRES
RUE DU CHERCHE MIDI
Rennes
DE BRETEUIL
Duroc
St. Placide
RUE VAUGIRARD
BD DE MONTPARNASSE
RUE DE RENNES
RUE

Seventh Arrondissement

LEFT BANK
Assemblée Nationale, Champ-de-Mars, École Militaire, Eiffel Tower, Invalides, Musée d'Orsay, Rodin Museum, UNESCO

Known affectionately as "Seventh Heaven," this quiet, luxurious residential area is full of stately mansions built before the Revolution and now occupied by embassies, government offices, well-to-do Parisians, and expatriates. The Champ-de-Mars served as the parade ground for the École Militaire and is the backyard of the Eiffel Tower. Les Invalides is the home of four world-famous military museums and is the final resting place of Napoléon Bonaparte.

HOTELS IN THE SEVENTH ARRONDISSEMENT

GRAND HÔTEL LÉVÊQUE ★
29, rue Cler, 75007 (7th)
50 rooms, 35 with shower or bath and toilet

Committed Cheap Sleepers who like the seventh arrondissement love the Lévêque. Located among the colorful food shops that line the rue Cler, it is close to all the things that one often forgets are so important on a trip: banks, a post office, do-it-yourself laundries, cleaners, well-priced shops, cafés for a midmorning cup of hot chocolate, a street *marché,* and several exceptional cheese shops and *charcuteries* to tempt picnickers.

Despite the use of often-washed chenille, some marginal-quality furniture, and questionable color mixtures, the rooms are clean and the mattresses hard (read "cement"). If you have a bathless site, the showers in the hall are free and the toilets spotless. The hotel is always busy, so if you are interested, book ahead at least one month during peak periods.

English Spoken: Yes

Facilities and Services: Direct-dial phone; safe in office, no charge; no elevator or TV

Nearest Tourist Attractions (Left Bank): Champ de Mars Park, Eiffel Tower, good shopping, lively street *marché*

TELEPHONE
47-05-49-15

FAX
45-50-49-36

MÉTRO
École Militaire, Latour-Maubourg

CREDIT CARDS
MC, V

RATES
Single 200–350F, double 200–375F, triple 440F

BREAKFAST
30F extra per person, no croissants

HÔTEL AMÉLIE ★★

5, rue Amélie, 75007 (7th)

15 rooms, all with shower or bath and toilet

A favorite with female solo voyagers, as well as being cute and cheap for the area, the Amélie has none of the miscellaneous colors found in many two-star hotels in Paris. You will climb lots of stairs going up to the rooms, which are pocket-size but freshly decorated with white wicker furniture and colorful framed posters and sport tiled bathrooms. Breakfast is served in a miniature sitting room on the first landing, or in bed, if guests prefer. The owners, M. and Mme. Orville, speak English, and *en plus,* they love Americans. Good restaurants are in the neighborhood (see *Cheap Eats in Paris*), and tempting shopping on rue St-Dominique is a minute away. You are in the middle, between the Eiffel Tower and Invalides, and the area is very dignified.

English Spoken: Yes

Facilities and Services: Direct-dial phone; mini-bar; TV; safe in office, no charge; no elevator

Nearest Tourist Attractions (Left Bank): Invalides, Eiffel Tower, Champ-de-Mars Park, discount shopping

TELEPHONE
45-51-74-75

FAX
45-56-93-55

MÉTRO
Latour-Maubourg

CREDIT CARDS
AE, DC, MC, V

RATES
Single 375F, double 425–475F

BREAKFAST
35F extra per person

HÔTEL BERSOLY'S SAINT-GERMAIN ★★★

28, rue de Lille, 75007 (7th)

16 rooms, all with shower or bath and toilet

The old stone walls and floors in the lobby are clean and polished, and the two breakfast rooms downstairs—

TELEPHONE
42-60-73-79

FAX
49-27-05-55

MÉTRO
Rue de Bac, St-Germain-des-Prés

CREDIT CARDS
MC, V

RATES
1–2 persons 590–725F; two-room apartment 800F per night (sleeps 4)

BREAKFAST
55F extra per person

one in a bistro style and the other in an oriental motif—are attractive. I must be honest, however, and say that the addition of masses of fake flowers has added nothing to the character of the hotel. But gaudy fake flowers don't diminish the comfort of the hotel, so the hotel is still included.

Every bedroom has been named for a famous French artist. In each case, a reproduction of one of that artist's paintings hangs in the room, and the mood and color scheme of the room are taken from the painting. If you like bold reds and black, request the ground-floor Picasso room, with its entrance off the atrium. If you prefer pastels, the Seurat or Sisley room is the one to ask for. Small bathrooms, low seating in the rooms, and steep steps may discourage some. Others will love the location, only minutes away from the Musée d'Orsay, the Louvre, serious shopping, and equally serious restaurants (see *Cheap Eats in Paris*).

NEW! The hotel now has a two-room, fully fitted apartment in a quiet building about a five-minute walk from the hotel, on rue de Verneuil. It is nicely done with throw rugs on tile floors and furniture from the *rustique* school. The apartment would best serve a couple. The Murphy bed is comfortable, but the sofa bed looked back-breaking to me.

English Spoken: Yes

Facilities and Services: Direct-dial phone; hair dryer; elevator; TV with international reception; safe in office, no charge. Apartment: Direct-dial phone; dishwasher; hair dryer; elevator; fitted kitchen; iron and ironing board; washer and dryer; TV; private safe, no charge

Nearest Tourist Attractions (Left Bank): Musée d'Orsay, Louvre, Tuileries, shopping

HÔTEL DE L'ACADÉMIE ★★★
32, rue des Saints-Pères, 75007 (7th)
34 rooms, all with shower or bath and toilet

TELEPHONE
45-48-36-22

FAX
45-44-75-24

MÉTRO
St-Germain-des-Prés

CREDIT CARDS
AE, DC, MC, V

Sheltered in yet another deftly restored 17th-century building on the Left Bank, Gerard Chekroun's attractive hotel was once the residence for the private guards of the Duc du Rohan. Intact in the public areas are the original ceilings and stone halls, highlighted by Oriental rugs, country French furniture, and dried floral arrangements. A statue of Diane stands at the entrance to the formal dining room, which is color coordinated down to the last lampshade in greens and roses. The small but well-detailed rooms have window treatments and bedspreads in either pink or blue floral print. The bathrooms are nicely tiled and supplied with French toiletries and good towels. None of the suites have views, but the marble baths with gold terra-cotta detailing and whirling Jacuzzis and the lush fabrics—including damask bedspreads—add the needed luxurious touches. The hotel is on the edge of St-Germain-des-Prés and within a brisk walk of the Musée d'Orsay, Notre-Dame, and many restaurants listed in *Cheap Eats in Paris.*

English Spoken: Yes

Facilities and Services: Air-conditioning in some rooms; bar; direct-dial phone; hair dryer; elevator; Jacuzzi in some suites; mini-bar; private parking, 140F per night; radio; TV with international reception; safe in office, no charge

Nearest Tourist Attractions (Left Bank): Fitness walk to Musée d'Orsay, islands, St-Germain-des-Prés, Rodin Museum

RATES
Single 740F, double 860F, suite 1,350F; lower off-season rates upon request

BREAKFAST
50F extra per person, buffet

HÔTEL DE LONDRES ★★★

1, rue Augereau, 75007 (7th)

30 rooms, all with shower or bath and toilet

Realistic prices, a very quiet location in the tony seventh arrondissement, easy walking distance to the Eiffel Tower, colorful shopping, and a good Métro connection add up to make this a fine selection. A soothing color scheme of beiges, browns, and soft blues creates a tranquil mood in the exceptionally clean and well-kept bedrooms. Management is ever vigilant, always repainting, recovering, or rewallpapering the minute necessary . . . never waiting until shabbiness sets in. Closet space can be limited, and the tiled baths are functional but on the small side. Room nos. 62 and 64 on the top floor have Eiffel Tower views. Nos. 101 and 102 are quiet ground-floor picks overlooking the garden. Off the reception area is an airy breakfast room, where you will probably see Elza, a Belgian griffon dog, snoozing and dreaming the morning away. The owners of the hotel are sweet and always helpful, and they do their utmost to make your stay here as comfortable and pleasant as possible.

English Spoken: Yes

Facilities and Services: Direct-dial phone; hair dryer; elevator to most floors (not in the back building); laundry service; mini-bar; TV with international reception; safe in office, no charge

TELEPHONE
45-51-63-02

FAX
47-05-28-96

MÉTRO
École Militaire

CREDIT CARDS
AE, DC, MC, V

RATES
1–2 persons 340–700F, triple 500–700F; extra bed 140F

BREAKFAST
40F extra per person

Nearest Tourist Attractions (Left Bank): Champ-de-Mars Park, Eiffel Tower, Invalides, good shopping

HÔTEL DE NEVERS ★★
83, rue de Bac, 75007 (7th)
11 rooms, all with shower or bath and toilet

TELEPHONE
45-44-61-30
FAX
42-22-29-47
MÉTRO
Rue de Bac
CREDIT CARDS
None, cash only
RATES
Single 370F, double 400–440F; extra bed 90F
BREAKFAST
30F extra per person

For price, location, and a sense of *vieux* Paris, this neat little hotel of dollhouse proportions stands head and shoulders above its nearest rival. If you do decide to stay here, you can have all sorts of fun spending the money you saved in one of the boutiques or antique shops for which this neighborhood is famous.

Appealing to fashionable and pretty guests on their way up, the tiny bedrooms are individually named after country flowers. I like no. 11, "Clématite," on the fourth floor with a private terrace and a view of slate roofs and red chimney pots that seems to go on forever. No. 10, "Campanule," is also appealing, with a small patio and a big skylight opening from the pitched roof. "Rose" looks onto rue de Bac and has one of the best bathrooms. There is no elevator, and *le petit déjeuner* is served in a miniscule top-floor salon that is a nice climb up a winding stone stairwell.

English Spoken: Yes

Facilities and Services: Direct-dial phone; no elevator; mini-bar in some rooms; safe in office, no charge

Nearest Tourist Attractions (Left Bank): Musée d'Orsay, St-Germain-des-Prés, good shopping

HÔTEL DU CADRAN ★★★
10, rue Champ de Mars, 75007 (7th)
42 rooms, all with shower or bath and toilet

TELEPHONE
40-62-67-00
FAX
40-62-67-13
MÉTRO
École Militaire
CREDIT CARDS
MC, V
RATES
1–2 persons 850–950F, suite 1,400F
BREAKFAST
45F extra per person, buffet or Continental

Architect and interior designer Marie Hélèn Chaine realized her lifelong dream when she opened the Cadran in 1994. In so doing, she took an old hotel and café, completely gutted them, and created her 42-room showplace that is a model of charm, comfort, and convenience.

The hotel lobby is focused on a large, 17th-century fireplace and Dauphine clock standing next to it. Oriental carpets arranged on the stone floors give the room warmth and complement the blue leather couches. A full bar is available and so is a bookshelf lined with current periodicals and books. The arched breakfast room doubles as an art gallery for changing exhibitions. A generous buffet breakfast is served here, or a Continental will be delivered to your room. The bedrooms have whitewashed, built-in furniture, which maximizes space beautifully, and air-conditioning, which soundproofs them from street noise. Colors are harmonized around either yellow-and-blue- or green-and-red-striped curtains and spreads. Prints by Czech artist Werner Reinisch, a friend of Mme. Chaine, hang on the walls. Tiled baths and showers offer Roger and Gallet soaps and lotions, excellent lighting, and ample sink space. A few rooms have glimpses of the Eiffel Tower. A chair and table positioned by the elevator on each floor add a thoughtful touch. Nonsmoking floors (not just rooms) are a welcome relief for many guests, as is the excellent service provided by Mme. Chaine and her courteous staff.

English Spoken: Yes

Facilities and Services: Air-conditioning; bar; direct-dial phone; elevator; mini-bar; TV with international reception; room safe, no charge; nonsmoking floors; conference facilities; fax and secretarial services

Nearest Tourist Attractions (Left Bank): Invalides, Eiffel Tower, shopping

HÔTEL DU CHAMP DE MARS ★★
7, rue du Champ de Mars, 75007 (7th)
25 rooms, all with shower or bath and toilet

TELEPHONE
45-51-52-30

FAX
None

MÉTRO
École Militaire

CREDIT CARDS
MC, V

RATES
Single 380F, double 380–440F, triple 525F

BREAKFAST
40F extra per person

French tourists visiting their capital have discovered this remarkable hotel value located between the Eiffel Tower and Invalides. This modest but modern, fastidiously maintained hotel reflects great pride of ownership. When I visited the hotel this time, the owner told me he was thinking of selling and retiring. Oh, I hope not . . . it is just perfect the way it is. Proudly displayed in the lobby is his impressive collection of begonias and staghorn ferns. You will see other signs of his green thumb scattered throughout the hotel.

The quiet, generally updated rooms have simple, harmonious color schemes, wooden furniture, and firm mattresses. Room nos. 2 and 4 have their own small garden and are especially pleasant during the summer months. The rooms along the back are very quiet, but have little light and depressing views of blank walls. Avoid these if you can. The homey downstairs breakfast room, with tapestry-covered high-back chairs placed around three tables, has a color TV where you can catch up on the morning news by watching *Bonjour France.* Excellent discount shopping, several banks, a main post office, the Métro, a wonderful street *marché* on rue Cler, and lots of favorite Cheap Eats in Paris are all close at hand.

English Spoken: Generally, no

Facilities and Services: Direct-dial phone; elevator; no TV or safe

Nearest Tourist Attractions (Left Bank): Champ-de-Mars Park, Eiffel Tower, Invalides, good discount shopping, interesting daily street *marché*

HÔTEL DU PALAIS BOURBON ★★
49, rue de Bourgogne, 75007 (7th)
32 rooms, 29 with shower, bath, and toilet

TELEPHONE
45-51-63-32, 47-05-29-26

FAX
45-55-20-21

MÉTRO
Varenne, Invalides, Assemblée Nationale

CREDIT CARDS
MC, V

RATES
Single 290–490F, double 340–580F, triple 700F, quad 790F; extra bed, add 30 percent to the cost of the room

BREAKFAST
40F extra per person

The Palais Bourbon has long been a favorite with readers of *Cheap Sleeps in Paris* who are looking for a cheap, clean, and respectable hotel suitable for the entire family. Located in a quiet residential area of Paris, only one-half block from the Rodin Museum, five minutes from Invalides, and about ten minutes from the Musée d'Orsay, the hotel is just across the Seine from the Tuileries.

The Claudon family has owned, managed, and lived in the hotel for more than 50 years and runs it with a steely eye out for anything, or anyone, out of line. Recent improvements include a stark new entrance with rough stuccoed walls. The breakfast room, with its six square and oblong tables and one large round one in the center, is softened by a tall green plant in the window and another sharing space on the sideboard with stacks of magazines. Black-and-white prints of the Sorbonne and the Palais Bourbon hang on the white walls. Other improvements include the addition of a few new bathrooms. Some of the rooms are definitely faded and in dire need of redoing: specifically nos. 6, 18, 23, and 26 are drooping. Best bets for the moment are the rooms with new bathrooms.

English Spoken: Limited

Facilities and Services: Direct-dial phone; elevator; some mini-bars; TV in rooms with bathtubs; room safes in rooms with bathtubs and in office, no charge

Nearest Tourist Attractions (Left Bank): Rodin Museum, Invalides, Musée d'Orsay, Tuileries

HÔTEL DUC DE SAINT-SIMON ★★★

14, rue de Saint-Simon, 75007 (7th)

34 rooms, all with shower or bath and toilet

Everyone has their first hotel in Paris, and this was mine. Of course in those days, it bore about as much resemblance to what it is today as the bicycle does to the Rolls Royce. Over the years, and through many changes, my enthusiasm for the hotel has not dimmed, and it still tops my short list of ideal small Parisian hotels.

I am drawn to the Duc de Saint-Simon for many reasons, especially its intimately romantic feeling, wonderful sense of privacy, overall beauty, and high degree of personalized service. Built around a courtyard garden, many of the rooms open onto this green view, while several larger rooms and suites open onto their own private terraces. I like *all* the rooms, but a favorite has always been no. 11, decorated in rich floral fabrics with a corner sitting area and view windows that open onto the gardens and seem to bring them inside. Another beautiful room is no. 17, with a king-size bed covered in a bright tropical print. Interesting hand-painted detailing accentuates lighted closets that frame the bed. A huge dresser with a mirror above, comfortable chairs, and a view of the green garden make this room one you never want to leave.

The owners of the hotel, M. and Mme. Lindqvist, have been antique collectors of note for many years and have used their handsome collection throughout the hotel, from the beautiful grandfather clock in the lobby to the graceful marble-topped dressers in the bedrooms. The downstairs cellar bar has pillowed niches and quiet corners just big enough for two to sip drinks and talk about life and love.

The prices for a stay here are high, no doubt about it. But for those seeking a quietly elegant, discreet stay in Paris, this should be *the* hotel of choice.

English Spoken: Yes

Facilities and Services: Air-conditioning in some rooms; bar; direct-dial phone; hair dryer in some rooms; elevator; TV by request; safe in room, no charge; room service for light snacks

Nearest Tourist Attractions (Left Bank): Musée d'Orsay, Tuileries, St-Germain-des-Prés, Rodin Museum, excellent browsing and shopping

TELEPHONE
45-48-35-66, 42-22-07-52 for reservations

FAX
45-48-68-25

MÉTRO
Rue du Bac

CREDIT CARDS
None, cash only

RATES
1–2 persons 1,100–1,600F, suite 1,600–1,850F; extra bed 30 percent of room rate

BREAKFAST
75F extra per person

HÔTEL ÉLYSÉES MAUBOURG ★★★
35, boulevard Latour-Maubourg, 75007 (7th)
35 rooms, all with shower or bath and toilet

TELEPHONE
45-56-10-78; toll-free from U.S. and Canada 1-800-528-1234

FAX
47-05-65-08

MÉTRO
Latour-Maubourg

CREDIT CARDS
AE, DC, MC, V

RATES
Single 580F, double 680–740F; extra bed 200F

BREAKFAST
50F extra per person

The Best Western–aligned Élysées Maubourg is a favorite stopping place for those seeking services from a professional hotel staff. In addition to the 30 well-fitted rooms, it boasts a Finnish sauna that is free for guests to use at their leisure. The traditionally styled rooms are decorated without much originality, but they are superbly comfortable, with plenty of space and good bathrooms with modern accessories. In addition to the location, which has good bus and Métro connections, as well as taxi stands close by, business people will appreciate the 15-seat conference room and the secretarial services available. The nicely appointed lobby and the stone cellar breakfast room—with its marble-topped bistro tables and matching chairs—are additional pleasures. And so are the many Cheap Eats in Paris that are within a five- to ten-minute walk from the hotel door.

English Spoken: Yes

Facilities and Services: Bar; conference room; direct-dial phone; hair dryer; elevator; mini-bar; secretarial services; TV with international reception; room safe, no charge; free sauna

Nearest Tourist Attractions (Left Bank): Invalides, Rodin Museum, discount shopping on rue St-Dominique

HÔTEL LA BOURDONNAIS ★★★
111, 113, avenue de la Bourdonnais, 75007 (7th)
60 rooms, all with shower or bath and toilet

TELEPHONE
47-05-45-42

FAX
45-55-75-54

MÉTRO
École Militaire

CREDIT CARDS
DC, MC, V

RATES
Single 490F, double 570–630F, triple 680F, quad 740F, suite 975F

BREAKFAST
35F extra per person

Hôtel la Bourdonnais is a personal favorite that over the years has never failed to please. The location could not be better. It is five minutes from a Métro and only ten from an RER stop. The area is filled with good shopping, from discount clothing boutiques to a colorful daily street *marché* on rue Cler. There are many inexpensive restaurants within easy walking distance (see *Cheap Eats in Paris*). The beautiful Champ-de-Mars Park, with the Eiffel Tower at one end and the impressive École Militaire at the other, is only two blocks away and a great place for a picnic, people-watching, or a morning jog.

The lobby and reception rooms are accented by velvet-covered furniture, soft lighting, bouquets of flowers, and nice paintings. A small breakfast corner and bar overlook a glassed-in garden where drinks and breakfast are served. The traditional rooms are tastefully decorated with excellent reproduction furnishings and soft fabrics. All have very generous closet and drawer space, comfortable chairs, large writing desks, and hidden combination safes to store valuables. The ample marble bathrooms feature big mirrors, hair dryers, and plenty of towels. This outstanding hotel is the choice of many international travelers who seek good value, so to avoid disappointment, book way ahead.

English Spoken: Yes

Facilities and Services: Bar; direct-dial phone; hair dryer; elevator; mini-bar; porter; radio; TV with international reception; room safe, no charge

Nearest Tourist Attractions (Left Bank): Champ-de-Mars Park, Eiffel Tower, Invalides, Trocadéro, good shopping

HÔTEL LATOUR-MAUBOURG ★★
150, rue de Grenelle, 75007 (7th)
10 rooms, all with shower or bath and toilet

TELEPHONE
47-05-16-16

FAX
47-05-16-14

MÉTRO
Latour-Maubourg

CREDIT CARDS
AE, DC, MC, V

RATES
Single 500–650F, double 700–725F, suite 980F; extra bed 130F

BREAKFAST
Included, cannot be deducted

For many years, the Hôtel Latour-Maubourg was an elegant pension-hotel that guests never wanted to leave. In fact, one guest arrived when it first opened and was one of the last to leave when it closed in 1993. Facing the Invalides across a small park, this town house was in the Klein family for more than 150 years. It was their home until they opened it to paying guests. Now the Klein family is gone, replaced by young, dynamic new owners, Victor and Maris Orsenne, their three children, and their dog Faust.

When the Orsennes took over, they closed the hotel in order to totally redo it. They reopened in the spring of 1994, with exceptionally graceful results. They wisely kept the best pieces of furniture, recovering them to give a more up-to-date look. The beautiful wooden staircase has been shined and polished, and the gorgeous high ceilings cleaned and repainted. All of the landscape paintings and Anonymous Ancestors have been dusted and rehung. The former dining room, with a large fireplace, now doubles as a sitting room and breakfast area. The rooms display uniformity and a warm sense of color. The furniture in the bedrooms reflects the 1930s and 1940s and has been custom crafted for the hotel. Soundproof doors have also been installed. Some of the bathrooms are new. I wondered about those that seem to me to be definitely dated. In talking with a guest, she told me that the 1930s-style tubs are long and deep, so you can stretch out and have the bubbles come right up to your chin. She also appreciated the size and shelf space and was glad they had not been changed. The marble fireplaces are still in place and so are the tall, double French windows that open onto the tiny park across the street where you can watch pensioners in berets feeding the pigeons or discussing the latest political scandal. Beds are covered with pillowy duvets or blankets . . . it is your choice, just be sure to state your preference.

While the hotel is now dramatically different, it is still full of character, and the spirit of friendliness is here in full force, as always. I hope you will like it as much as I do.

English Spoken: Yes, and German

Facilities and Services: Direct-dial phone; fax in the suite; hair dryer; no elevator; mini-bar; TV with international reception; safe in office, no charge

Nearest Tourist Attractions (Left Bank): Invalides, Rodin Museum, Musée d'Orsay

HÔTEL LES JARDINS D'EIFFEL ★★★

8, rue Amélie, 75007 (7th)

80 rooms, all with shower or bath and toilet

TELEPHONE
47-05-46-21

FAX
45-55-28-08

MÉTRO
Latour-Maubourg, Invalides

CREDIT CARDS
AE, DC, MC, V

RATES
Single 600–775F, double 700–900F, triple 980F, quad 1,300F; private parking 95F per 24-hour period

BREAKFAST
Included, but will deduct 60F per person (!) if not taken

Les Jardins d'Eiffel has built a solid reputation as a fine small hotel offering many four-star features at three-star prices.

After a hard day, you can park your car in the private hotel garage, work out at the hotel gym or relax in the sauna, and then wander a block in almost any direction and find a wonderful restaurant serving food you will love at prices you can afford (see *Cheap Eats in Paris*).

The quiet rooms and suites are not flashy or fancy, but simply coordinated and well-appointed with wooden built-ins and the latest in modern bathrooms, including telephones and lighted magnifying mirrors. A new wing will add 30 rooms, making a total of 40 with views of the Eiffel Tower. The existing lobby, breakfast room, and garden will be redone to be more in keeping with the new look of the hotel. Several times a year, owner Rene Rech selects works from local artists and displays them in the main salon. Of course guests are welcome to purchase any that capture their fancy. The competent desk staff will book reservations, organize sightseeing trips, rent a car for you—with or without driver—and confirm airline tickets. There is a one-day laundry and cleaning service and a doctor is on call 24 hours a day.

English Spoken: Yes

Facilities and Services: Air-conditioning; bar; baby sitting; direct-dial phone; hair dryer; elevator; laundry and cleaning services; mini-bar; private parking; radio; TV with international reception; room safe, no charge; trouser press; concierge; doctor on 24-hour call; laundry and cleaning

Nearest Tourist Attractions (Left Bank): Champ-de-Mars Park, Invalides, Eiffel Tower, shopping

HÔTEL LE TOURVILLE ★★★
16, avenue de Tourville, 75007 (7th)
30 rooms, all with shower or bath and toilet

The renovation of Le Tourville has infused a breath of fresh air into the conservatively staid seventh arrondissement, known best for its diplomatic missions and upper bourgeois lifestyle, not for anything *avant-garde.* A stay here in any room will certainly encourage you to settle right in, open a bottle of champagne, and rejoice in what Paris is all about.

If the Hôtel le Saint Grégoire appeals to you (see page 101), you will adore le Tourville, the newest creation by that team. Magnificently orchestrated interiors, again by designer David Hicks, suggest a more sedate mood here, but one that is just as appealing. M. Hicks has knowingly mixed antiques, beautiful fabrics, original prints, and a collection of North African tribal rugs, blending them around late-20th-century comforts. Beautiful fresh roses are everywhere, from a bowl of miniature buds floating on the reception desk, to a fragrant bouquet welcoming guests to one of the suites. The lobby has a deep green, velvet-tufted couch with four blue linen chairs nicely positioned around a circular table. A collection of books and an oil painting behind the couch give the room an old-world feel. To keep the room contemporary, tables covered with blue and yellow fabric are placed on either side of a linen sofa.

The rooms are air-conditioned and exceptional in every detail. The suites have Jacuzzis, and all rooms and suites feature antiques and nicely framed prints in a background of sand, pink, or golden yellow. Room no. 16 has its own terrace, and no. 104, on the ground floor, opens onto a garden. No. 60, a top-floor suite, sleeps four and is done in white wicker. No. 62, another top-floor suite with dormer windows, houses three and has an old-fashioned washstand.

English Spoken: Yes

TELEPHONE
47-05-62-62

FAX
47-05-43-90

MÉTRO
École Militaire

CREDIT CARDS
AE, DC, MC, V

RATES
1–2 persons 760–1,390F, suite 2,000F; extra bed 100F

BREAKFAST
50F extra per person

Facilities and Services: Air-conditioning in all rooms; bar; direct-dial phone; hair dryer; elevator; TV with international reception; safe in office and in suites, no charge; video in one suite

Nearest Tourist Attractions (Left Bank): Invalides, Eiffel Tower, Champ-de-Mars Park, shopping (see Cheap Chic, page 215).

HÔTEL MUGUET ★★
11, rue Chevert, 75007 (7th)
45 rooms, all with shower or bath and toilet

TELEPHONE
47-05-05-93
FAX
45-50-25-37
MÉTRO
Latour-Maubourg, École Militaire
CREDIT CARDS
AE, MC, V
RATES
Single 390F, double 425–475F, triple 625F
BREAKFAST
40F extra per person

Hidden on an out-of-the-way, peaceful side street, the Muguet used to be my favorite "vintage" hotel. I knew something had changed when I heard from a reader who wrote telling me how much she enjoyed the new and modern rooms. At the Muguet? A 1950s-style Cheap Sleep making no pretences at modernization or *haute* decor? Maybe they just changed one or two rooms, but all 45? This I had to see.

I am happy to tell you that the Muguet has indeed changed . . . all 45 rooms. It has taken on a totally new look inside and now sings with style from head to toe. Staying here will make anyone feel like a privileged budget traveler, especially in the suite, with its lovely tiled bathroom. Rooms are outfitted in country-style furniture with different color schemes in either pink, yellow, or blue. Everything is well coordinated; mirrored wardrobes are generous; and from nos. 61 and 62 on the sixth floor, you can see the Eiffel Tower. From no. 63, your vista is over Invalides. On the fifth floor, ask for no. 51, with a balcony and good Eiffel Tower view.

Thankfully, everything was not thrown away during the renovation. The facade of black and gray-green marble is intact, and so is the lovely grandfather clock standing next to the reception desk. No one replaced the colorful flowers and lush green plants in the garden with plastic versions, and, more important, the owners are still here with their welcoming smiles.

The immediate neighborhood could hardly be dubbed "the miracle mile," but it is quiet both day and night. After a nice 10-minute stroll, you can be at the Invalides viewing Napoléon's tomb or on a park bench at the Champ-de-Mars Park admiring the Eiffel Tower while eating a gourmet picnic put together from the food shops that line rue St-Dominique and rue Cler. Good restaurants abound (see *Cheap Eats in Paris*), and so does discount shopping (see Cheap Chic, page 215).

English Spoken: Yes

Facilities and Services: Air-conditioning on the sixth floor; direct-dial phone; hair dryer; elevator to five floors; TV; safe in office, no charge

Nearest Tourist Attractions (Left Bank): Champ-de-Mars Park, Invalides, Eiffel Tower, Rodin Museum

HÔTEL RELAIS BOSQUET ★★★

19, rue du Champ de Mars, 75007 (7th)

40 rooms, all with shower or bath and toilet

The Relais Bosquet offers guests comfort, space, and peacefulness in a renovated 40-room hotel built around a courtyard. Each room has all the three-star perks, as well as an iron and ironing board, an electric fan, and an assortment of current periodicals. Decor is uniform in all the rooms, with creamy wall coverings and furnishings that are of good quality. Brass poles, artistically hung with soft pillows covered in the same material as the curtains, are mounted as headboards behind the beds. Baths have three-tiered rolling carts and nice towels. Top room picks include no. 51, a large twin on the back; no. 54, which can serve as a small double or generous single; and no. 32, a big room for two with double sinks in the well-lighted bathroom. The upscale residential area of the seventh arrondissement offers some of the best Cheap Eats in Paris, casual discount shopping, and easy access by Métro or bus to the rest of Paris.

English Spoken: Yes

Facilities and Services: Direct-dial phone; hair dryer; elevator; electric fan; iron and ironing board; mini-bar; TV with international reception; room safe, no charge

Nearest Tourist Attractions (Left Bank): Eiffel Tower, Invalides, Champ-de-Mars Park

TELEPHONE
47-05-25-45; toll-free in the U.S. 1-800-448-8355

FAX
45-55-08-24

MÉTRO
École Militaire

CREDIT CARDS
AE, DC, MC, V

RATES
Single 660–760F, double 710–810F; extra bed 150F

BREAKFAST
55F extra per person

HÔTEL SAINT-DOMINIQUE ★★

62, rue Saint-Dominique, 75007 (7th)

34 rooms, all with shower or bath and toilet

In the 1700s, this building housed Dominican nuns. Today, it is a quaint hotel on a busy shopping street. An English country theme is carried out from the beamed lobby to the snug rooms, which are furnished in pine and wicker, with soft, billowing curtains dressing the windows. Matching bedspreads, coordinated wall coverings, and a pretty provincial-style breakfast room,

TELEPHONE
47-05-51-44

FAX
47-05-81-28

MÉTRO
Latour-Maubourg

CREDIT CARDS
AE, DC, MC, V

RATES
Single 425–455F, double 455–495F, triple 600–700F; extra bed 100F

BREAKFAST
40F extra per person

reached via a winding, wooden staircase, are other positive points. My favorite rooms are the two that open onto the terrace, where breakfast is served on warm spring and summer mornings. I also like no. 8, a twin on the back, and although the floors slant a bit, the roomy bedroom and bathroom, with a rolling cart for toiletries, save the day. The rooms do not boast exciting views, the elevator does not service all floors, and not all rooms have a chair . . . only a backless stool. While these may be deterrents for some, many Cheap Sleepers in Paris overlook them in favor of a tranquil stay in a hotel with reasonable rates and friendly management.

English Spoken: Yes

Facilities and Services: Direct-dial phone; hair dryer in some rooms; TV with French cable; safe in office and rooms, no charge

Nearest Tourist Attractions (Left Bank): Invalides, Champ-de-Mars Park, Eiffel Tower, Rodin Museum, discount shopping

HÔTEL SAINT-THOMAS D'AQUIN ★★

3, rue du Pre aux Clercs, 75007 (7th)

21 rooms, all with shower or bath and toilet

TELEPHONE
42-61-01-22

FAX
42-61-41-43

MÉTRO
St-Germain-des-Prés

CREDIT CARDS
AE, DC, MC, V

RATES
Single 450–530F, double 455–535F

BREAKFAST
40F extra per person

In an area where prices and noise are generally quite high, the Saint-Thomas d'Aquin is a moderate choice. The lobby and sitting room have been redone, replacing the uninviting Naugahyde and stark walls with upholstered barrel chairs and soft salmon wall covering. Even if everything does not always match perfectly, the glistening rooms are efficiently arranged and exceptionally well kept. The competent English-speaking owners, Christiane and Claude Carcanague, are diligent and friendly, which has encouraged repeat guests, who have been loyal to the hotel for many years. The location could not be better. The Musée d'Orsay, Louvre, Tuileries, and all of St-Germain-des-Prés are within a 10- to 20-minute walk. The shopping is wonderful, and so are many restaurants in the neighborhood (see *Cheap Eats in Paris*).

English Spoken: Yes

Facilities and Services: Bar; direct-dial phone; elevator; TV; office safe, no charge

Nearest Tourist Attractions (Left Bank): Musée d'Orsay, Louvre, St-Germain-des Prés, shopping

HÔTEL SOLFÉRINO ★★

91, rue de Lille, corner of rue de Solférino, 75007 (7th)

32 rooms, 27 with shower or bath and toilet

Cheap Sleepers in search of a sedate location should consider the Hôtel Solférino, delightfully situated just off the Seine and near the Musée d'Orsay. Decorated with an eclectic flair, the hotel mixes antiques, paintings, and curios in an unconventional way. Dining in the sunny pink-and-green breakfast room, with its skylight, display of hand-painted ceramics, and potted plants and flowers is like eating in a spring garden. The sitting room reminds me of a maiden auntie's parlor at the turn of the century. A curved, tapestry-covered sofa, complete with fringe, dominates, along with what seems to be a 12-foot mirror. The large *jardinière* with purple lilacs on it matches the lamp in the window.

The original cage elevator takes guests to the bedrooms. All are adequate, from the tiny top-floor, bathless singles to the large doubles equipped with showers and toilets. Avoid anything on the fifth floor. Seating in many rooms is limited to a folding metal chair, and age is catching up to the hallways. It is not the Ritz or the George V, but neither are the prices. The long-time owner and her multilingual staff are congenial, and as a result, there are many Cheap Sleep readers who return.

English Spoken: Yes

Facilities and Services: Direct-dial phone; elevator to fourth floor; TV in some rooms; safe in office (access 8 A.M.–3 P.M.), no charge

Nearest Tourist Attractions (Left Bank): Musée d'Orsay, Louvre, Tuileries

TELEPHONE
47-05-85-54

FAX
45-55-51-16

MÉTRO
Solférino, RER-Musée d'Orsay

CREDIT CARDS
MC, V

RATES
Single 275–475F, double 485–670F

BREAKFAST
40F extra per person

LIBERTEL BELLECHASSE ★★★

8, rue de Bellechasse, 75007 (7th)

41 rooms, all with shower or bath and toilet

Located on an interesting street in one of the nicest areas of Paris, the Libertel Bellechasse allows guests to walk easily to the Musée d'Orsay or across the Seine to the Tuileries and the Louvre. The hotel looks quite basic from the outside, but as soon as you step inside you will be struck by the bold entry done in dark green-blue-and-red-striped fabrics. The breakfast room is down an impressive wide stairway with a large mural to one side. Comfortably spaced round tables, dressed in fruit prints, sit under the tentlike ceiling. The small bedchambers

TELEPHONE
45-50-22-31; central reservation 44-70-24-24

FAX
45-51-52-36; central reservation 44-70-24-51

MÉTRO
Solférino

CREDIT CARDS
AE, DC, MC, V

RATES
Single 720F, double 820F, suite 1,000F

BREAKFAST
65F extra per person

are artfully arranged to take advantage of every inch of space. They have a military-Directoire theme, carried out by using strong colors and hanging a collection of military prints throughout. Some of the rooms are done in drab shades of brown and green and tend to be depressing. Better choices would be any of those in red, yellow, or blue.

English Spoken: Yes

Facilities and Services: Direct-dial phone; hair dryer; elevator; mini-bar; TV with international reception; office safe, no charge

Nearest Tourist Attractions (Left Bank): Musée d'Orsay, Tuileries, Louvre

LIBERTEL SÈVRES VANEAU ★★★

86, rue Vaneau, 75007 (7th)

39 rooms, all with shower or bath and toilet

TELEPHONE
45-48-73-11; central reservation 44-70-24-24

FAX
45-49-27-74; central reservation 44-70-24-51

MÉTRO
Vaneau

CREDIT CARDS
AE, DC, MC, V

RATES
Single 675F, double 750F, suite 850F

BREAKFAST
60F extra per person, buffet

The location is slightly off-center, but the trade-off is the good-size rooms, all with fireplaces. Actually, you can walk to the Rodin Museum or to La Pagode, Paris's most unusual cinema theater, built around a Japanese temple that was shipped to Paris in the 1920s. It has flying cranes and a tearoom and shows films of all vintages and tastes.

As you enter the hotel under a black wrought-iron awning, you are greeted by a whimsical wooden English butler holding a vase of flowers. The lobby, outfitted with softly upholstered love seats and chairs, is welcoming, and so is the breakfast room with four vibrant posters by Walasse Ting. A buffet breakfast is served on Pillivuyt porcelain set on gray tables surrounded by chairs with floral seat cushions.

Closet and drawer space is sparse in some of the bedrooms, but only if you arrive with everything but the kitchen sink in your luggage. All are coordinated in pleasing colors and have nicely framed prints. I could take up residence in no. 405, with a rosy brown marble fireplace, white bamboo furniture, and floral wallpaper that matches the curtains and quilted, custom-made bedspread. The white-tiled bathroom, with a tub and shower, has a nice supply of toiletries and a heated towel rack. No. 402 is a warm and cozy single facing the street. Dark mauve coloring accents the soft pinks that dominate. This room is appealing because it offers more space.

English Spoken: Yes

Facilities and Services: Direct-dial phone; hair dryer; elevator to fourth floor; mini-bar; TV with international reception; office safe, no charge; room service for light meals

Nearest Tourist Attractions (Left Bank): Rodin Museum

SPLENDID HÔTEL ★★★

29, avenue de Tourville and 1 avenue Dusquene, 75007 (7th)

48 rooms, all with shower or bath and toilet

Before 1992, the Splendid was anything but . . . now it lives up to its name on almost every count. Done in an Art Deco theme with soft blond wood and pastel wall colorings, the modernized rooms and serviceable baths offer all the comforts three-star sleepers demand. Balconies on the fifth and sixth floors offer views of the École Militaire. While sitting by the window in the suite (no. 507), you will be looking directly at *La Tour* Eiffel. If you would rather work, there is a fax and a computer plug. Windows are double-glazed to shield against the nonstop traffic at this busy intersection, but on hot nights, better have those earplugs handy, or swelter behind shut windows.

A large downstairs bar is a good place to go for a relaxing drink, and don't fret over the purple wall covering, green chairs with black accents, and the chrome bar stools . . . they all work to make the room contemporary in an offbeat way. The hotel is minutes from rue Cler, a pedestrian market street where well-dressed, basket-toting locals shop for their vegetables, flowers, meats, cheeses, and fresh morning croissants. Close to the hotel are several excellent restaurants (see *Cheap Eats in Paris*), and the Métro is a two-minute walk.

English Spoken: Yes

Facilities and Services: Bar, direct-dial phone; hair dryer; elevator; mini-bar; parking per day, 40F outside, 100F underground; radio; TV with international reception; room safe, no charge; fax and computer outlet in suites

Nearest Tourist Attractions (Left Bank): Eiffel Tower, Champ-de-Mars Park, discount shopping (See Cheap Chic, page 215)

TELEPHONE
45-51-24-77

FAX
44-18-94-60

MÉTRO
École Militaire

CREDIT CARDS
AE, DC, MC, V

RATES
Single 640–690F, double 740–880F, suite 1,000F

BREAKFAST
45F extra per person

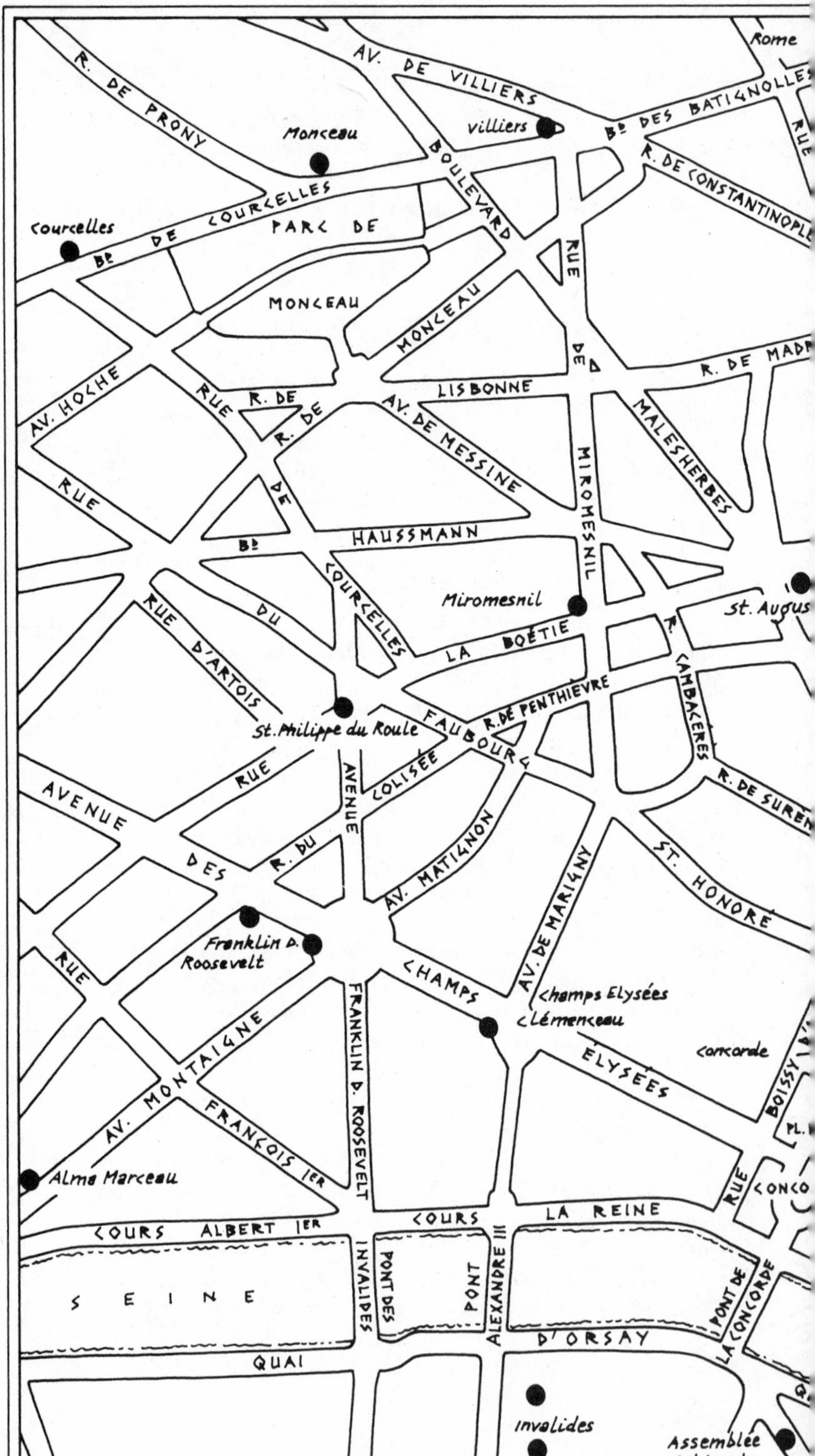

R. DE PRONY
AV. DE VILLIERS
Rome
Villiers
Monceau
Bd DES BATIGNOLLES
R. DE CONSTANTINOPLE
Courcelles
Bd DE COURCELLES
PARC DE MONCEAU
BOULEVARD
RUE
MONCEAU
DE LA
R. DE MADR
AV. HOCHE
RUE
R. DE
R. DE
LISBONNE
AV. DE MESSINE
MALESHERBES
MIROMESNIL
RUE
DE
Bd HAUSSMANN
COURCELLES
Miromesnil
St. Augus
RUE D'ARTOIS
DU
LA BOÉTIE
R.
CAMBACÉRÈS
R. DE PENTHIÈVRE
St. Philippe du Roule
FAUBOURG
AVENUE
COLISÉE
RUE
AVENUE
R. DE SURÈN
DES
R. DU
AV. MATIGNON
ST. HONORÉ
AV. DE MARIGNY
Franklin D. Roosevelt
CHAMPS
Champs Elysées Clémenceau
RUE
ÉLYSÉES
Concorde
BOISSY
FRANKLIN D. ROOSEVELT
AV. MONTAIGNE
FRANÇOIS 1ER
PL.
Alma Marceau
RUE
CONCO
COURS ALBERT 1ER
COURS LA REINE
SEINE
INVALIDES
PONT DES
PONT
ALEXANDRE III
PONT DE LA CONCORDE
D'ORSAY
QUAI
Q
Invalides
Assemblée Nationale

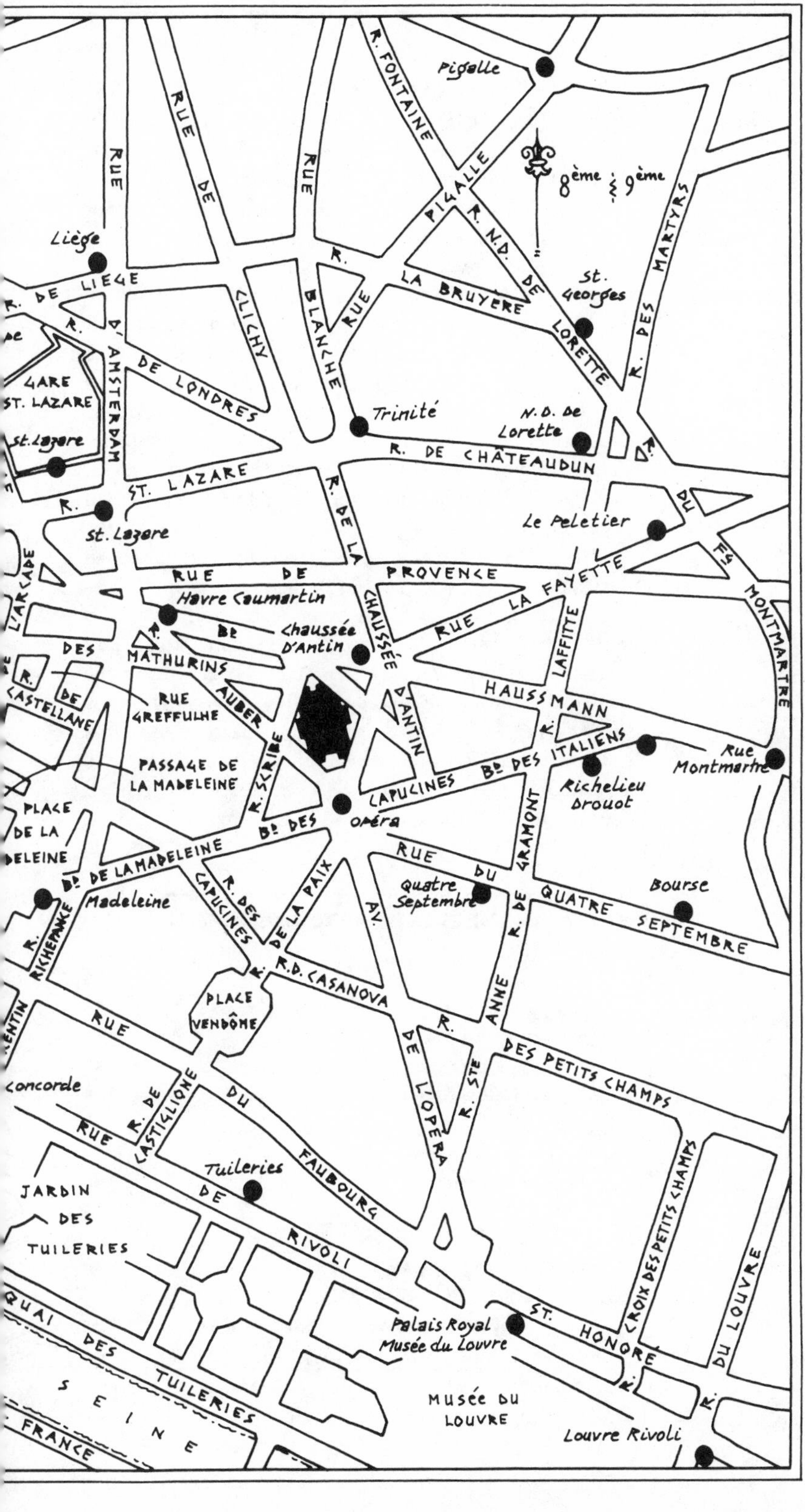

Pigalle
8ème & 9ème
R. FONTAINE
PIGALLE
R. N.D. DE LORETTE
RUE DE CLICHY
RUE BLANCHE
RUE
Liège
R. DE LIEGE
R. LA BRUYERE
RUE
St. Georges
R. DES MARTYRS
R. D'AMSTERDAM
R. DE LONDRES
GARE ST. LAZARE
St. Lazare
Trinité
N.D. DE Lorette
R. DE CHÂTEAUDUN
ST. LAZARE
R.
St. Lazare
R. DE LA CHAUSSÉE D'ANTIN
Le Peletier
R. DU FG MONTMARTRE
L'ARCADE
RUE DE PROVENCE
RUE LA FAYETTE
Havre Caumartin
BD HAUSSMANN
Chaussée D'Antin
LAFFITTE
DES MATHURINS
R. AUBER
R. DE CASTELLANE
RUE GREFFULHE
PASSAGE DE LA MADELEINE
R. SCRIBE
BD DES ITALIENS
Rue Montmartre
Richelieu Drouot
BD DES CAPUCINES
Opéra
PLACE DE LA MADELEINE
BD DE LA MADELEINE
R. DES CAPUCINES
R. DE LA PAIX
RUE DU QUATRE SEPTEMBRE
Quatre Septembre
R. DE GRAMONT
Bourse
Madeleine
R. RICHEPANCE
R. D. CASANOVA
AV. DE L'OPERA
R. STE ANNE
PLACE VENDÔME
RUE DU FAUBOURG ST. HONORÉ
R. DES PETITS CHAMPS
Concorde
R. DE CASTIGLIONE
RUE DE RIVOLI
Tuileries
R. CROIX DES PETITS CHAMPS
JARDIN DES TUILERIES
RUE DU LOUVRE
Palais Royal Musée du Louvre
QUAI DES TUILERIES
SEINE
MUSÉE DU LOUVRE
Louvre Rivoli

Eighth Arrondissement

RIGHT BANK
American Embassy, Arc de Triomphe, Étoile, Champs-Élysées, elegant shopping on rue du Faubourg St-Honoré, Petit Palais, Grand Palais, place de la Concorde, Madeleine Church

The 10-lane Champs-Élysées, sweeping dramatically from the Arc de Triomphe to the place de la Concorde, is the most famous avenue and parade ground in the world, and it is definitely worth a serious look and stroll. But save the shopping, partying, and eating for less touristy and unspoiled areas. This is the traditional watering hole for showbiz celebrities, glamour girls on the way up and down, tourists in baseball caps, heavy-set men and their young companions, and anyone else who wants to hide behind dark glasses 24 hours a day. The flame on the tomb of the unknown soldier burns under the Arc de Triomphe, and the view from the top is inspiring. Twelve avenues radiate from the Arc de Triomphe, forming the world-famous, death-defying traffic circle known as *l'Étoile.*

The place de la Concorde is the largest square in Paris. Two of its most famous occupants are the luxurious Hôtel Crillon and the American Embassy. It is thrilling to stand on this strikingly beautiful square and be surrounded by some of the greatest landmarks in the world; the Tuileries Gardens, the Louvre, and the view up the Champs-Élysées to the Arc de Triomphe, across the Seine to the Palais Bourbon, and up the rue Royale to the Madeleine Church. In the evening, when it is all illuminated and the fountains are playing, it is a sight you will never forget.

HOTELS IN THE EIGHTH ARRONDISSEMENT

GALILEO HÔTEL ★★★
54, rue Galilée, 75008 (8th)
27 rooms, all with shower or bath and toilet

For years, contented guests with sophisticated, artistic temperaments have flocked to Roland and Elisabeth Buffat's popular hotels on the Île St-Louis: Hôtel de

Lutèce and Hôtel des Deux-Îles. Now they have a third one to tempt them, the Galileo. The Buffat's newest hotel re-creates an elegant French town home in an oasis of calm, only a few steps from the Champs-Élysées.

Like the flowers in the boutique-lobby and garden, guests are beautifully arranged in the elegantly pristine rooms, all fashioned alike in comforting colors of beige, brown, and cocoa. No. 403, a double with two armchairs, a desk, and gray marble bath, has a *Rear Window*–type view onto the life within the apartments in the building across from it. Two rooms on the fifth floor have balconies, and no. 402, a single, has excellent space. Butcher-block tables adorn the underground mirrored dining room, and green plants and posters of familiar Paris landmarks and buildings give it interest.

English Spoken: Yes

Facilities and Services: Air-conditioning; direct-dial phone; hair dryer; elevator; mini-bar; radio; TV with international reception; office safe, no charge

Nearest Tourist Attractions (Right Bank): Champs-Élysées, Arc de Triomphe

TELEPHONE
47-20-66-06

FAX
47-20-67-17

MÉTRO
George-V

CREDIT CARDS
AE, MC, V

RATES
1–2 persons 825–975F

BREAKFAST
55F extra per person; buffet downstairs, Continental in rooms

HÔTEL DES CHAMPS-ÉLYSÉES ★★

2, rue d'Artois, 75008 (8th)

36 rooms, all with shower or bath and toilet

During World War II, this hotel housed Dutch and American soldiers. It now houses savvy Cheap Sleepers in Paris who want a moderate, reliable nest near the Champs-Élysées and the Arc de Triomphe.

I like the hotel for many reasons, especially because it is owned and run by M. Delfau, who inherited it from his father and grandfather. Five years ago the hotel underwent renovation, and since then maintenance has been consistent. Thirty-six attractive rooms and modern baths have coordinated colors, good space usage, and most importantly, provide many three-star amenities for two-star prices. The downstairs provincial dining room, a small atrium garden, and the warm hospitality of M. Delfau and his staff add further to the hotel's popularity.

English Spoken: Yes

Facilities and Services: Bar; direct-dial phone; hair dryer; elevator; mini-bar; TV with international reception; room safe, no charge

Nearest Tourist Attractions (Right Bank): Champs-Élysées, Arc de Triomphe, shopping along rue Faubourg du St. Honoré

TELEPHONE
43-59-11-42

FAX
45-61-00-61

MÉTRO
St-Philippe-du-Roule

CREDIT CARDS
MC, V

RATES
1–2 persons 470–540F; extra bed 100F

BREAKFAST
40F extra per person

HÔTEL DU MINISTÈRE ★★

31, rue de Surene, 75008 (8th)

28 rooms, all with shower or bath and toilet

TELEPHONE
42-66-21-43

FAX
42-66-96-04

MÉTRO
Madeleine

CREDIT CARDS
AE, MC, V

RATES
Single 410–570F, double 600F, triple 750F

BREAKFAST
45F extra per person

When asked to provide the names of two-star winners on the Right Bank near the American Embassy and the Champs-Élysées, the Hôtel du Ministère always tops my list. Just between us, it is the sort of hotel guidebook writers want to keep to themselves, or share with only a few select friends . . . as I will with you. Now into its fourth generation of running the hotel, the Blanc family continues to provide their guests with every comfort and convenience. Someone from the family is always available; either the young Blancs, with their three daughters, or M. Blanc's parents, who live at the hotel.

The rooms have been individually decorated by several members of the family. It would be impossible to go far wrong in any of the perfectly tailored choices, with their oak beams, attractive Italian lights, family antiques, generous closets, beautiful baths, and coordinated color schemes and fabrics. My sentimental favorite is no. 3, because the furniture M. Blanc's grandmother received as a bride is used, and it is still in mint condition. His father painted the picture in this room, as well as those that hang in many other bedrooms. In addition to the well-tended rooms, the reasonable prices and hospitable atmosphere combine to make this an excellent choice. It is warmly recommended by all who stay here.

Note: The prices quoted here are special for *Cheap Sleeps in Paris* readers who mention the book when reserving.

English Spoken: Yes

Facilities and Services: Direct-dial phone; hair dryer; elevator; mini-bar; radio; TV with international reception; office safe, no charge

Nearest Tourist Attractions (Right Bank): Champs-Élysées, place de la Concorde, Madeleine, shopping on rue St-Honoré, Tuileries

HÔTEL FOLKESTONE ★★★

49, rue Castellane, 75008 (8th)

49 rooms, all with shower or bath and toilet

The Folkestone is one of the brightest stars of the Best Western chain in Paris and definitely one of the better choices in an area where prices are usually over the top. A stay here puts you in the middle of the business, high fashion, and entertainment precinct of the city.

The contemporary bedrooms are decorated in peach, pale gray, and cream, with polished cotton fabrics on the beds and hanging at the windows. The smallest doubles, at the back, have miniature bathrooms and no view. The bright, cheerful rooms on the street have good general space and double windowpanes to buffer noise.

Breakfast is very special here. Every morning one of the maids, whose hobby is cooking, rises at dawn to prepare luscious *tartes,* cakes, quiches, and a fresh fruit compote. These are placed on the buffet breakfast table along with yogurt, boiled eggs, hot brioches, *pain au chocolate,* croissants, sweet butter, and assorted jams. English tea, American or French coffee, and hot chocolate are also served. For my money, this sumptuous meal is reason enough to stay at the Folkestone.

English Spoken: Yes

Facilities and Services: Air-conditioning in first-floor rooms; bar; direct-dial phone; hair dryer; elevator; minibar; radio; TV with international reception; room safe, 30F per stay

Nearest Tourist Attractions (Right Bank): Madeleine Church, old Opéra, shopping on rue Faubourg du St-Honoré and at Au Printemps and Galeries Lafayette department stores

TELEPHONE
42-65-73-09; toll-free from the U.S. and Canada 1-800-528-1234

FAX
42-65-64-09

MÉTRO
Madeleine, Havre-Caumartin

CREDIT CARDS
AE, DC, MC, V

RATES
Single 765F, double 850F, triple 965F, quad 1,080F

BREAKFAST
50F extra per person

HÔTEL LA SANGUINE ★★

6, rue de Surène, 75008 (8th)

31 rooms, all with shower or bath and toilet

The upstairs lobby and reception room promise an intimacy in a rather impersonal business district between the Madeleine Church and the Champs-Élysées. Rooms deliver three- and four-star comforts, such as fax plugs, room safes in most, and telephones in all the bathrooms. Unfortunately there is no elevator for the four floors, and back views are nothing short of grim. These are *not* reasons to ignore this good-value hotel. The neighborhood is tomblike at night and on the weekends, when offices are closed, so an uninterrupted night's rest is assured from a front-facing room. All the rooms have pleasing colors and fabrics, and most of the showers have curtains. The Continental breakfast includes orange juice and homemade croissants along with coffee, tea, or rich hot chocolate. The warm welcome and friendliness extended by assistant manager Claudine Chalande is the reason many regulars return on a regular basis.

TELEPHONE
42-65-71-61

FAX
42-66-96-77

MÉTRO
Madeleine

CREDIT CARDS
AE, MC, V

RATES
Single 440F, double 525F; extra bed 75F

BREAKFAST
40F extra per person

During the week, when the hotel caters to business people, the hotel is generally full, but when they go home for the weekend, last-minute reservations are possible.

English Spoken: Yes

Facilities and Services: Direct-dial phone (and one in the bathroom); hair dryer; no elevator; mini-bar; TV with international reception; safe in double rooms, no charge; fax plugs

Nearest Tourist Attractions (Right Bank): Madeleine Church, shopping on rue St-Honoré, place de la Concorde, Tuileries, Louvre

HÔTEL LIDO ★★★
4, passage de la Madeleine, 75008 (8th)
32 rooms, all with shower or bath and toilet

TELEPHONE
42-66-27-37; toll-free from the U.S. and Canada 1-800-528-1234

FAX
42-66-61-23

MÉTRO
Madeleine

CREDIT CARDS
AE, DC, MC, V

RATES
Single 850F, double 970F; extra bed 100F

BREAKFAST
Included, cannot be deducted

For the ultimate center-city location, close to almost everything by foot or Métro, the Lido is a stellar choice. Window boxes filled with bright red geraniums set the hotel apart on the little *passage* off place de la Madeleine. An 18th-century tapestry dominates the reception and lobby. Exposed beams, magnificent, hand-rubbed antiques, a miniature garden, and masses of fresh flowers complete the charming beginning. Even the smallest, red-linen-lined rooms have enough living space. Minibars are hidden in heavy wooden furniture, and delicate lace spreads cover the large beds. Extras such as full-length mirrors, sewing kits, scented soaps, and the personalized service by the cordial staff make the Lido one of the top selections in the eighth arrondissement.

English Spoken: Yes

Facilities and Services: Air-conditioning in 15 rooms; bar; direct-dial phone; hair dryer; elevator; mini-bar; TV with international reception; room safe, 50F per stay

Nearest Tourist Attractions (Right Bank): Madeleine Church, Fauchon, place de la Concorde, Tuileries, Louvre, Palais-Royal, old Opéra, shopping at Galeries Lafayette and Au Printemps department stores, Champs-Élysées

HÔTEL MARIGNY ★★
11, rue de l'Arcade, 75008 (8th)
32 rooms, 26 with shower or bath and toilet

Only a few hundred yards from the Madeleine Church and a bracing 10 minutes from Gare St-Lazare and place de la Concorde is this reliable Cheap Sleep owned and ably run by the Maugars family. The neighborhood is dull as dishwater after 7 P.M. and on weekends, but the prices are right and the Métro is close. The spotless rooms are reached by the same antique bird-cage elevator that Marcel Proust used when he lived and wrote in the hotel. Most of the rooms are sunny, several connect, and some on the top floor have balconies where you can step outside and enjoy the view. Renovated rooms are naturally preferred, especially no. 61, a double with a shower. The room is simply decorated in textured white wallpaper, with a matching peach floral fabric for the bedspread and curtains.

English Spoken: Yes

Facilities and Services: Direct-dial phone; elevator; mini-bar; TV; office safe, no charge

Nearest Tourist Attractions (Right Bank): Madeleine Church, Tuileries, place Vendôme, place de la Concorde, old Opéra, shopping at Galeries Lafayette and Au Printemps department stores

TELEPHONE
42-66-42-71

FAX
47-42-06-76

MÉTRO
Madeleine, Havre-Caumartin

CREDIT CARDS
MC, V

RATES
Single 235–475F, double 480F; extra bed 150F

BREAKFAST
35F per person

HÔTEL QUEEN MARY ★★★
9, rue Greffulhe, 75008 (8th)
35 rooms, all with shower or bath and toilet

Visitors to Paris with champagne tastes but a Perrier budget, who desire a distinguished hotel in the center of the city between the old Opéra and the Madeleine Church, will never do better than the completely redone Queen Mary. The new British owner, David Byrne (who also owns Hôtel du Bois in the 16th, see page 168), has used only the finest materials in refurbishing his newest hotel acquisition.

Beautiful ceiling details and thick moldings soften the rooms, uniformly done with English carpeting, rich fabrics, and built-in furniture in pale wood tones. Luxury accessories such as air-conditioning, double-glazed windows, 20-channel TV, FM radio and alarm clock, room safe, and beautiful bathrooms with a hair dryer and separate telephone add to the appreciation of the rooms. Breakfast is served in a yellow-and-green basement dining room, where you have your choice of a regular Continental repast, one for slimmers, or a no-calorie-barred buffet that includes bacon, eggs, and cornflakes, along with your croissants, butter, and jam.

Many thoughtful touches make the difference here: a decanter of sherry in each room; happy hour from 6–8 P.M. in the friendly blue-and-white bar off the entry; and

TELEPHONE
42-66-40-50

FAX
42-66-94-92

MÉTRO
Madeleine, Havre Caumartin, Opéra, RER-Auber

CREDIT CARDS
MC, V

RATES
Single 725F, double 825–900F, suite 1,200F; extra bed 180F

BREAKFAST
65F per person, three choices: Continental, slimmer, buffet

breakfast service in a tiny fountain garden when weather permits.

Shoppers take serious note: You are in ultrachic Fashion Country here. The names Lanvin, Yves St-Laurent, Jean-Paul Gaultier, and many more are on the boutiques that are no less than a 10- to 15-minute browse from the hotel door.

English Spoken: Yes

Facilities and Services: Air-conditioning; bar; direct-dial phone; hair dryer; elevator; mini-bar; radio; TV with international reception; room safe, 10F per day; trouser press; decanter of sherry in room

Nearest Tourist Attractions (Right Bank): Madeleine Church, old Opéra, designer shopping, and shopping at Galeries Lafayette and Au Printemps department stores

TIMHÔTEL ST-LAZARE ★★

113, rue Saint Lazare, 75008 (8th)

92 rooms, all with bath or shower and toilet

TELEPHONE 43-87-53-53
FAX 43-87-66-25
MÉTRO Saint-Lazare
CREDIT CARDS AE, DC, MC, V
RATES Single 460F, double 550F, triple 695F
BREAKFAST 55F extra per person

See page 49 for general information about Timhôtels.

English Spoken: Yes

Facilities and Services: Bar; conference room; direct-dial phone; hair dryer; elevator; TV with international reception; office safe, no charge

Nearest Tourist Attractions (Right Bank): Grand boulevards, shopping at Galeries Lafayette and Au Printemps department stores, old Opéra

Ninth Arrondissement

(See map, pages 132–133.)

In the southern part of this arrondissement is the old Opéra with its famous Chagall ceiling, many large banks, and shopping at Galeries Lafayette and Au Printemps. At the northern end is the infamous Pigalle, a sleazy 24-hour neighborhood lined with peep shows, bordellos, "ladies of the night," and everything else you can imagine that walks on the seamy side of life. Avoid the Métro stops Anvers, Pigalle, and Barbès-Rochechouart after dark.

RIGHT BANK
Grands magazins (Au Printemps and Galeries Lafayette), old Opéra, Pigalle

HOTELS IN THE NINTH ARRONDISSEMENT

HÔTEL DES ARTS ★★

7, Cité Bergère, entrance at No. 6, rue de Faubourg Montmartre, 75009 (9th)

26 rooms, all with shower or bath and toilet

The Cité Bergère is a *passage* in central Paris that has eight hotels offering more than 400 rooms to weary travelers. I have seen them all, and the Hôtel des Arts, filled with pretty pink and white flowers, is the best of the bunch by far. While it is nothing fancy, the rooms are spotless and have price tags that appeal to couples on budgets who are happy in a busy city location. The rooms all display a wondrous mixture of period furniture, including some family pieces such as an old dressing table on the fifth floor that belonged to the owner's *grand'mère.* Flocked and flowered wallpaper, chrome, plastic, fringe, ruffles, and chenille are also used with abandon. A lifetime collection of posters lines the stairs and hallways and now almost reaches the top floor. The pretty glass dining room has a wagon filled with flowers and green plants. In one corner, Babar, a colorful 30-year-old bird talks and whistles a happy tune. While hardly a tourist mecca, the location is within walking distance of the Folies Bergère and a Métro stop or two away from Montmartre. Motorist take note: The hotel has four *free* parking spaces. In any part of Paris, that convenience and savings alone are worth double the price of the room.

English Spoken: Yes

TELEPHONE
42-46-73-30

FAX
48-00-94-42

MÉTRO
Rue Montmartre, exit Faubourg Montmartre

CREDIT CARDS
AE, DC, MC, V

RATES
Single 370–390F, double 390–420F, triple 550F

BREAKFAST
30F extra per person

Facilities and Services: Bar; direct-dial phone; elevator; hair dryer; TV; office safe, no charge; four free parking spaces

Nearest Tourist Attractions (Right Bank): Folies Bergère, old Opéra, shopping at Galeries Lafayette and Au Printemps department stores

MONDIAL HÔTEL EUROPÉEN ★★

21, rue Notre-Dame-de-Lorette, 75009 (9th)

36 rooms, all with shower or bath and toilet

TELEPHONE
48-78-60-47

FAX
42-81-95-58

MÉTRO
St-Georges

CREDIT CARDS
MC, V

RATES
1–2 persons 375F, triple 480F, quad 500F

BREAKFAST
30F extra per person

Anyway you look at it, staying in and around Pigalle is a tough call. You either settle for a dump with questionable guests and nonstop street noise, or you wind up in a tour-bus hotel filled with revelers in from the sticks for a few laughs. However, all hope is not lost. The Mondial Hôtel Européen, a Métro stop away from all the earthy activities associated with Pigalle, is a nonthreatening choice in a decent area. It is a clean renovated budget hotel that is cheery and packs all the basic comforts. Pinks and peach are the colors of choice, and chenille the fabric used in the nondescript rooms that remind me of a Motel 6. The owners have been here for 15 years or more and are extremely nice.

English Spoken: Yes

Facilities and Services: Direct-dial phone; hair dryer; elevator; TV; office safe, no charge

Nearest Tourist Attractions (Right Bank): Pigalle, Montmartre

Eleventh and Twelfth Arrondissements

These arrondissements are known as the *quartiers populaires* because they are traditionally working-class neighborhoods where many foreigners settle. These are not hotbeds of tourist activity, but they provide interesting glimpses of both the blue-collar Parisian way of life and the new-wave artists. The neighborhoods around the Bastille and the futuristic new Opéra are the city's new bohemia, full of art galleries, lofts, cafés, nightclubs, and boutiques featuring the craze of the week. This area hums night and day and is definitely the "in" place to see and be seen for anyone in the thirty-something category who likes to walk on the wild side.

RIGHT BANK
Place de la République, rue de Paradis, Gare du Nord, Gare de l'Est, Bastille, new Opéra, nightlife around rue de Lappe

HOTELS IN THE ELEVENTH ARRONDISSEMENT

HOTELS IN THE TWELFTH ARRONDISSEMENT

DAVAL HÔTEL ★★
21, rue Daval, 75011 (11th)
23 rooms, all with shower or bath and toilet

M. Gonod runs his Bastille budget hotel with good sense, good humor, and kindness. Valued mainly for its "in" location and price, the Daval Hôtel occupies a platinum position in the white-hot Bastille area, only a short promenade from the new Opéra and all the cafés, bars, boutiques, and galleries that characterize this newly popular *quartier.* The rooms are done in the same minimalistic style: open closets, compact baths, built-in

TELEPHONE
47-00-51-23
FAX
40-21-80-26
MÉTRO
Bastille, Bréguet-Sabin
CREDIT CARDS
AE, MC, V

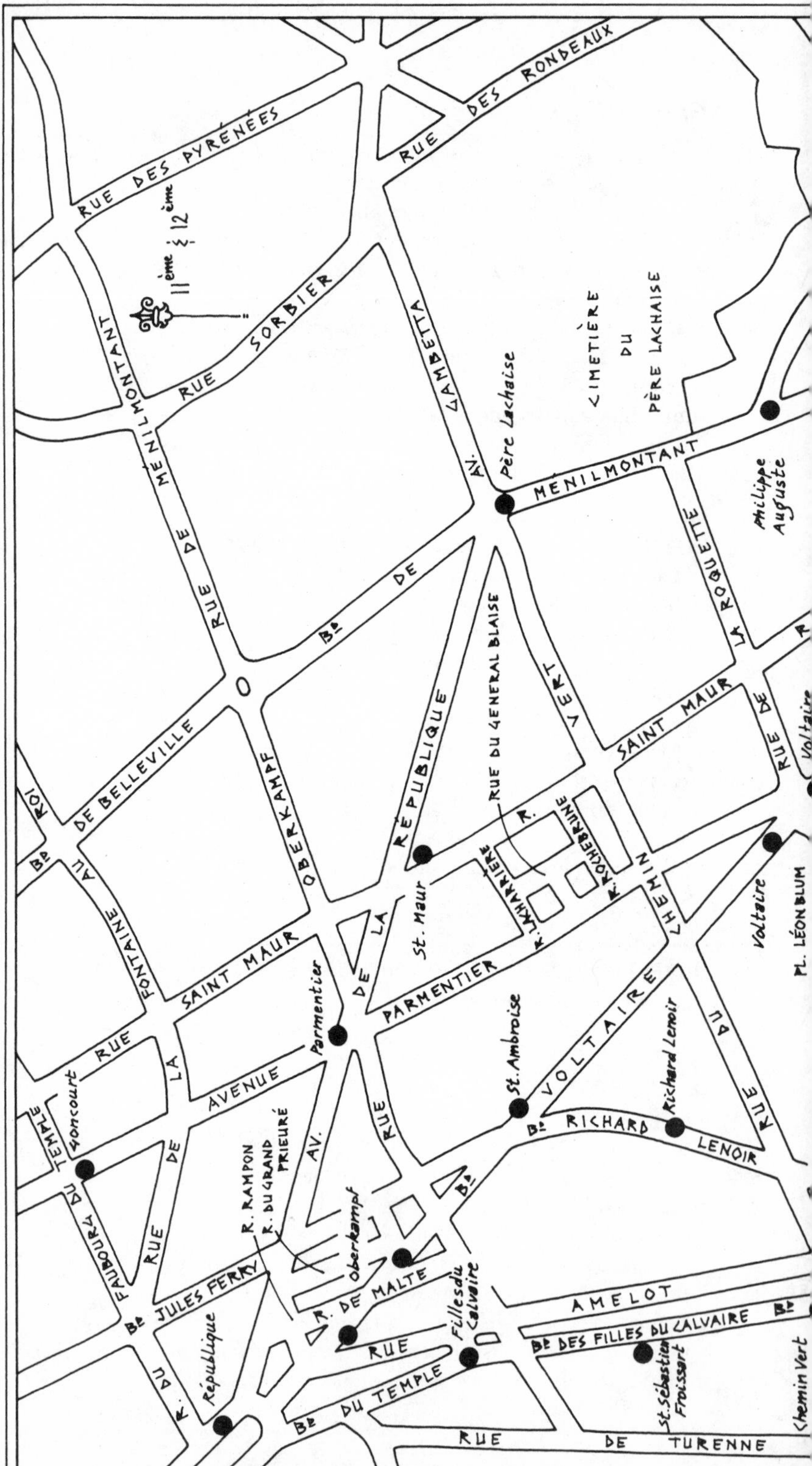

RUE DES PYRÉNÉES
RUE DES RONDEAUX
11ème & 12ème
RUE SORBIER
RUE DE MÉNILMONTANT
AV. GAMBETTA
CIMETIÈRE DU PÈRE LACHAISE
Père Lachaise
MÉNILMONTANT
Philippe Auguste
LA ROQUETTE
BD DE BELLEVILLE
OBERKAMPF
AV. DE LA RÉPUBLIQUE
RUE DU GENERAL BLAISE
VERT
SAINT MAUR
RUE DE
Voltaire
BD
FONTAINE AU ROI
RUE SAINT MAUR
Parmentier
PARMENTIER
St. Maur
R. LACHARRIÈRE
R. ROCHEBRUNE
CHEMIN
PL. LÉON BLUM
Voltaire
St. Ambroise
VOLTAIRE
Richard Lenoir
BD RICHARD LENOIR
RUE DU
Goncourt
FAUBOURG DU TEMPLE
RUE DE LA
AVENUE
R. RAMPON
R. DU GRAND PRIEURÉ
AV.
Oberkampf
RUE
BD JULES FERRY
R. DE MALTE
Filles du Calvaire
AMELOT
BD DES FILLES DU CALVAIRE
St. Sébastien Froissart
Chemin Vert
République
R. DU
BD DU TEMPLE
RUE DE TURENNE

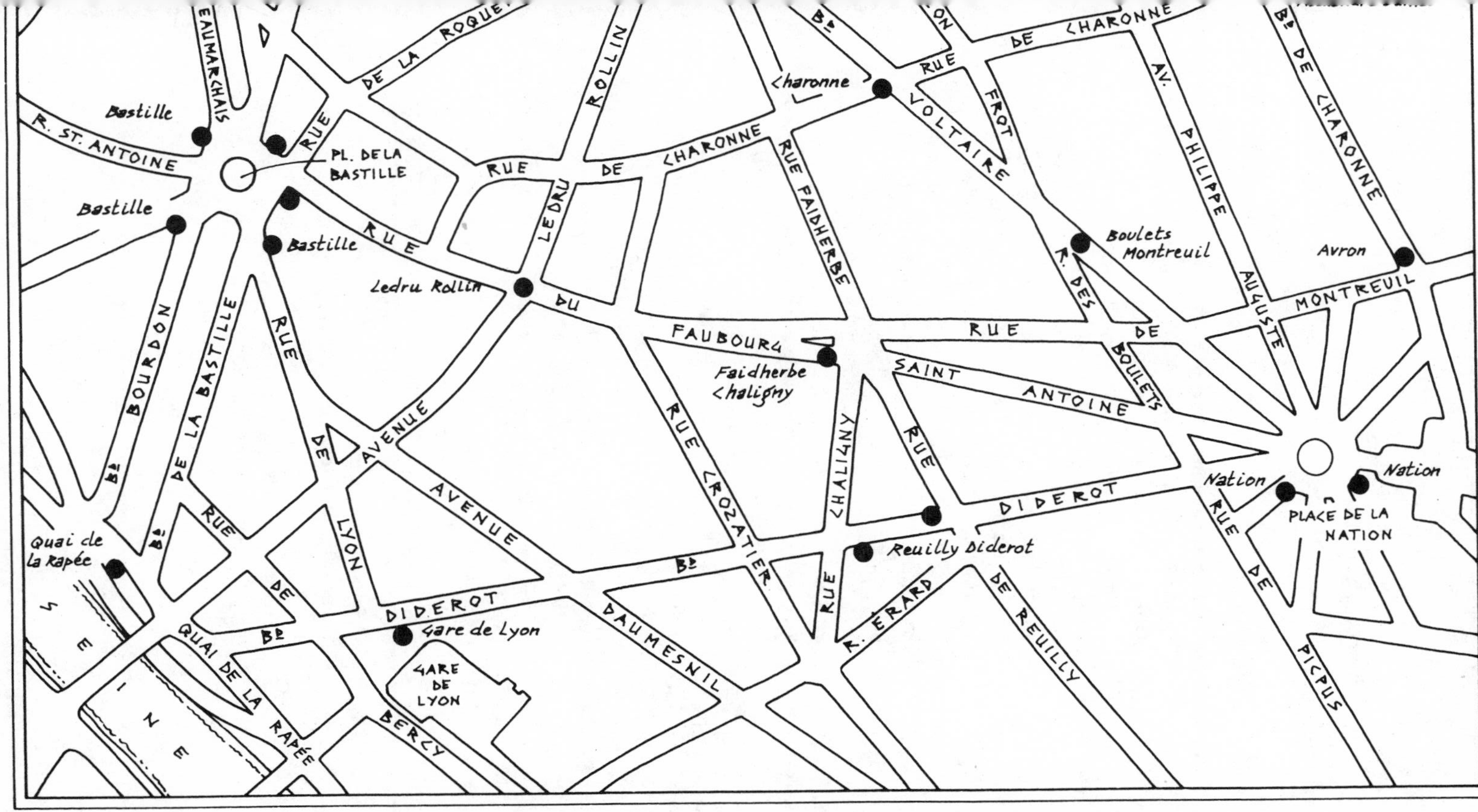
EAUMARCHAIS
Bastille
R. ST. ANTOINE
Bastille
RUE DE LA ROQUE
PL. DE LA BASTILLE
Bastille
ROLLIN
RUE DE CHARONNE
RUE LEDRU
Ledru Rollin
RUE DU FAUBOURG SAINT ANTOINE
Charonne
RUE VOLTAIRE
Bd
RUE FROT
AV. PHILIPPE AUGUSTE
Bd DE CHARONNE
RUE FAIDHERBE
Boulets Montreuil
R. DES BOULETS
Avron
MONTREUIL
Faidherbe Chaligny
Bd BOURDON
Bd DE LA BASTILLE
RUE DE LYON
AVENUE
AVENUE
RUE CROZATIER
CHALIGNY
RUE
DIDEROT
Nation
Nation
PLACE DE LA NATION
RUE DE PICPUS
Quai de la Rapée
Bd
Reuilly Diderot
RUE
R. ERARD
DE REUILLY
RUE DE
DIDEROT
Bd
Gare de Lyon
DAUMESNIL
SEINE
QUAI DE LA RAPÉE
GARE DE LYON
BERCY

RATES
Single 340F, double 390–490F, triple 490F, quad 600F
BREAKFAST
45F extra per person

beds and side tables, and no chairs or stools for seating. A few dings and nicks remind you that the rooms have been well lived-in. Mercifully, the walls are thick enough to buffer the neighbor's snoring or late-night television viewing. The Continental breakfast may seem expensive, but it does include orange juice and a piece of cheese.

English Spoken: Yes

Facilities and Services: Direct-dial phone; elevator; hair dryer; TV; room safe, no charge

Nearest Tourist Attractions (Right Bank): Bastille area, new Opéra

HÔTEL DE NEVERS ★

53, rue de Malte, and 8, rue Rampon, 75011 (11th)
34 rooms, 10 with shower or bath and toilet

TELEPHONE
47-00-56-18
FAX
43-57-77-39
MÉTRO
Oberkampf, République
CREDIT CARDS
MC, V
RATES
Single 155–260F, double 175–275F, triple 350F, quad 385F
BREAKFAST
25F extra per person

For a one-star Cheap Sleep in the 11th arrondissement, the Hôtel de Nevers gets two thumbs up. Alain and Sophie Bourderau lived in Williamsburg, Virginia, and helped her sister run a French restaurant. Now they are back in Paris, running their shiny one-star hotel. As you walk in, you will be greeted by either Alain or Sophie, and their ink-black cat Jo, who loves to sit right on top of the reception desk and chew on pens . . . so watch out! Green trellis wallpaper enhances the profusion of green plants that sit in planter boxes around the room. Bedrooms are reached via a metal stairway with the original brass handrail in place. The less athletic can step into the mirrored cage elevator. Cleanliness is a priority, sophisticated decor is not, so please do not expect rooms to bear the *Architectural Digest* seal of approval. You won't like living in no. 21, which faces an air shaft, but in no. 18 you will have plenty of sun, a stall shower, and wallpaper with iris flowers on it. Breakfast is served in your room and includes a croissant . . . which most one-star morning meals do not.

English Spoken: Yes

Facilities and Services: Direct-dial phone; elevator to four floors; no TV; safe in office, no charge

Nearest Tourist Attractions (Right Bank): Nothing; must use public transportation

HÔTEL DU GRAND-PRIEURÉ ★★

20, rue du Grand-Prieuré, 75011 (11th)

32 rooms, all with shower or bath and toilet

When people ask for a hotel near place de la République, I now have an answer: the Hôtel du Grand-Prieuré. Someone had great fun at the fake flower *marché,* because they are everywhere: outside in window boxes, inside in pots and bouquets, wrapped around standing trees, stuffed in an atrium. Fake floral displays aside, the hotel has merit and value. First of all, it is very clean . . . always a good sign. Next, the management is on the ball and makes sure that the hotel runs well. Each floor sports a different color, and all 32 rooms and adjoining baths are acceptable. No. 501, on the top floor, is a good selection because it has sun, more space, and a bathroom with a bidet, which is hard to find these days in modest two-star hotels. On the same floor, no. 502 has linen-covered walls, a nice desk, and the toilet apart from the bathroom. Bright red doors greet guests staying in no. 604. A utilitarian dining room, brightened by red bentwood bistro chairs placed around white square tables, is where you will be served a reasonably priced Continental breakfast.

English Spoken: Limited

Facilities and Services: Direct-dial phone; hair dryer; elevator; mini-bar; radio; TV; office safe, no charge

Nearest Tourist Attractions (Right Bank): None; must use public transportation

TELEPHONE
47-00-74-14

FAX
49-23-06-64

MÉTRO
République, Oberkampf

CREDIT CARDS
AE, MC, V

RATES
1–2 persons 340–380F, triple 480F; extra bed 80F

BREAKFAST
35F extra per person

HÔTEL RÉSIDENCE ALHAMBRA ★★

11 bis & 13, rue de Malte, 75011 (11th)

58 rooms, all with shower or bath and toilet

Here is a textbook example of getting what you pay for. Out of the way? Yes, more than a New York minute to get to what's really happening. Close to the Métro? Yes, five major lines serve place de la République. Cheap? Absolutely, when you consider you will receive a 10 percent discount if you mention you are a faithful reader of this bible for all Cheap Sleepers in Paris.

The hotel is better than the neighborhood suggests. Automatic doors lead from the street into the leather-clad lobby. Blue or orange colors, open closets, no drawers, a built-in desk, and one chair sum up the rooms. Plumbing is of recent vintage. Eight of the rooms overlook what has to be the prettiest hotel garden on the Right Bank . . . at least in an out-of-the-way two-star. If

TELEPHONE
47-00-35-52

FAX
43-57-98-75

MÉTRO
République, Oberkampf

CREDIT CARDS
MC, V

RATES
Single 325F, double 345–375F, triple 420–550F; 10 percent discount for readers of *Cheap Sleeps in Paris,* must mention when reserving

BREAKFAST
30F extra per person

you are lucky and secure one of these prime spots, you will overlook rose bushes, seasonal flowers, and trees, all lovingly tended by the owner's sister. Tables and chairs are set outside in the summer, making it an especially nice place to have your morning croissant.

English Spoken: Yes

Facilities and Services: Direct-dial phone; some TVs; safe in office, no charge

Nearest Tourist Attractions (Right Bank): None; must use public transportation

HÔTEL RHETIA ★

3, rue du General Blaise (near avenue Parmentier), 75011 (11th)

24 rooms, 16 with shower or bath and toilet

TELEPHONE
47-00-47-18

FAX
42-61-23-17

MÉTRO
Saint-Ambroise, Saint-Maur

CREDIT CARDS
None, cash only

RATES
1–2 persons 180–240F, triple 250–290F; extra bed 50F; shower 10F

BREAKFAST
10F extra per person (a steal!)

Keep the prices cheap enough and people will come back again and again, just as they do from Sweden, Belgium, Singapore, Australia, England, the U.S., and Canada. As one Sydney, Australia, guest put it, "It is neat, clean, tidy, homey . . . all you need." I agree. Not all the rooms have private bathrooms, and only four have a television. Most are minimally furnished in the usual one-star collection that has been used well over the years. At only 10 francs per person, breakfast can be considered a gift. Grab it! The red hall carpets are worn but clean; the neighborhood is safe and quiet (for Paris); and the rooms along the front face the square Maurice Gardet. You are within reasonable walking distance to all the nightlife the area is known for and a Métro ride to everything else interesting.

English Spoken: None

Facilities and Services: Direct-dial phone (for Paris only); four rooms with a TV

Nearest Tourist Attractions (Right Bank): Not much other than nightlife about a 15-minute walk from the hotel; must use public transportation for everything else

PARIS BASTILLE ★★

14, rue de la Roquette, 75011 (11th)

29 rooms, all with shower or bath and toilet

TELEPHONE
48-05-62-47

FAX
49-23-07-58

MÉTRO
Bastille

Once a worn-out, old hotel, the Paris Bastille has been refurbished and redecorated, and new bathrooms have been installed along with color televisions that you can tune into for CNN and your news fix. At the Paris Bastille, don't expect gold trimmings and designer linens; do look for rooms for savings in a popular location. Singles are nice, even on the back. Rooms with double beds get claustrophobic, but mattresses are top quality and so are the shiny white tiled baths. No smoking rooms are available, and the climb up the stairs is not too taxing. The area is filled with fast-track nightlife, cafés to hang out in for hours, and boutiques showing next year's fashion fads.

English Spoken: Yes

Facilities and Services: Direct-dial phone; hair dryer; no elevator; mini-bar; TV with international reception; office safe, no charge

Nearest Tourist Attractions (Right Bank): Bastille, Marais

CREDIT CARDS
MC, V

RATES
Single 450F, double 525F, suite 600F; extra bed 50 percent of room rate

BREAKFAST
50F extra per person

PAX HÔTEL ★

12, rue de Charonne, 75011 (11th)

47 rooms, 37 with shower or bath and toilet

If the dark red carpet, orange chenille spreads, and lavender-tiled bathroom don't grab you in room no. 204, surely the low price will. Low Cheap Sleeping prices also prevail in the rest of the hotel, which is kept spotlessly clean and beauitfully maintained, despite the tacky colors. There is no elevator, but you will have a television, and if you are in a bathless roost for more than a week, your shower will be free. If you receive your mail and retirement checks at a Leisure World address, this is not your Paris stomping ground. You will undoubtedly run into wine-guzzling *chochards* relaxing in doorways and old ladies in fuzzy slippers tossing baguettes to pigeons. It is not all residentially challenging . . . not by a long shot. This is the "with-it" *quartier* that boasts everything on the wild side—from late-night disco palaces to cafés and wine bars of the moment. The area is close to the new Opéra Bastille, but a Métro ride away from almost everything else, unless walking 15 or 20 minutes is something you don't mind doing.

English Spoken: Generally

Facilities and Services: Direct-dial phone; hair dryer; no elevator; TV; no safe

Nearest Tourist Attractions (Right Bank): Opéra Bastille

TELEPHONE
47-00-40-98

FAX
43-38-57-81

MÉTRO
Ledru Rollin, Bastille

CREDIT CARDS
AE, MC, V

RATES
1–2 persons 200–250F, triple 360F, quad 400F; shower 20F (no charge if you stay a week)

BREAKFAST
30F extra per person

LE PAVILLON BASTILLE ★★★

65, rue de Lyon, 75012 (12th)

24 rooms, all with shower or bath and toilet

TELEPHONE
43-43-65-65

FAX
43-43-96-52; toll free 800-233-2552

MÉTRO
Bastille

CREDIT CARDS
AE, DC, MC, V

RATES
1–2 persons 950F, suite 1,400F (see Special Package Deals, following)

BREAKFAST
78F extra per person

The Pavillon Bastille is not only a perfect gem of a hotel, smack-dab across from the Opéra Bastille, but the most artistically imaginative hotel to open in Paris for some time.

The entire hotel is a creative study in blue and yellow by noted architectural designer Jean-Pierre Heim, whose commissions include Christian Lacroix boutiques and the French embassies in New York and Riyadh. His work at the hotel received the American magazine *Hotel Restaurant Design International* "Award of Excellence" for the best hotel design under 300 rooms. You can imagine the competition!

Yellow and blue are used exclusively on everything from the awning hanging over the granite courtyard, with a 17th-century fountain, to the bonbons placed on your pillow at night. Taking his cue from music, Heim wove harmonious details into the design of the hotel: doorknobs shaped like flutes, wall and furniture details adapting the five-line pattern of written music, and rugs with the lines of grand pianos. A mirrored entry reflects the lounge, which was planned "as a dreamy landscape of light and dark objects floating within space," says Heim. Upon arrival, guests are served refreshments here or escorted to their rooms . . . there is no formal registration area.

The 24 bedrooms are all slightly different in design, but they have the same custom-made furniture to make the most of their limited space. A mirrored wall behind the bed shows the hand-painted Venetian-style yellow walls. Framed prints in each room were gleaned from flea markets. The rooms, either queen or twin bedded, offer all the amenities, including air-conditioning, international TV, a VCR, *free* beverages from the mini-bar, and a personal printed guide to Paris. Bathrooms are beautifully fitted with magnifying mirrors, Porthault robes, and plenty of soft towels.

The vaulted cellar is now Le Orchestra, a breakfast room where bleached oak chairs and paneling blend with blue-and-yellow upholstery and table linens. Hand-painted blue walls complement the dark blue carpeting. A large buffet with yogurt, cereal, fruit, and fresh orange juice is served every morning.

Owners Chantal and Michel Arnaud and their English-speaking staff do everything they can to insure guests are happy and cared for. Special weekend and summer packages make this wonderful hotel even better.

Special Package Deals at Le Pavillon Bastille: *Une Soiree Exceptionelle (One of a kind evening)* includes an evening at the Opéra Bastille, first-category seating, accommodation and breakfast at Le Pavillon Bastille, and a preopera drink in the hotel lounge. Depending on performance, the rates are from 815–1,035F per person, double occupancy, 465F extra for single occupancy.

Paris with Pleasure in Mind includes two nights and two breakfasts at Le Pavillon Bastille, a boat trip along the Seine, two days free Métro tickets, one-day complimentary passes to some museums, dinner for two (including wine) at Bofinger, and candy for the children left at home. The rate is 1,260F per person in a double room.

Alternate: Between July 1 and August 31, bring the children and you can stay three nights for the price of two. Daily rate for first two nights: 925F per room. Also available without children.

English Spoken: Yes

Facilities and Services: Air-conditioning; bar; direct-dial phone; hair dryer; elevator; mini-bar with free beverages; radio; TV with international reception; room safe, no charge; room service for light meals; no charge for ironing guests' clothes; office services; laundry and dry cleaning services

Nearest Tourist Attractions (Right Bank): Opéra Bastille, Marais

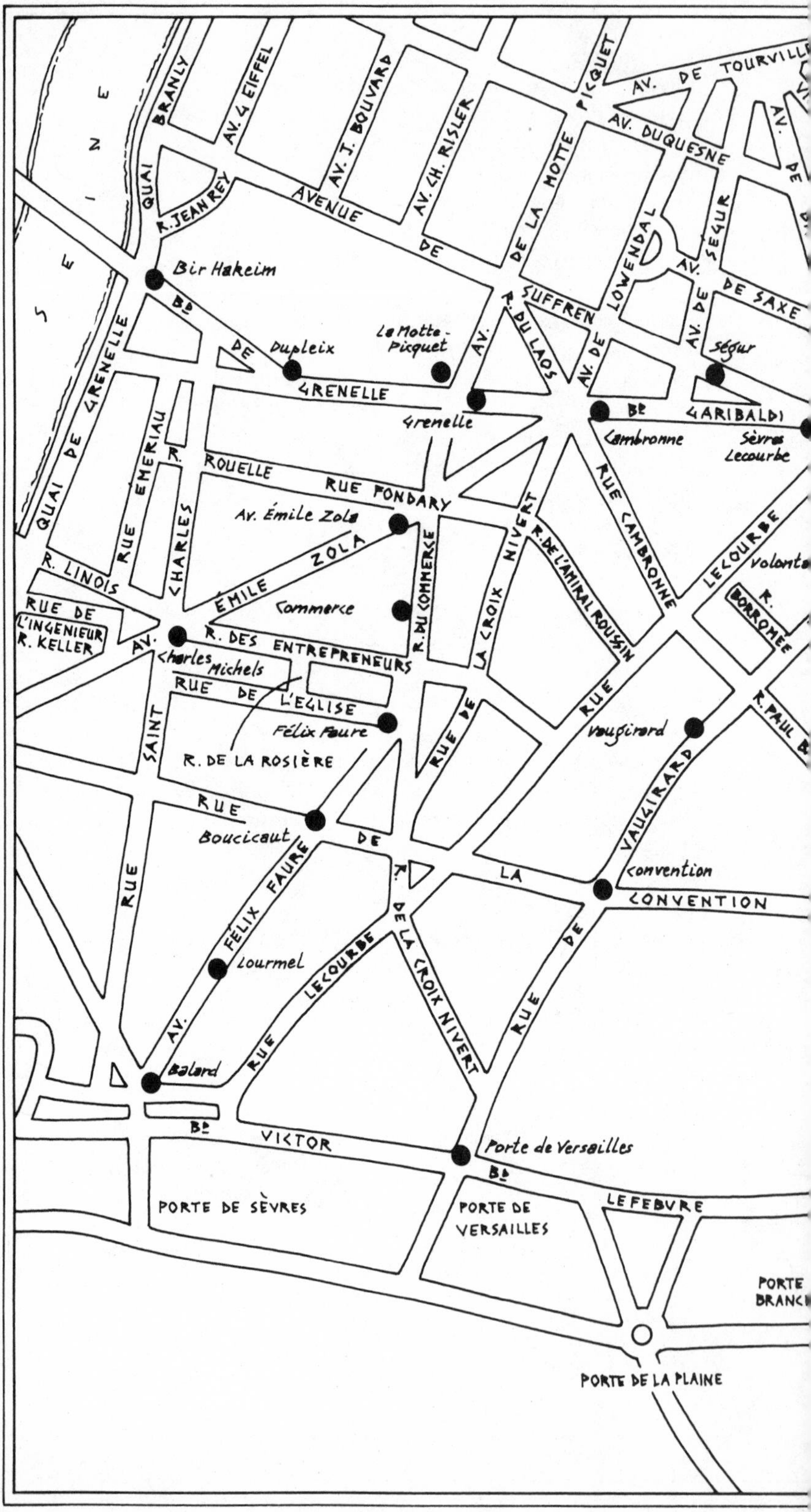
SEINE
QUAI BRANLY
AV. G. EIFFEL
AV. J. BOUVARD
AV. CH. RISLER
PICQUET
AV. DE TOURVILLE
AV. DUQUESNE
R. JEAN REY
AVENUE DE SUFFREN
DE LA MOTTE
LOWENDAL
AV. DE SÉGUR
AV. DE SAXE
Bir Hakeim
Bd DE GRENELLE
Dupleix
La Motte-Picquet
AV.
R. DU LAOS
AV. DE
Ségur
QUAI DE GRENELLE
Grenelle
Bd GARIBALDI
Cambronne
Sèvres Lecourbe
R.
RUE EMERIAU
ROUELLE
RUE FONDARY
Av. Émile Zola
CHARLES
AV. ÉMILE ZOLA
R. LINOIS
RUE DE L'INGENIEUR R. KELLER
Commerce
R. DU COMMERCE
LA CROIX NIVERT
R. DE L'AMIRAL ROUSSIN
RUE CAMBRONNE
LECOURBE
Volonta
R. BORROMÉE
AV. Charles Michels
R. DES ENTREPRENEURS
RUE DE L'EGLISE
Félix Faure
R. DE LA ROSIÈRE
SAINT
RUE DE
RUE Vaugirard
VAUGIRARD
R. PAUL B
RUE Boucicaut
DE LA CONVENTION
convention
RUE
AV. FÉLIX FAURE
R. DE LA CROIX NIVERT
Lourmel
RUE LECOURBE
RUE DE
Balard
Bd VICTOR
Porte de Versailles
Bd LEFEBVRE
PORTE DE SÈVRES
PORTE DE VERSAILLES
PORTE BRANC
PORTE DE LA PLAINE

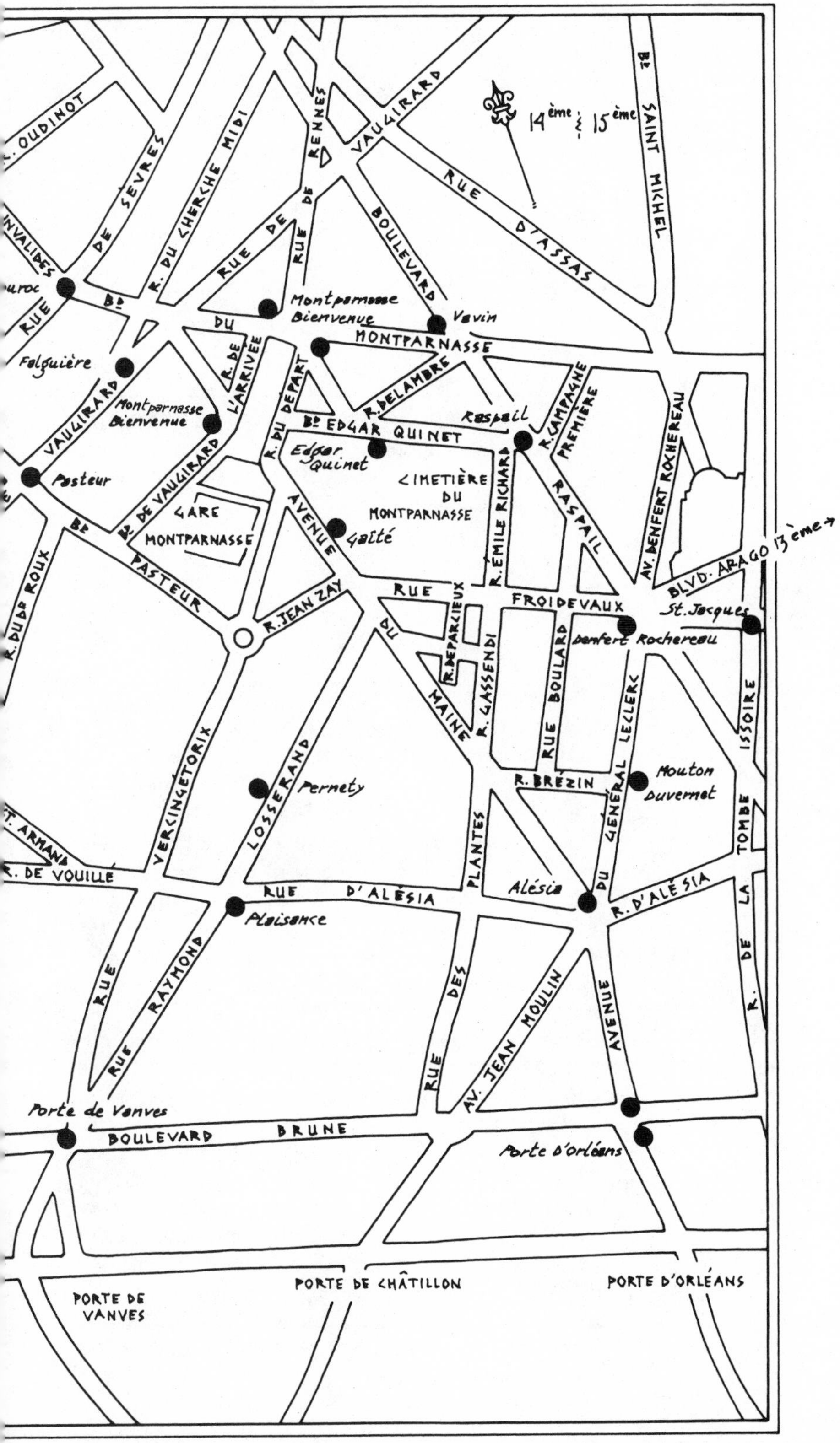
14ème & 15ème
Bd SAINT MICHEL
RUE D'ASSAS
RUE DE VAUGIRARD
BOULEVARD
RUE DE RENNES
R. DU CHERCHE MIDI
DE SEVRES
R. OUDINOT
INVALIDES
Duroc
RUE
Bd DU MONTPARNASSE
Montparnasse Bienvenue
Vavin
Falguière
R. DE L'ARRIVÉE
R. DU DÉPART
R. DELAMBRE
Bd EDGAR QUINET
Raspail
R. CAMPAGNE PREMIÈRE
AV. DENFERT ROCHEREAU
Montparnasse Bienvenue
VAUGIRARD
Pasteur
Bd DE VAUGIRARD
Edgar Quinet
CIMETIÈRE DU MONTPARNASSE
R. EMILE RICHARD
RASPAIL
GARE MONTPARNASSE
AVENUE
Gaîté
BLVD. ARAGO 13ème →
Bd PASTEUR
R. DUBOUX
R. JEAN ZAY
RUE FROIDEVAUX
St. Jacques
Denfert Rochereau
R. DEPARCIEUX
R. GASSENDI
RUE BOULARD
DU MAINE
ISSOIRE
VERCINGETORIX
LOSSERAND
Pernety
R. BRÉZIN
DU GÉNÉRAL LECLERC
Mouton Duvernet
T. ARMAND
R. DE VOUILLE
RUE D'ALÉSIA
Alésia
R. D'ALÉSIA
Plaisance
RUE RAYMOND
RUE
RUE DES PLANTES
AV. JEAN MOULIN
AVENUE
R. DE LA TOMBE
Porte de Vanves
BOULEVARD BRUNE
Porte d'Orléans
PORTE DE VANVES
PORTE DE CHÂTILLON
PORTE D'ORLÉANS

Fourteenth Arrondissement

LEFT BANK
Montparnasse, Les Catecombs

In recent years Montparnasse has become the victim of a tragically insensitive redevelopment policy exemplified by the Tour Montparnasse. During the 1920s and 1930s, the 14th was well-known as the artistic headquarters of the modern art and literary worlds. Nostalgia buffs return today and head for the historic brasseries Le Dôme and La Coupole to rekindle memories of the famous who ate and drank there, but they find the spirit is just not the same.

HOTELS IN THE FOURTEENTH ARRONDISSEMENT

GRAND HÔTEL DU SQUARE (no stars)
2, rue Boulard, 75014 (14th)
30 rooms, none with shower or bath and toilet

TELEPHONE
43-22-50-09

FAX
None

MÉTRO
Denfert-Rochereau

CREDIT CARDS
None, cash only

RATES
Single 125–170F, double 190F; extra bed 50F for child up to 16, otherwise must have own room; shower 10F

BREAKFAST
Not served

The Grand Hôtel du Square is certainly *not* grand—in fact, it has not had a face-lift in years, but then neither have the rates, which can be described as almost prehistoric. In addition, its location far from the bright lights and excitement is not what I would call thrilling. But for Cheap Sleepers who find adventure in offbeat, low-budget digs, this could be the right hotel. The bare-bones rooms are done in the attic school of decorating, without carpets or bedside lamps, only an overhead light of questionable wattage. Some rooms have ornate marble fireplaces and sunny views over the nearby square; others display lovely old armoires. Most have chenille spreads that barely fit the slept-in mattresses, none of which are twins. All the rooms are spacious and clean as a whistle. Each floor has a toilet, and there are three showers in the hotel, all of which are clean enough to leave the Lysol in the suitcase. There is no breakfast served, and no one makes any attempt to speak English, unless you happen to run into the owner's daughter, who stops by now and then to visit her mother. The Métro stop is not far and bus connections are good.

English Spoken: None

Facilities and Services: None

Nearest Tourist Attractions (Left Bank): Montparnasse

HÔTEL DE BLOIS ★

5, rue des Plantes, 75014 (14th)

25 rooms, 15 with shower or bath and toilet

This seems to be about two blocks east of nowhere, and it better be very, very good, I thought, as I walked to my final hotel stop after a long, rainy day. As you can see, I needed to be impressed, and Mme. Fontange's Hôtel de Blois turned out to be an impressive winner in the one-star *Cheap Sleeps in Paris* sweepstakes. Cozy and homey are the words that spring to mind when I think of her cheery sitting room with windows overlooking the street. Breakfast is served here in the morning. Around the room, you will see fresh flowers, never dusty plastic ones (which you know by now that I definitely do not like). Her bedrooms are coordinated, none of this rainbow color approach with Garage Sale Gothic furniture. Ask for room no. 2, with a double bed, polished armoire, tiny floral print wallcovering, and a pink-tiled bathroom with new fittings and a shower curtain. No. 6 has a shower with doors, a double bed, and no view, but it does have space to live in. Oriental runners on white painted stairs and a different mural on each of the floors make climbing up to your room a pleasant exercise. Shopaholics take note: what you save on your room you can spend along rue Alésia, the discount shopping mecca for savvy Parisians. It is about a five-minute walk away. See page 231 in Cheap Chic for details.

English Spoken: Limited

Facilities and Services: Direct-dial phone; no elevator; TV; office safe, no charge

Nearest Tourist Attractions (Left Bank): Discount shopping on rue Alésia; must take public transportation to everything else

TELEPHONE
45-40-99-48

FAX
45-40-45-62

MÉTRO
Alésia, Mouton-Duvernet

CREDIT CARDS
MC, V

RATES
Single 220–350F, double 220–350F, triple 260–360F; shower 20F

BREAKFAST
30F extra per person (includes croissant)

HÔTEL DE GRANVILLE ★★

29, rue Deparcieux, 75014 (14th)

20 rooms, all with shower or bath and toilet

On a quiet cul-de-sac, just off the end of the shopping street rue Daguerre, is this Cheap Sleep. The genuine Paris neighborhood is relatively untouched by tourists or trends, so it retains its authenticity. It provides a good

TELEPHONE
43-22-29-57

FAX
43-27-22-02

MÉTRO
Denfert-Rochereau

CREDIT CARDS
V

RATES
Single 250F, double 380–420F, triple 450F

BREAKFAST
30F extra per person, but included at no extra charge in July and August

look at day-to-day life for the working Parisian who has little time or money for many extras. I found the hotel by accident and was attracted by the bright geraniums blooming in all 12 flower boxes under each window along the facade.

On the main floor is a functional breakfast room and lounge with a big leather sofa, two chairs, and a television set. A small elevator, geared to one person carrying one small suitcase, eliminates stair climbing with heavy bags. The clean rooms offer all the necessities and are done according to the two-star school of decorating: rust brown-and-orange textured walls, blue-and-brown carpeting, and ordinary furniture. For the most light and a cheerful outlook, ask for a room facing the front. Bathrooms excel; soap and shampoo are provided. Prices are fair, and during the dog days of summer (July and August), the owners toss in breakfast at no additional cost, saving you 30F per person.

English Spoken: Yes

Facilities and Services: Direct-dial phone; elevator; radio; TV; no safe

Nearest Tourist Attractions (Left Bank): Montparnasse

HÔTEL ISTRIA ★★

29, rue Campagne Première, 75014 (14th)
26 rooms, all with shower or bath and toilet

TELEPHONE
43-20-91-82

FAX
43-22-48-45

MÉTRO
Raspail

CREDIT CARDS
AE, MC, V

RATES
Single 470F, double 520–570F; extra bed 120F

BREAKFAST
40F extra per person

From this address you can wander the tree-lined boulevards and sit in the famous cafés that were the watering holes of Hemingway, Fitzgerald, and Henry Miller when they dominated the Montparnasse literary scene. In the 1920s and 1930s, when this was *the quartier* for artists and writers, the Istria was home to many of them, including Man Ray and his mistress Kiki, Marcel Duchamp, and the poet Maiakowsky. Now under the direction of Philippe Leroux and his delightful wife Danièle, the hotel was been renovated and is a favorite for those seeking a convenient Montparnasse location. A pretty tiled entry with country antiques and Oriental rugs leads to a postage-stamp garden along the back of the hotel. Some of the rooms that overlook the garden are confining for two persons with any luggage. To avoid being cramped, request a third-floor nest. Remember though, this building is old, and spacious rooms are not its strong suit; charm and friendliness are.

English Spoken: Yes

Facilities and Services: Direct-dial phone; hair dryer; elevator; radio; TV; room safe, no charge

Nearest Tourist Attractions (Left Bank): Montparnasse

HÔTEL L'AIGLON ★★★
232, boulevard Raspail, 75014 (14th)
47 rooms, all with shower or bath and toilet

The Hôtel l'Aiglon is a refined choice, about a one-minute walk from the Raspail Métro stop. A formal tone pervades, from the faux-book-lined bar to the beautifully redecorated rooms, all of which have been planned with discretion and good taste. Don't miss seeing the original stained-glass windows over the stairway, which takes guests from the ground floor to a formal dining room with large sideboard and mahogany tables covered in starched white linen. The rooms all face outward and many have peaceful views over the Cimetière Montparnasse. They are color-coordinated, with textured fabrics, firm mattresses, good closet and luggage space, and bathrooms with windows . . . something you do not see often in today's hotels. The suites are dreams come true, especially no. 55, with its soft beige walls and carpets. The sitting room is comfortably furnished with a desk, sofa bed, and easy chair, and it has a half-bath to one side. Twin beds in the bedroom—with its own balcony—and a double-sink bathroom make up the rest. No. 16 is a new room, in bright yellow and green colors that are carried out on the quilted bedspread and curtains. The gray bathroom has gold and beige accents and a floral design in the shower. If you are *tout seul,* it is a perfect choice.

Motorists will appreciate the private parking, and everyone will enjoy the brand of service and hospitality provided by Jacques Rols (who also own Le Notre-Dame Hôtel, see page 83) and his staff.

English Spoken: Yes

Facilities and Services: Bar; direct-dial phone; hair dryer; elevator; mini-bar; private parking; TV; office safe, no charge; laundry service

Nearest Tourist Attractions (Left Bank): Montparnasse

TELEPHONE
43-20-82-42

FAX
43-20-98-72

MÉTRO
Raspail

CREDIT CARDS
AE, DC, MC, V

RATES
Single 550F, double 605–680F, suite (1–4 persons) 1,000–1,575F; extra bed 120F; garage 80F (must request when reserving)

BREAKFAST
40F extra per person

HÔTEL LENOX MONTPARNASSE ★★★

15, rue Delambre, 75014 (14th)

36 rooms, all with shower or bath and toilet

TELEPHONE
43-35-34-50
FAX
43-20-46-64
MÉTRO
Vavin, Edgar-Quinet
CREDIT CARDS
AE, DC, MC, V
RATES
1–2 persons 550–675F, suite 950–985F
BREAKFAST
50F extra per person

The atmosphere is engaging and the clientele an international blend at the Lenox Montparnasse. The collection of furniture suggests Art Deco and the 1930s in both the lobby and large bar to one side. Green plants bring life to the rooms and beautiful sprays of fresh orchids give them wonderful color.

Rooms are nice, with just enough personality to set them apart from other mainstream Montparnasse hotels. If you want more leg room, reserve no. 69, a big twin with a corner sitting room, a tiny fireplace, and a rooftop view. It is softly decorated in blue and light gray. The bathroom has a rolling toiletry cart and blue-and-green inserts of flowers set against the white-tiled walls. No. 49 is a back double in yellow with good closet space and a nice bath, but not much light. The top-floor, two-room suite, with its marble fireplace, period furniture, and geometric upholstery, shows that an eclectic combination of styles and patterns can work if done correctly. Amusing etchings of French ladies of leisure with their dogs or coyly wrapped in fur—and not much else—are on the walls. The narrow bathroom has all the extras, including Roger and Gallet products.

English Spoken: Yes

Facilities and Services: Bar; direct-dial phone; hair dryer; elevator; radio; TV with international reception; office safe, no charge; room service for light snacks

Nearest Tourist Attractions (Left Bank): Montparnasse

HÔTEL NOVANOX ★★★

155, boulevard du Montparnasse, 75014 (14th)

27 rooms, all with shower or bath and toilet

TELEPHONE
46-33-63-60
FAX
43-26-61-72
MÉTRO
Vavin, Raspail
CREDIT CARDS
AE, DC, MC, V

From the outside it doesn't inspire. But inside, the future beckons. What used to be a basic budget hotel in Montparnasse is now the smart Novanox, an impressive example of what a sense of style and a great imagination—with a little money thrown in—can do with an old hotel. Hats off to owner Bernard Plasmans, who gambled everything on creating a modern fantasy hotel, which displays the latest in hotel design and contemporary craftsmanship. The yellow-and-blue lobby, with dangling mobile lights and the faces of Greek gods and goddesses softly painted on the walls and depicted on the upholstered chairs and couches, reminds me of a playful fairyland. At one end of the lobby is a breakfast area overlooking an enclosed sidewalk terrace. Dainty croissants and buttery brioches fill the breakfast baskets and are accompanied by an assortment of jams and a pot of sweet butter. A portion of cheese and kiwi perched in an egg cup complete the meal.

The rooms upstairs have a pastel color scheme, with contemporary furniture especially built to fit the design of each room. The toiletries are from the esteemed Roger and Gallet, the fresh flowers from the owner's mother's garden, the lamps from Spain, the carpet imported from Germany, and the ideas all from M. Plasmans. The result of it all? Still *magnifique!*

English Spoken: Yes

Facilities and Services: Bar; direct-dial phone; some hair dryers; elevator; mini-bar; radio; TV; room safe, no charge

Nearest Tourist Attractions (Left Bank): Montparnasse

RATES
1–2 persons 695F; extra bed 150F; ask for special weekend rates

BREAKFAST
55F extra per person

TIMHÔTEL LE MAINE ★★
146, avenue du Maine, 75014 (14th)
91 rooms, all with bath or shower and toilet

See page 49 for general information about Timhôtels.

English Spoken: Yes

Facilities and Services: Conference rooms; direct-dial phone; elevator; TV; office safe, no charge

Nearest Tourist Attractions (Left Bank): Montparnasse

TELEPHONE
43-35-57-60

FAX
40-47-01-49

MÉTRO
Gaieté

CREDIT CARDS
AE, DC, MC, V

RATES
Single 410F, double 495F, triple 615F

BREAKFAST
55F extra per person

Fifteenth Arrondissement

(See map, pages 152–153.)

The fifteenth is the biggest arrondissement and has few tourist attractions. If you enjoy seeing how the average Parisian lives, this is the perfect vantage point.

LEFT BANK
Nothing from a tourist's standpoint, but depending on the location, walking distance to La Tour Montparnasse, UNESCO, the Eiffel Tower, Champ-de-Mars

HOTELS IN THE FIFTEENTH ARRONDISSEMENT

HÔTEL BEAUGRENELLE ST-CHARLES ★★
82, rue Saint-Charles, 75015 (15th)
51 rooms, all with shower or bath and toilet

TELEPHONE
45-78-61-63
FAX
45-79-04-38
MÉTRO
Charles-Michels
CREDIT CARDS
AE, DC, MC, V
RATES
Single 380–430F, double 410–450F; extra bed 150F
BREAKFAST
40F extra per person

This hotel is just as unassuming as its neighborhood, which offers a comfortable niche for a look at what life is really all about in Paris, once you are away from the glittery and artsy *quartiers* that draw most visitors. You can spot the hotel from the Square St-Michels . . . just look for the bright red awning and the boxwood bushes framing the entry. The lobby has Art Deco–style leather love seats and armchairs. A modern breakfast room with black laminated tables and chairs is set apart by a bank of green plants. A glassed-in walkway joins the two buildings that make up the 51-room hotel. Several ground-floor rooms open onto the garden and are some of the best. All the rooms are small, but decent closet space rescues them from feeling too cramped. Light, pastel-colored fabrics and blond furniture lend a modern touch. Peace and quiet prevails when the sidewalks roll up about 9 or 10 P.M. Owner M. Colliot and his staff work hard to please their guests.

English Spoken: Yes

Facilities and Services: Direct-dial phone; hair dryer; elevator in front building only; TV with international reception; room safe, 20F per night; trouser press

Nearest Tourist Attractions (Left Bank): Shopping at the Centre Beaugrenelle; otherwise must use public transportation to all tourist destinations

HÔTEL CHARLES QUINZE ★★

37, rue St-Charles, corner of 36, rue Rouelle, 75015 (15th)

30 rooms, all with shower or bath and toilet

TELEPHONE
45-79-64-15

FAX
45-77-21-11

MÉTRO
Charles-Michels, Dupleix

CREDIT CARDS
AE, DC, MC, V

RATES
Single 420F, double 450–540F; extra bed 130F

BREAKFAST
45F extra per person

To some, the Charles Quinze might be considered to be in a tourist backwater. For others, it represents a change of pace and is a safe bet for those insisting on peace in noisy Paris. I like it not only because it is well maintained and executed, but because its location offers a glimpse of everyday life that you do not always see in more congested *quartiers.* As you walk by the place St-Charles, you will see old men quietly sitting under the shade of the chestnut trees reading their newspapers and talking about old times. Pretty young girls with long ribbons and smocked dresses roller-skate along the sidewalks, and matrons walk their little dogs. Hurrying housewives carrying brimming shopping baskets go from shop to shop picking just the right ingredients for their evening meal. For trips away from the hotel, a good Métro line is only a 10-minute walk, and the Eiffel Tower is about 20 if you window-shop along the way.

The hotel is done simply but with great style. Blue-and-white Chinese porcelain creates an oriental theme in the small, whitewashed lobby. Be sure to notice the framed needlepoint in the reception area. One dates from 1907, done by the owner's grandmother when she was a little girl. Another by the fireplace was done by her brother-in-law, and her son Vincent stitched the one hanging by the door when he was eight.

Each floor of the hotel is coordinated in a different color. The concise rooms have country-style, built-in furniture and matching draperies and bedspreads.

The hospitable owners, Claire and Martial Fournerie, also own the café/tabac next door. For a typical working-class lunch, drop in between noon and 2 P.M. and order the daily special. They are open for business from 7 A.M.–8 P.M. weekdays and serve drinks and cold sandwiches when lunch is not in progress.

English Spoken: Yes

Facilities and Services: Direct-dial phone; hair dryer; elevator; mini-bar; TV with international reception; office safe, no charge

Nearest Tourist Attractions (Left Bank): A 20-minute walk from the Eiffel Tower; otherwise, not much

HÔTEL FONDARY ★★
30, rue Fondary, 75015 (15th)
20 rooms, all with shower or bath and toilet

TELEPHONE
45-75-14-75
FAX
45-75-84-42
MÉTRO
Emile Zola
CREDIT CARDS
AE, MC, V
RATES
1–2 persons 425–475F
BREAKFAST
40F extra per person

If you do not require much space and will not rebel at an address in a tourist desert, then the Fondary is a quiet budget choice. Were it in a more tourist-inspired setting, the hotel would command higher prices and probably be full all the time with yuppies. The surrounding neighborhood provides a glimpse into Parisian bourgeois life that can be interesting, especially on your third or fourth trip, when you want to see more of the "real" Paris. On Wednesday and Sunday there is an enormous outdoor *marché* along boulevard de Grenelle, and every day along rue du Commerce you can watch daily life as shoppers crowd the stores and the open stalls that sell everything from housedresses, lampshades, and junk jewelry to food, fresh flowers, and car parts. The hotel is actually much better than outward appearances would suggest. On the main floor there is a pretty terrace off the dining room and a bar next to reception where you can buy a soft drink or a beer. Upstairs, the rooms are decorated in white bamboo, grass cloth, and pretty fabrics. Prices match the size of the hotel: small.

English Spoken: Yes

Facilities and Services: Bar (soft drinks and beer); direct-dial phone; elevator; mini-bar; TV; office safe, no charge

Nearest Tourist Attractions (Left Bank): Twenty-five-minute walk to Eiffel Tower through interesting blue-collar neighborhood; must use Métro for anything else

HÔTEL FRANTOUR-SUFFREN ★★★
20, rue Jean Rey, 75015 (15th)
407 rooms, all with shower or bath and toilet

TELEPHONE
45-78-50-00
FAX
45-78-91-42
MÉTRO
Bir-Haikeim
CREDIT CARDS
AE, DC, MC, V
RATES
Single 850F, double 895F, triple 1,050F, communicating rooms 2,000F, suites 2,000–3,400F

Featuring mauve-and-pink bedrooms and suites, with air-conditioning and free parking, the Frantour-Suffren is one of the five Frantour properties in Paris and the best of the lot by far. Possessing all the zip of an Elks Club in Kansas, and almost devoid of French zest, it is reminiscent of any large downtown hotel found in most major U.S. cities. Next door to the Hilton and in the shadow of the Eiffel Tower, it is a good choice for business travelers, groups, or those desiring many hotel conveniences. The rooms are spacious and include excellent closet and shelf space, large desks, and big bathrooms. The eighth floor is reserved exclusively for nonsmokers. The choicest rooms are on the top two or three floors, facing the Eiffel Tower. Here you can almost reach out and touch the moon as it floats by.

Be sure to avoid the mediocre (and high-priced) food in the hotel dining room and eat instead at one of the interesting small restaurants or cafés listed in *Cheap Eats in Paris.*

Rates run high. To get around this, reserve through a travel agent and insist that the price be negotiated or go with a package deal through one of the airlines.

English Spoken: Yes

Facilities and Services: Air-conditioning; bar; conference room; direct-dial phone; nonsmoking floor (eighth); mini-bar; radio; TV with international reception; rooms for handicapped; restaurant; duty-free shop; free parking; porters; special group check-in lobby

Nearest Tourist Attractions (Left Bank): Eiffel Tower, Champ-de-Mars Park, Trocadéro

BREAKFAST
75F extra per person! *Please,* don't pay this outrageous price. Eat at the corner café or pâtisserie.

LE NAINVILLE HÔTEL (no stars)
53, rue de l'Église, entrance at 17, rue de la Rosière, 75015 (15th)
37 rooms, 5 with shower or bath and toilet

Perched over a bar and café in a pedestrian corner of the 15th arrondissement is the budget-lovers' Nainville. Considering the logistics, you would hardly expect it to offer the comforts it does. Let's start with breakfast. You have your choice of seating—smoking or nonsmoking—in the corner bar. The table is set with a neatly pressed linen napkin, and the meal includes orange juice and a croissant, along with bread and jam. Most no-star hotels would not *think* of serving breakfast, let alone provide linens and juice. Next, in the fancy rooms (i.e., with a bathtub) you will find a *peignoir.* Want to take a break and catch up on the news around the world? Then just flip the TV to CNN news and you have it all . . . in English. Remember, this is a no-star hotel. Okay, so there are no twin beds or elevator, and the toilet paper is square. Then there is the matter of the interior decoration, which in some rooms literally screams at you with wild wallpaper and carpets that have no intention of matching. The semiantique furniture is comfortably worn, but it isn't shabby. Back to the good points, which I think far outweigh the bad. The rooms and the bathrooms—both private and those down the hall—are clean; rooms with private toilets and showers overlook

TELEPHONE
45-57-35-80

FAX
None

MÉTRO
Charles-Michels, Felix-Faure

CREDIT CARDS
None, cash only

RATES
1–2 persons 210–370F; shower 25F

BREAKFAST
35F extra, served only in the bar

the pretty Square Violet; the neighborhood is quiet all the time; the owners, Mme. Dupux and her husband, who runs the bar, are accommodating; and bottom line . . . the price is right for budget-watching Cheap Sleepers in Paris. Some of the best bets include no. 41, which overlooks a rose garden; no. 10, with a double-beveled glass armoire; and no. 16, on the street, but which has the best use of color. Avoid nos. 23 (bad shower), 13 (too small), and 24 (peeling paint).

English Spoken: No

Facilities and Services: Direct-dial phone; no elevator or safe; TV with international reception

Nearest Tourist Attractions (Left Bank): None; must use public transportation

PRACTIC HÔTEL (no stars)
20, rue de l'Ingénieur Robert Keller, 75015 (15th)
34 rooms, 27 with shower or bath and toilet

TELEPHONE
45-77-70-58
FAX
40-59-43-75
MÉTRO
Charles-Michels
CREDIT CARDS
AE, MC, V
RATES
1–2 persons 235–385F, triple 460F; extra bed 80F
BREAKFAST
40F extra per person

For the best Cheap Sleep in the 15th arrondissement, the Practic Hôtel, just behind the Centre Beaugrenelle shopping complex, is head and shoulders above the closest competitor. I would not want to go too far out on a limb and say it is the best no-star in Paris, but believe me, it is right up there in the top one percent.

While definitely not a candidate for those who revel in Louis XV surroundings, the hotel displays none of those depressing, exhausted, faded, and snagged interiors that plague almost every other budget dig in the city. The entry—in dull brown with industrial-strength carpeting, a vase of fake flowers, and old prints of Paris scattered around—could use a new look. But you are not living here, so just keep on going. The rooms are amazing, and spotless besides. I am a fan of no. 50, a double with soft gray-and-blue carpet, two desks, a view of the skyscraper apartments that line the Seine, and a beautiful bathroom with a stall shower. Double-glazed windows help to keep the noise levels down. No. 17, redone in blue with only a sink and bidet, is a steel at 220F for one or two people. On the fifth floor is a two-room suite (don't forget we are in a no-star here) with blond furniture. One room has twin beds, the other just one twin. The bathroom comes with soap and shampoo and shower doors . . . all for under $100. What a deal! The third floor, still outfitted in chenille with browns and beiges reminiscent of the 1960s, has yet to be redone, but the rooms are just as clean and the prices even a little lower.

Eight rooms have *cour* views, but they are not *too* bad. Breakfast is served in a blue-and-white first-floor dining room and includes cheese, fruit compote, juice, croissants, bread, jam, and a bonbon. Mme. Bihan is the sweetest manageress this side of heaven, and her faithful regulars know to reserve as far in advance as they can. Please do the same.

English Spoken: Yes

Facilities and Services: Direct-dial phone; elevator; TV in 29 rooms; no safe

Nearest Tourist Attractions (Left Bank): None; must use public transportation. Across from the Centre Beaugrenelle is one of the best Monoprix stores in Paris. See Cheap Chic, page **XX**, for details about these stores, which are the K-Marts of France.

TIMHÔTEL MONTPARNASSE ★★

20–22, rue de l'Arrivée, 75015 (15th)

80 rooms, all with bath or shower and toilet

TELEPHONE
45-48-96-62

FAX
45-48-77-30

MÉTRO
Montparnasse

CREDIT CARDS
AE, DC, MC, V

RATES
Single 410–500F, double 500F; extra bed 100F

BREAKFAST
55F extra per person

See page 49 for general information about Timhôtels.

English Spoken: Yes

Facilities and Services: Direct-dial phone; elevator; TV with international reception; office safe, no charge

Nearest Tourist Attractions (Left Bank): Montparnasse

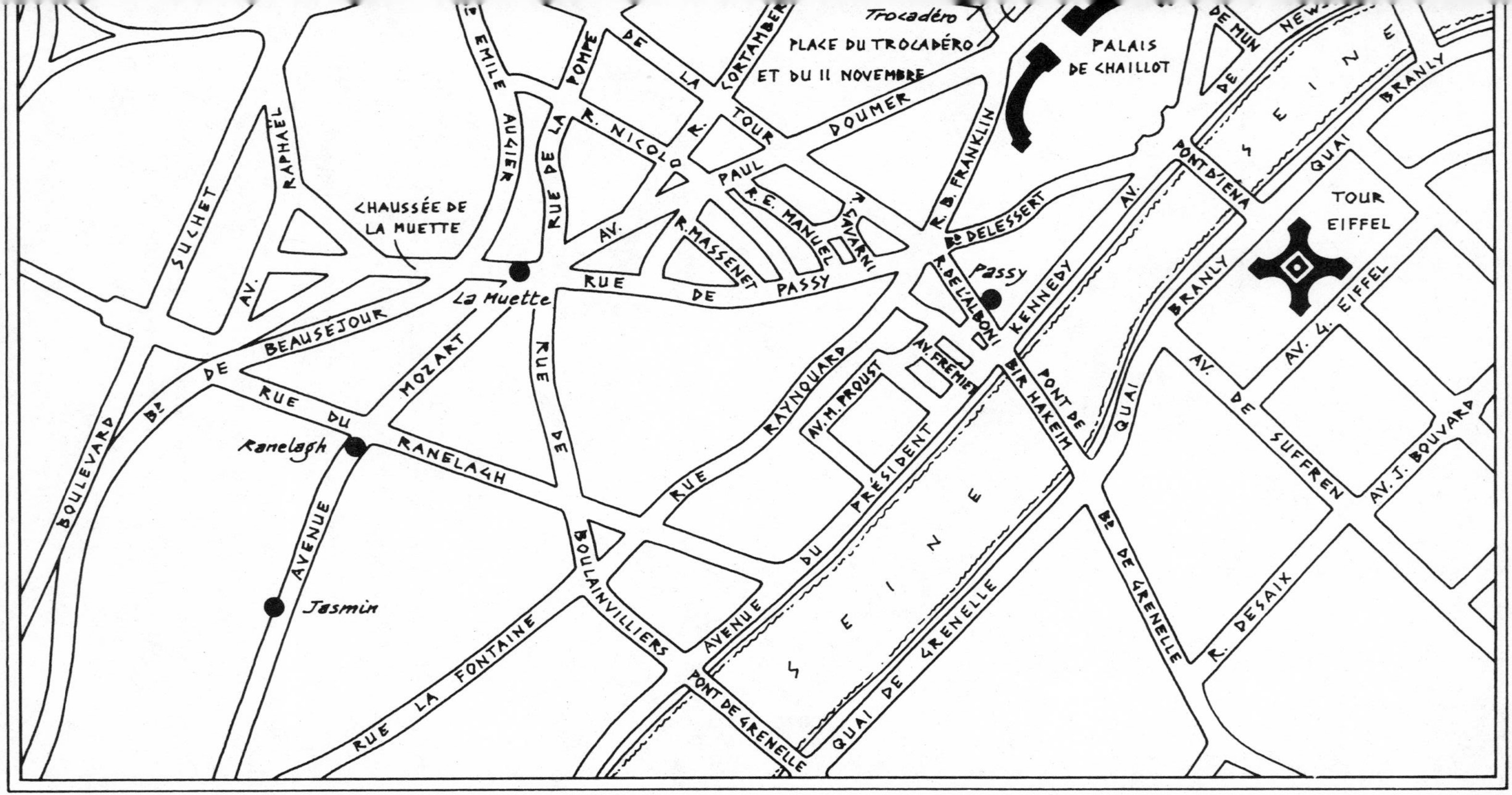
BOULEVARD
SUCHET
AV. RAPHAËL
CHAUSSÉE DE LA MUETTE
AV. EMILE AUGIER
RUE DE LA POMPE
R. NICOLO
R. DE LA TOUR
CORTAMBERT
PLACE DU TROCADÉRO ET DU 11 NOVEMBRE
Trocadéro
PALAIS DE CHAILLOT
AV. PAUL DOUMER
R. B. FRANKLIN
R. E. MANUEL
R. SAVARNI
R. MASSENET
Bd DELESSERT
La Muette
RUE DE PASSY
Passy
R. DE L'ALBONI
Bd DE BEAUSEJOUR
AV. MOZART
RUE DE RANELAGH
RUE DU RANELAGH
Ranelagh
AVENUE
Jasmin
RUE DE BOULAINVILLIERS
RUE RAYNOUARD
AV. M. PROUST
AV. FREMIET
AV. KENNEDY
AVENUE DU PRÉSIDENT
PONT DE BIR HAKEIM
PONT D'IENA
SEINE
QUAI BRANLY
AV. DE NEW-
DE MUN
TOUR EIFFEL
AV. G. EIFFEL
AV. DE SUFFREN
AV. J. BOUVARD
R. DESAIX
Bd DE GRENELLE
RUE LA FONTAINE
PONT DE GRENELLE
QUAI DE GRENELLE

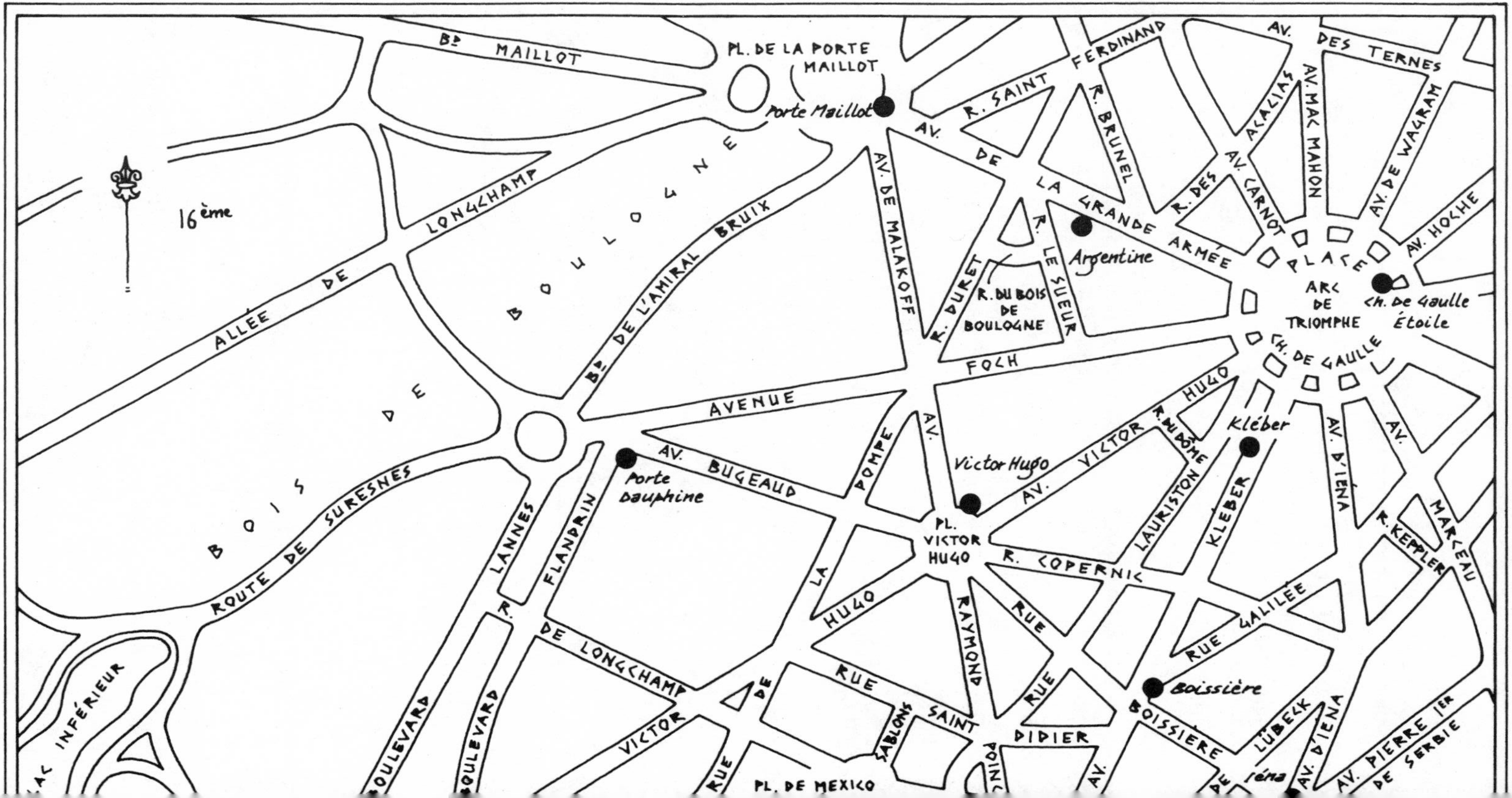

Bd MAILLOT
PL. DE LA PORTE MAILLOT
Porte Maillot
AV. DES TERNES
R. SAINT FERDINAND
AV. DE LA GRANDE ARMÉE
R. BRUNEL
R. DES ACACIAS
AV. CARNOT
AV. MAC MAHON
AV. DE WAGRAM
AV. HOCHE
16ème
ALLÉE DE LONGCHAMP
BOIS DE BOULOGNE
Bd DE L'AMIRAL BRUIX
AV. DE MALAKOFF
R. DURET
R. DU BOIS DE BOULOGNE
R. LE SUEUR
Argentine
PLACE CH. DE GAULLE
ARC DE TRIOMPHE
Ch. De Gaulle Étoile
AVENUE FOCH
ROUTE DE SURESNES
LANNES
R. FLANDRIN
AV. BUGEAUD
Porte Dauphine
AV. DE LA POMPE
Victor Hugo
PL. VICTOR HUGO
AV. VICTOR HUGO
R. DU DÔME
Kléber
AV. KLEBER
R. LAURISTON
R. COPERNIC
AV. D'IÉNA
R. KEPPLER
AV. MARCEAU
LAC INFÉRIEUR
BOULEVARD
BOULEVARD
R. DE LONGCHAMP
VICTOR HUGO
RUE DE LA
RUE DES SABLONS
RUE SAINT DIDIER
RAYMOND
POINC
RUE
RUE GALILÉE
Boissière
BOISSIERE
LÜBECK
AV. D'IÉNA
AV. PIERRE 1er DE SERBIE
PL. DE MEXICO
AV.
DE Iéna

Sixteenth Arrondissement

RIGHT BANK
Avenue Foch, Boid de Boulogne, Jardin d'Acclimitation, Marmottan Museum, Musée Guimet, Passy, Trocadéro

Known as a sedate, posh, and old-moneyed sector, the 16th is the home of the BCBG *(bon chic bon genre)* crowd, otherwise known as French yuppies. This is stylish territory, bordered by the Bois de Boulogne and the river Seine. Here you will see luxurious apartments and prostitutes in BMWs on the avenue Foch and fashionable shops in Passy and along the boulevard Victor Hugo. Trocadéro, directly across from the Seine and the Eiffel Tower, is the name of the gardens around the Palais de Chaillot, an imposing two-winged building that houses four museums. The spectacular view from the steps of Trocadéro at night, across the Seine to the Eiffel Tower, with the illuminated pools, fountains, and statues between, is one you must not miss.

HOTELS IN THE SIXTEENTH ARRONDISSEMENT

HÔTEL DU BOIS ★★

11, rue du Dome, corner of 29, avenue Victor-Hugo, 75016 (16th)

41 rooms, all with shower or bath and toilet

TELEPHONE
45-00-31-96
FAX
45-00-90-05
MÉTRO
Charles-de-Gaulle-Étoile, Kléber

For a stay on the exclusive avenue Victor-Hugo, with all of its lovely shops, consider the Hôtel du Bois, a friendly establishment that has dedicated guests who enjoy being only a few minutes' walk from the Champs-Élysées. The entrance to the hotel is in a passageway reached on foot by steep steps from the street level, or by car on an upper level through one-way streets from behind. You will recognize the hotel by the pretty planter boxes under each window. Owner David Byrne (see Hôtel Queen Mary, page 139) has shined, polished, and gradually redone the tired rooms, worn reception, and old bathrooms. The hotel is now up to speed in most areas. A host of useful information in English is also provided about everything from what to see and do to where to eat and shop in the immediate neighborhood. Rates are low for this expensive area.

English Spoken: Yes

Facilities and Services: Direct-dial phone; no elevator; mini-bar; TV with international reception; office safe, no charge

Nearest Tourist Attractions (Right Bank): Champs-Élysées, Arc de Triomphe

CREDIT CARDS
AE, MC, V

RATES
Single 450F, double 520–600F; extra bed 145F; lower off-season rates available

BREAKFAST
50F extra per person

HÔTEL DU ROND-POINT DE LONGCHAMP ★★★
86, rue de Longchamp, 75016 (16th)
57 rooms, all with shower or bath and toilet

The area around the hotel dates back to the 13th century, when Longchamp was an austere abbey surrounded by fields and meadows belonging to a few farms. One of them was located right next to the hotel, and there is a plaque to commemorate Boileau and La Fontaine, great French writers, who came here to buy their fresh milk. Today the area is known as one of the most prestigious residential areas in the capital.

The owner of this wonderful hotel, Gerard Dumontant, is the president of the independent hoteliers in France, so you can imagine that his hotel reflects only the best . . . and let me assure you it does. The hotel appeals to the traditionalists looking for exceptional value, classic service, and a multitude of facilities. The ground floor consists of a plant-filled lounge, a bar, and a billiards room with soft leather armchairs. Some of the rooms are decidedly Louis XIV, with four-poster beds and heavy curtains swooping from floor to ceiling. Others reflect more modern tastes. Several are superbly planned for business people. These rooms double as an office and sitting room during the day and have a comfortable Murphy pull-down bed for the night. All rooms have international television reception, air-conditioning, and fabulous marble bathrooms. Room service from Angelina's Tearoom on the corner is just a phone call

TELEPHONE
45-05-13-63

FAX
47-55-12-80

MÉTRO
Trocadéro

CREDIT CARDS
AE, DC, MC, V

RATES
Single 560–950F, double 810–1,100F (ask about low season rates)

BREAKFAST
70F extra per person

away. Angelina's is world famous for the thickest, most decadently rich, hot chocolate you will ever taste.

English Spoken: Yes

Facilities and Services: Air-conditioning; bar; direct-dial phone; hair dryer; elevator; mini-bar; radio; TV with international reception; business facilities; office safe, no charge; laundry services; room service

Nearest Tourist Attractions (Right Bank): Trocadéro, shopping on avenue Victor Hugo

HÔTEL ÉTOILE-MAILLOT ★★★

10, rue de Bois de Boulogne, corner of rue Duret, 75016 (16th)

28 rooms, all with shower or bath and toilet

TELEPHONE
45-00-42-60

FAX
45-00-55-89

MÉTRO
Argentine

CREDIT CARDS
AE, DC, MC, V

RATES
Single 610–750F, double 660–800F, suite 930–970F

BREAKFAST
Included, but will take 40F off per person if you do not want it; must say so when reserving

The Étoile-Maillot is a haven of comfort and tranquillity in the fashionable district around avenue Foch and the Bois de Boulogne. It is the type of small, personally run hotel that is hard to find in today's world, which seems to favor cutting-edge modern or retro Art Deco rehabs that are nice but don't necessarily say Paris. For elegant living on an expanded budget, it is difficult to find higher quality than this hotel. Although it is a bit far, the nearest Métro line is direct to the Champs-Élysées, the place de la Concorde, and the Louvre. In 15 minutes you can be at the new Opéra Bastille seeing how the wilder half lives and plays.

The atmosphere of the Étoile-Maillot is that of a gracious French home. The rooms are beautifully furnished with an impressive collection of genuine Louis XV and XVI antiques, tapestry-covered chairs, Oriental rugs, silk wall coverings, and inlaid chests. The suite consists of a sitting room, bedroom with a king-size bed, and a marble bath, and is a wonderful choice for anyone who wants to work and entertain in a hotel room setting. The management's efforts show on a daily basis, from the bouquets of fresh flowers in the lobby to the white-glove cleanliness of the hotel in general.

English Spoken: Yes

Facilities and Services: Direct-dial phone; hair dryer; elevator; mini-bar; TV with international reception; office safe, no charge

Nearest Tourist Attractions (Right Bank): Bois de Boulougne, Arc de Triomphe, Champs-Élysées, Palais des Congrès

HÔTEL FRÉMIET ★★★
6, avenue Frémiet, 75016 (16th)
36 rooms, all with shower or bath and toilet

The Frémiet is in a neighborhood that was designed and built by Emmanuel Frémiet, a noted architect who has many of his works of art on display at the Musée d'Orsay. Quietly positioned on avenue du President Kennedy, this large hotel has been owned and run for 30 years by Claude Fourmond. From the pleasant lobby and polite desk staff, ably headed by M. Mitri, to the seventh-story singles nested under the eaves, everything sails along in good order and is done in unobtrusive taste. Eighty percent of the hotel's bedrooms have been redone, so be sure to specify one of these. For instance, no. 61, a two-room suite with blue furniture and upholstery set against a backdrop of soft yellow, has its original fireplace and ceiling detail to remind you of days gone by. To keep you posted in the present, there is a phone in the bathroom.

The hotel is not within easy walking distance to much, but the no. 72 bus, which follows the river and passes all the major monuments and sites, stops a half block away, and the Passy Métro stop is only a five-minute walk. Motorists driving into Paris can get off the *periphérique* at Porte St-Cloud and be at the hotel in under 10 minutes without suffering the trauma of crossing town in wild traffic. Public parking is nearby. Another plus: Reservations can be made from the U.S. and Canada by calling Best Western's toll-free 800 number.

English Spoken: Yes

Facilities and Services: Air-conditioning in 17 rooms; bar; direct-dial phone; hair dryer; elevator; rooms for handicapped; mini-bar; radio in some rooms; TV; office safe, no charge

Nearest Tourist Attractions (Right Bank): Passy, Seine

TELEPHONE
45-24-52-06; toll-free from the U.S. and Canada 1-800-528-1234

FAX
42-88-77-46

MÉTRO
Passy

CREDIT CARDS
AE, DC, MC, V

RATES
Single 550–715F, double 720–915F, triple 915–975F, suite 1,050–1,700F

BREAKFAST
45F extra per person

HÔTEL GAVARNI ★★
5, rue Gavarni, 75016 (16th)
30 rooms, all with shower or bath and toilet

Here is an attractive choice on a quiet street in the center of Passy, one of Paris's most sought-after residential and shopping *quartiers.* The hotel is expertly run by the Mornands, whose backgrounds include extensive hotel experience in both France and the United States. They are a friendly couple who go out of their way to

TELEPHONE
45-24-52-82

FAX
40-50-16-95

MÉTRO
Passy

CREDIT CARDS
AE, DC, MC, V
RATES
Single 450–530F, double 550–570F; extra bed 80F
BREAKFAST
35F extra per person

welcome American guests and take a personal interest in their needs.

Both the breakfast room and lobby are smartly done with cane furniture and bright floral murals. Upstairs, everything is always kept in top shape and is sparkling clean. For the Mornands, there is no such thing as peeling paint, threadbare carpets, or nicks and tears in the furniture or upholstery. The cozy singles at the back of the hotel have corner marble fireplaces and are popular with many repeat visitors. No. 603 is a favorite because it has a view of the Eiffel Tower from both windows, which is especially beautiful when illuminated at night.

English Spoken: Yes

Facilities and Services: Direct-dial phone; elevator; TV with international reception; office safe, no charge

Nearest Tourist Attractions (Right Bank): Passy, Trocadéro

HÔTEL KEPPLER ★★
12, rue Keppler, 75016 (16th)
49 rooms, all with shower or bath and toilet

TELEPHONE
47-20-65-05
FAX
47-23-02-29
MÉTRO
George V, Kléber
CREDIT CARDS
AE, MC, V
RATES
1–2 persons 475F; extra bed 100F
BREAKFAST
35F extra per person

For a two-star, family-run hotel, the Keppler offers much more than just a Cheap Sleep in a quiet location. It has, for one thing, honest-to-goodness room service, an unheard-of feature in almost all three-star hotels in Paris, let alone a two-star. Improvements have been made, and they have added even further to the overall recommendation of this hotel. The new lobby shows off a pretty fireplace and a small corner bar. The large dining room has been redecorated and now has mahogany upholstered chairs, blue walls, and Levelor blinds along the streetside windows. For the prices, you cannot expect luxury with deep-pile carpeting. The rooms are, however, efficiently modern with sturdy Swedish-style desks and chairs and ample closet and drawer space. Four rooms have balconies. A team of uniformed maids wearing beepers keeps everything shipshape, and management keeps an ear tuned to inappropriate noise. There are many repeat guests, and it is easy to understand their loyalty to this hidden Parisian value, where reservations and a deposit are required far, far in advance of your stay.

English Spoken: Yes

Facilities and Services: Bar; direct-dial phone; some hair dryers; elevator; TV; room safe, no extra charge; room service

Nearest Tourist Attractions (Right Bank): Arc de Triomphe, Champs-Élysées, Guimet Museum

HÔTEL MASSENET ★★★
5 bis, rue Massenet, 75016 (16th)
41 rooms, all with shower or bath and toilet

For a beautiful stay in Paris on a tranquil street in Passy, I like the formal Massenet. The well-heeled French executive clientele appreciates the quiet neighborhood close to the Passy shopping district, the professional services of the uniformed hotel staff, and, above all, the prices. These travelers know that if the Massenet were in a more mainstream location, the prices would be nearly doubled.

Downstairs, the public rooms are paneled in a rich walnut. Soft seating and a small library along one wall create an appealing English intimacy. Morning croissants are served in a little alcove overlooking a colorful patio. All the rooms are well furnished and impeccably maintained. No. 70 has its own balcony and walk-in closet that is almost as large as some hotel rooms I have stayed in. If traveling alone, request no. 71, a top-floor single with a view terrace. If quiet and space are top priorities, no. 25, a back twin, has a triple-drawer marble dresser, workable desk, three chairs, double luggage rack, and two sinks, a large tub, and oversize towels in the bathroom.

English Spoken: Yes

Facilities and Services: Bar; direct-dial phone; hair dryer; elevator; mini-bar; TV with international reception; office safe, no charge

Nearest Tourist Attractions (Right Bank): Passy, 20-minute walk to Trocadéro and the Eiffel Tower

TELEPHONE
45-24-43-03

FAX
45-24-41-39

MÉTRO
Passy

CREDIT CARDS
AE, DC, MC, V

RATES
Single 575–760F, double 900F; extra bed 175F, baby bed 100F

BREAKFAST
Included, but can be deducted at 40F per person

HÔTEL NICOLO ★★
3, rue Nicolo, 75016 (16th)
28 rooms, all with shower or bath and toilet

Join diplomats visiting their nearby embassies, delegates to the OECD, and other smart, money-saving travelers anxious to maximize their daily travel allowances by staying at the hidden Nicolo in the center of Passy. What you save here you can spend engaging in guilt-free shopping at the discount shops on rue de la Tour (see Cheap Chic, page 225) or rue de Passy, one of Paris's shopping meccas for traditional, well-made clothing. If shopping doesn't appeal to you, surely one of the

TELEPHONE
42-88-83-40

FAX
42-24-45-41

MÉTRO
Passy, La Muette

CREDIT CARDS
MC, V

RATES
Single 380F, double 410–460F, triple 490F
BREAKFAST
40F extra per person

nearby restaurants recommended in *Cheap Eats in Paris* will.

The owner of the Nicolo is an American woman who is gradually making changes, with an eye to attracting more guests from the U.S. Almost all rooms have a small entry, giving the feeling of spaciousness. Rooms are color-friendly, and many look onto a small garden that has a lovely tree. Bathrooms are dated in terms of tile, but certainly spotless and serviceable. True, the hotel is old, but it has enough Galic charm to draw many repeats. Another plus in its favor is the desk staff, which has improved greatly.

English Spoken: Yes

Facilities and Services: Direct-dial phone; elevator; TV; no safe

Nearest Tourist Attractions (Right Bank): Passy, 20-minute walk to Trocadéro and the Eiffel Tower

HÔTEL PASSY EIFFEL ★★★
10, rue de Passy, 75016 (16th)
50 rooms, all with shower or bath and toilet

TELEPHONE
45-25-55-66
FAX
42-88-89-88
MÉTRO
Passy
CREDIT CARDS
AE, DC, MC, V
RATES
Single 560–680F, double 630–700F, triple 800F
BREAKFAST
40F extra per person

The Hôtel Passy Eiffel, on the main street in Passy, provides a firsthand look at one of Paris's most exclusive neighborhoods and some of the best shopping to be found. The marbled foyer and lobby face onto a garden courtyard with six rooms facing it. Two salons are tucked along each side: one has a grand piano and inviting seating; the other is an airy, glass-enclosed breakfast room. Wood-beam ceilings add a sense of dimension to the variety of rooms. For the most part they are comfortable, but with a few faded overtones. All have pleasing views. From the top floor on the side street, guests can watch the elevator scale the Eiffel Tower as it takes tourists to the various levels. For breakfast, be sure to sample some of the honey bottled directly from the owner's beehives. During the week you can pet his dog Volga, who holds court in the reception area.

English Spoken: Yes

Facilities and Services: Bar; direct-dial phone; hair dryer; elevator; mini-bar; TV with international reception; office safe, no charge

Nearest Tourist Attractions (Right Bank): Shopping in Passy, Trocadéro

HÔTEL REGINA DE PASSY ★★★
6, rue de la Tour, 75016 (16th)
64 rooms, all with shower or bath and toilet

Built in 1930 for the International Exhibition, this wonderful hotel is high on the Right Bank of the Seine across from the Eiffel Tower. The almost-grand lobby has a graceful winding staircase framed by marvelous, signed stained-glass windows. Half of the hotel rooms have been restyled, and they are sophisticated and ultramodern with geometric prints, chrome and leather furniture, and modern bathrooms. The older rooms are still in excellent condition and retain a benign elegance from their faded past . . . as well as lower price tags. Fifteen rooms have small balconies where you can step out and look over the Passy neighborhood with the Eiffel Tower in the distance. The two penthouse apartments with private rooftop terraces boast impressive furnishings, marble bathrooms (one with a sunken tub), small bars, fully equipped kitchens, and enough wardrobe space for most of us to unpack and stay a year. These apartments would be the answer for a small family or anyone on an extended stay. The management and staff is anxious to please in every way, which should certainly enhance any visit to Paris.

English Spoken: Yes

Facilities and Services: Air-conditioning in one apartment; bar; direct-dial phone; elevator; hair dryer; minibar; room safe, no charge; radio; TV with international reception

Nearest Tourist Attractions (Right Bank): Passy, 20-minute walk to Trocadéro and Eiffel Tower

TELEPHONE
45-24-43-64

FAX
40-50-70-62

MÉTRO
Passy

CREDIT CARDS
AE, DC, MC, V

RATES
1–2 persons 630–900F, apartments 1,000–1,650F; extra bed 200F

BREAKFAST
45F extra per person

LE HAMEAU DE PASSY ★★
48, rue de Passy, 75016 (16th)
35 rooms, all with shower or bath and toilet

Hidden in a garden walkway off the busy rue de Passy, the Hameau de Passy is a snappy two-star addition to this posh pocket of Paris. The owners of the Hôtel Passy Eiffel (see page 174) took this rumpled hotel and transformed it into the modern, four-building structure it is today. All the rooms face the garden and are done in the same style, with stark white walls, open closets, soft sheer curtains at the windows, and harmonizing fabrics and carpets. Ground-floor rooms lack security, so I suggest asking for something on a higher floor. If you are lucky and land in building no. 4, the

TELEPHONE
42-88-47-55

FAX
42-30-83-72

MÉTRO
Passy, La Muette

CREDIT CARDS
AE, MC, V

RATES
Single 525F, double 570–590F, triple 670F

BREAKFAST
Included, cannot be deducted

elevator takes the strain out of climbing up several flights to your room. Otherwise, in buildings no. 1, 2, and 3, you will have to hike up a winding outdoor metal stairway. If this sort of exercise does not bother you, and you want to be only a whisper away from all the great shopping in Passy, then consider this hotel.

English Spoken: Yes

Facilities and Services: Direct-dial phone; elevator in building no. 4 only; TV with international reception; office safe, 30F per stay

Nearest Tourist Attractions (Right Bank): Passy, 20-minute walk to Trocadéro and the Eiffel Tower

LE PARC DE LA MUETTE HÔTEL ★
10, Chaussee de la Muette, 75016 (16th)
17 rooms, all with shower or bath and toilet

TELEPHONE
45-03-14-84
FAX
42-88-31-63
MÉTRO
La Muette
CREDIT CARDS
AE, MC, V
RATES
Single 250–290F, double 370–400F; extra bed 75F
BREAKFAST
35F extra per person

This stopover is not for everyone . . . but if you like this corner of the 16th, want to be closer to Monet's masterpieces in the Marmottan Museum, and don't have deep pockets with change to lay out for expensive stays, then consider this hotel/bar/brasserie.

I found it when I was eating at the Le Parc de la Muette brasserie downstairs. Both the hotel and brasserie are owned by a friendly man named M. Coudy, who seems to know everyone and be everywhere all at once. The Cheap Sleep has no lobby and no hotel atmosphere. Upon arrival, you check in at the brasserie bar, are given the key to your lodgings, and are then shown the stairs to this six-floor walk-up, which offers 17 rooms, all with private facilities. Colors are in reasonable sync with the plain rooms, and the furniture is uniform in its antiquity and well-used appearance. Room no. 5 has a marble fireplace and big bathroom. It faces the street, which should not be a noise nuisance, since the neighborhood is very staid after dark. It is probably not a destination guaranteed to be romantic or appeal to fussy Aunt Clara and her bridge club, but it is okay when considering the alternatives.

English Spoken: Some

Facilities and Services: Direct-dial phone; TV; no elevator or safe

Nearest Tourist Attractions (Right Bank): Marmottan Museum, Boise de Boulogne

RÉSIDENCE CHAMBELLAN MORGANE ★★★

6, rue Keppler, 75016 (16th)

20 rooms, all with shower or bath and toilet

TELEPHONE
47-20-35-72

FAX
47-20-95-69

MÉTRO
George-V

CREDIT CARDS
AE, DC, MC, V

RATES
1–2 persons 660–880F

BREAKFAST
55F extra per person

In 1984, when I began writing *Cheap Sleeps in Paris,* I fell in love with a little hotel in the 16th arrondissement called Résidence Morgane. It was run by a *petite grand'mère* who pampered her guests beyond the call of duty. She would make an omelet at midnight, keep your messages, forward your mail, and do your laundry and ironing if asked. When I returned a year later, Madame was gone and the hotel had been taken over by a gruff, uncaring owner. Four years ago, on a hunch, I decided to recheck the hotel. I am so glad I did. Although Madame is not back, the present owners do their utmost to please their international clientele. The new owners also masterminded a renovation that turned the hotel into the epitome of three-star elegance and classic luxury.

The stage is set by the entrance and lobby, done in American Southwest colors with white enamel woodwork and beautifully upholstered Louis XV–style antiques. Light, pumpkin-colored halls lead to stylishly outfitted bedrooms with silk wall coverings, matching quilted spreads and curtains, and efficient mirrored and marbled bathrooms. Now, as once before, I am happy to recommend this hotel for a quiet stay close to the golden triangle of Concorde, the Eiffel Tower, and the Champs-Élysées.

English Spoken: Yes

Facilities and Services: Bar; direct-dial phone; elevator; hair dryer; mini-bar; radio; room service after 6 P.M.; laundry service; TV with international reception; office safe, no charge

Nearest Tourist Attractions (Right Bank): Champs-Élysées, Arc de Triomphe

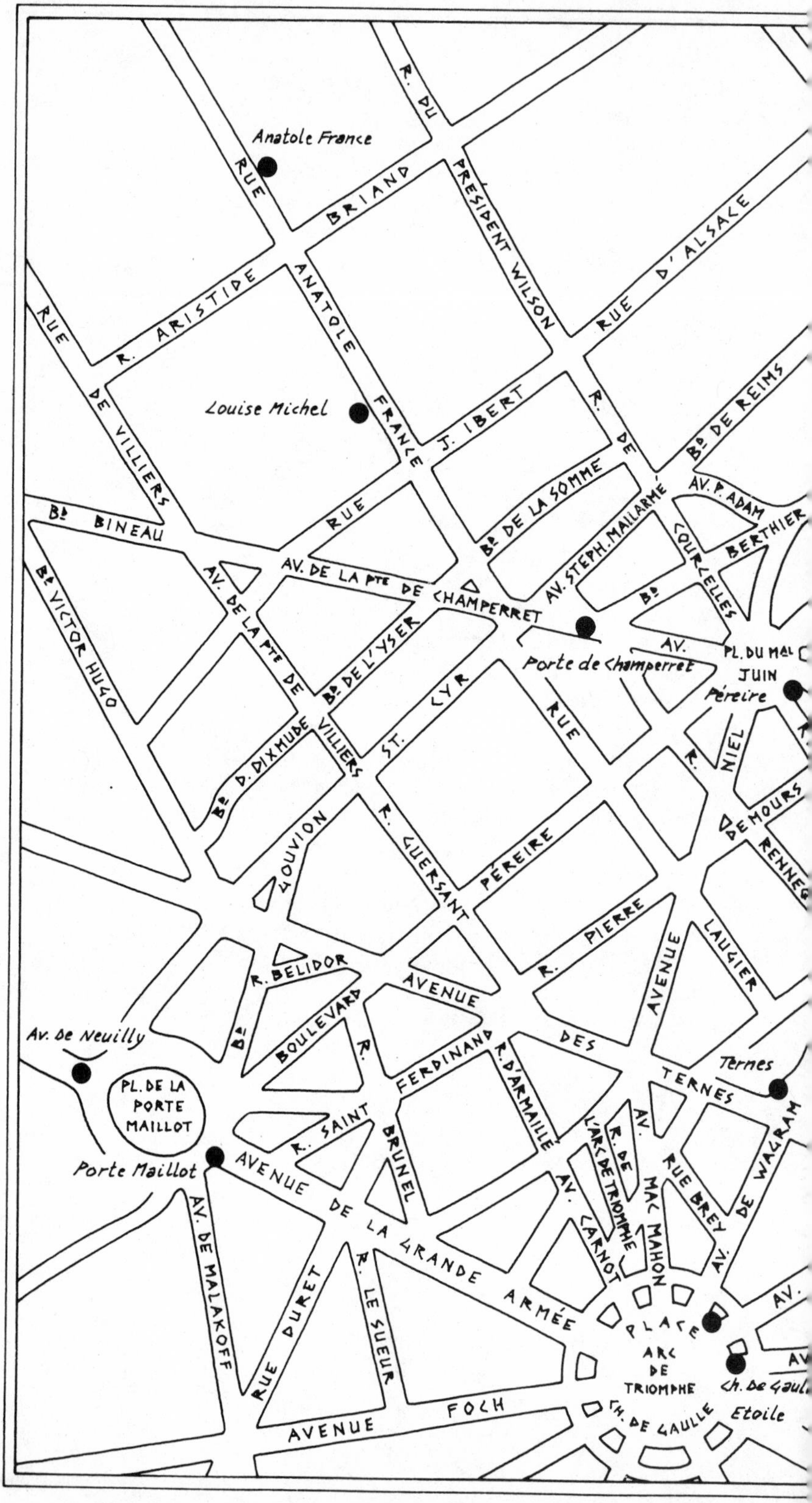
Anatole France
RUE
R. DU
PRESIDENT WILSON
BRIAND
RUE D'ALSACE
RUE
R. ARISTIDE
ANATOLE
FRANCE
RUE
DE VILLIERS
Louise Michel
J. IBERT
R. DE
Bd DE REIMS
Bd DE LA SOMME
Bd BINEAU
RUE
AV. STEPH. MALLARMÉ
AV. P. ADAM
COURCELLES
BERTHIER
Bd
Bd VICTOR HUGO
AV. DE LA PTE DE CHAMPERRET
AV. DE LA PTE DE VILLIERS
Bd DE L'YSER
Porte de Champerret
AV.
PL. DU Mal JUIN
Péreire
ST. CYR
RUE
Bd D. DIXMUDE
R.
NIEL
DEMOURS
GOUVION
R. GUERSANT
PÉREIRE
R. PIERRE
AVENUE
LAUGIER
R. BELIDOR
AVENUE DES TERNES
Bd
BOULEVARD
R.
FERDINAND
R. D'ARMAILLE
Av. De Neuilly
Ternes
PL. DE LA PORTE MAILLOT
Porte Maillot
R. SAINT
BRUNEL
L'ARC DE TRIOMPHE
R. DE
AV. MAC MAHON
RUE BREY
AV. DE WAGRAM
AV. CARNOT
AVENUE DE LA GRANDE ARMÉE
AV. DE MALAKOFF
RUE DURET
R. LE SUEUR
PLACE
ARC DE TRIOMPHE
Ch. De Gaulle
Etoile
CH. DE GAULLE
AVENUE FOCH

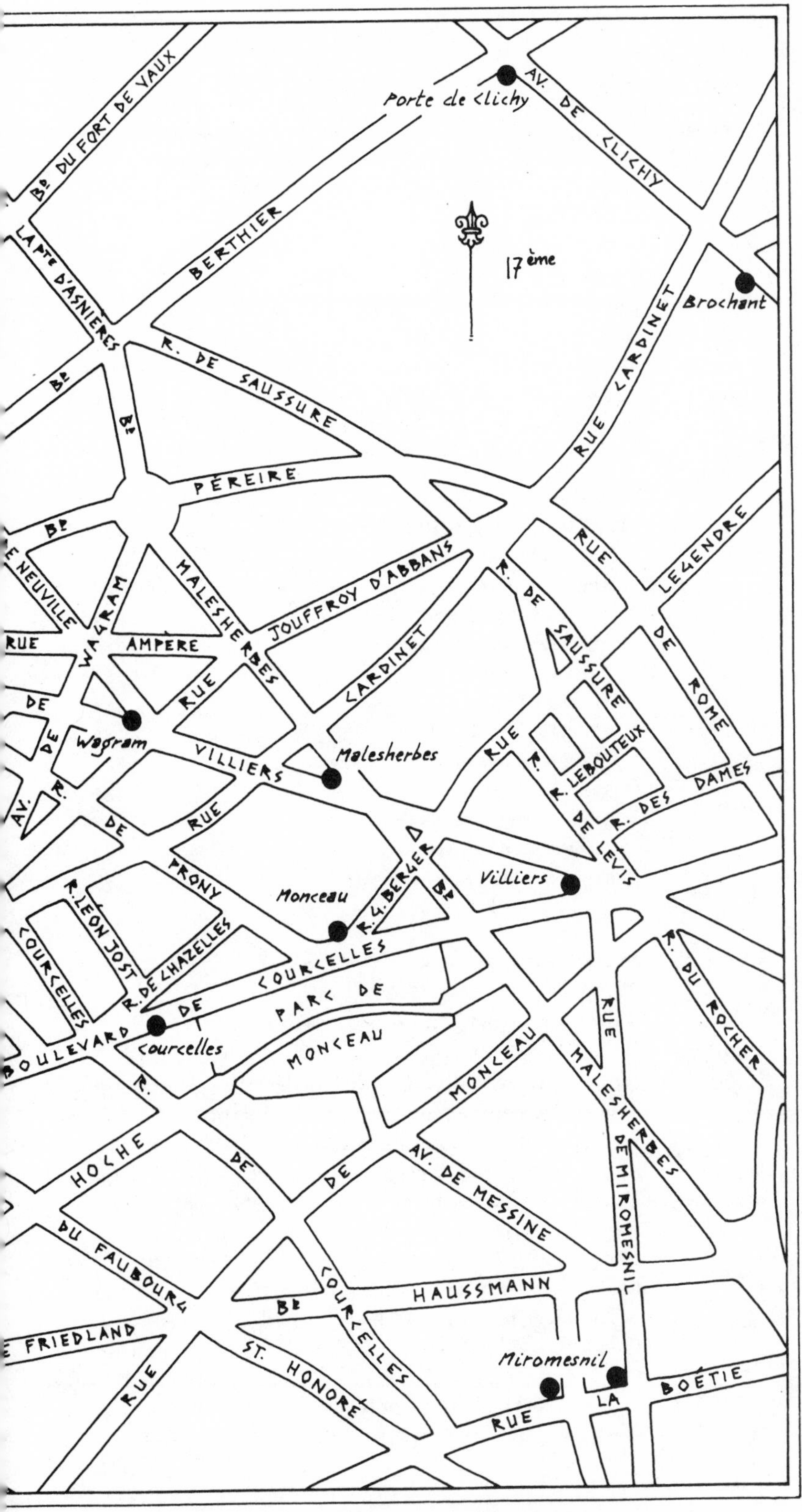

Porte de Clichy
AV. DE CLICHY
Bd DU FORT DE VAUX
BERTHIER
17ème
Brochant
RUE CARDINET
LA Pte D'ASNIERES
R. DE SAUSSURE
Bd
Bd PÉREIRE
Bd
E NEUVILLE
WAGRAM
MALESHERBES
JOUFFROY D'ABBANS
RUE LEGENDRE
R. DE SAUSSURE
RUE AMPERE
DE ROME
CARDINET
RUE
DE
Wagram
Malesherbes
VILLIERS
RUE
R. LEBOUTEUX
R. DES DAMES
AV. DE
R. DE LEVIS
RUE DE PRONY
Bd
R. G. BERGER
Villiers
Monceau
R. LEON JOST
COURCELLES
R. DE CHAZELLES
COURCELLES
PARC DE MONCEAU
BOULEVARD DE
Courcelles
R. DU ROCHER
RUE MALESHERBES
R. HOCHE
MONCEAU
DE
DE
AV. DE MESSINE
DE MIROMESNIL
DU FAUBOURG
HAUSSMANN
Bd
COURCELLES
E FRIEDLAND
ST. HONORÉ
RUE
Miromesnil
RUE LA BOÉTIE

Seventeenth Arrondissement

RIGHT BANK
Palais des Congrès

The better half of the 17th arrondissement extends west from boulevard Malesherbes to the Arc de Triomphe. To the east, it is full of questionable characters dealing in the shadier side of life. This is an area to avoid. The main attraction is the Palais des Congrès, a convention center with restaurants, movie theaters, and the pick-up and drop-off point for passengers going to and from Roissy-Charles-de-Gaulle Airport. There are many fine hotels in the better section of the arrondissement, and the areas around them are safe. Bus and Métro connections to more tourist-inspired parts of Paris are excellent.

HOTELS IN THE SEVENTEENTH ARRONDISSEMENT

HÔTEL ASTRID ★★★
27, avenue Carnot, 75017 (17th)
41 rooms, all with shower or bath and toilet

TELEPHONE
44-09-26-00
FAX
44-09-26-01
MÉTRO
Charles-de-Gaulle-Étoile
CREDIT CARDS
AE, MC, V
RATES
Single 450–530F, double 480–670F, triple 700F
BREAKFAST
60F extra

At the Guillet family's Hôtel Astrid, you will pay a moderate price for living in this top-drawer part of Paris. The colors throughout are cheerfully appropriate and blend well with the furnishings. Two of the nicest bedrooms have small balconies for viewing the Arc de Triomphe. The rooms are upgraded continually, and I recommend that you ask for one of the newest when reserving. No. 7, pictured on the hotel's brochure, is a nice choice because it is bigger. As you can see in the brochure, it has two armchairs, a marble fireplace, and twin brass beds. What you can't see in the brochure are the good closets and the bathroom, which has a tub, but no shower. The hotel is only about a five-minute walk from the Air France bus stop for Roissy-Charles-de-Gaulle Airport, so if you don't have much luggage, or if you have a luggage trolley, you can save money on cab fare.

English Spoken: Yes

Facilities and Services: Direct-dial phone; hair dryer; elevator; parking in front to hotel; TV with international reception; room safe, no charge

Nearest Tourist Attractions (Right Bank): Arc de Triomphe, Champs-Élysées

HÔTEL BÉLIDOR ★
5, rue Bélidor, 75017 (17th)
47 rooms, 18 with shower or bath and toilet

No serious Cheap Sleeper in Paris can afford to overlook the Bélidor. The only dramatic change lately is the weeding out of the old, knickknack-rich reception and breakfast areas so you can better appreciate the brick and marble fireplace and small window garden. The owner is still just as sweet as ever, and the room colors and patterns as mixed. A stay here will provide you with a clean bed in a decent area just around the corner from the Palais de Congrès. The rooms are neat as pins, and those with bathtubs are larger than many two- and three-star rooms that will cost twice the price. Don't let the orange chenille and nontouristy location deter you. After only a 10- or 15-minute Métro journey you can be standing under the new pyramid at the Louvre, floating down the Seine on a *bateau mouche,* or strolling through the most romantic streets in St-Germaine-des-Prés. It is crucial to remember to plan ahead for this one because it is booked weeks in advance all during the year.

English Spoken: Yes

Facilities and Services: Direct-dial phone; no elevator, TV, or safe

Nearest Tourist Attractions (Right Bank): Palais des Congrès exhibition and convention center; all other tourist attractions require public transportation

TELEPHONE
45-74-49-91

FAX
45-72-54-22

MÉTRO
Porte Maillot, *sorti côté pairs* (exit on the even-numbered side of the street)

CREDIT CARDS
None, cash only, paid in advance

RATES
Single 145–295F, double 200–440F; shower 20F

BREAKFAST
30F per person, included

HÔTEL DE BANVILLE ★★★
166, boulevard Berthier, 75017 (17th)
39 rooms, all with shower or bath and toilet

The classic Hôtel de Banville is my idea of a wonderful, personalized Parisian hotel. It was built in 1928 by architect Jerome Bellat, who designed many of the magnificent buildings the 17th arrondissement is famous

TELEPHONE
42-67-70-16

FAX
44-40-42-77

MÉTRO
Péreire, Porte-de-Champeret

CREDIT CARDS
AE, MC, V

RATES
Single 600–660F, double 785F, triple 880F, quad 975F

BREAKFAST
Continental 50F extra per person, *Dietetique* 75F extra, *Pleinform* 85F extra

for. From the beautiful lobby to the rooms filled with family antiques and heirlooms, you can tell immediately that this is a hotel where the owners know what they are doing. The hotel has developed a large following of appreciative guests who applaud the efforts of owner Mme. Lambert, her daughter, and their right-hand man, Jean-Pierre, who is also the talented artist who did all the paintings that hang throughout the hotel. Mme. Lambert grew up in the hotel business, and all of her family is involved in the industry in some way. Her background and expertise, combined with her impeccably good taste, are evident everywhere you look.

Every time I visit the hotel, I think this is it, what more can she possibly do to improve on perfection . . . and every time I am surprised. In addition to a recently redone lobby and dining area with hand-painted murals, a new sitting room has been added, with an eye to group usage. The bedrooms are on a revolving schedule of redecorating and upgrading. All are nice . . . there are no faded, gloomy rooms where you might be stuck. Those on the eighth floor have sweeping views, from the Arc de Triomphe to the Tour Montparnasse. Naturally these are in great demand. In no. 21, a small entry leads to a room papered in deep salmon and cream-colored miniature print. Twin beds have padded headboards that complement the beige-and-white quilt pattern used on barrel chairs. The mirrored closets provide plenty of move-in space, and the location in back guarantees calm. Other favorites include no. 22, done in white wicker; the pink-and-white no. 24, with a brass bed and sofa that converts into bunks for children; and either no. 75 or 85 for singles. If romance is on your agenda, reserve no. 83 with a view over all of Paris.

Even breakfast is special at the Banville. You can order a basic Continental, or the *dietetique,* which features wheat bread and yogurt, or go all out and have sausage, eggs, and fruit juice along with your croissants and coffee.

The hotel is located on a busy boulevard lined with plane trees. The Métro is close; you can take the RER to the Musée d'Orsay and St-Michel; the 92 bus puts you at Étoile and the 84 drops you at place de la Concorde.

English Spoken: Yes

Facilities and Services: Bar; direct-dial phone; hair dryer; elevator; TV with international reception; room safe, no charge

Nearest Tourist Attractions (Right Bank): None; must use public transportation

HÔTEL DES DEUX ACACIAS ★★

28, rue de l'Arc-de-Triomphe, 75017 (17th)

31 rooms, all with shower or bath and toilet

Never mind its rather plain atmosphere . . . this top-pick Cheap Sleep will please visitors wanting to keep within a certain budget and still be conveniently close to the Champs-Élysées. The hotel has been in the same family for generations and is now owned by Mme. Delmas, who took over from her parents when they retired 65 years ago. Her gentle demeanor permeates the entire operation, with the possible exception of the sometimes austere welcome from the manageress's unsmiling husband.

No one could ever call this modest place modern, but the spotless, large rooms are color coordinated, well ventilated, and have generous closet and luggage space. Two small student rooms on the top floor are in great demand for long stays and must be reserved months in advance. Enclosed public parking is available across the street for motorists.

English Spoken: Limited

Facilities and Services: Direct-dial phone; elevator; TV; office safe, no charge

Nearest Tourist Attractions (Right Bank): Champs-Élysées, Arc de Triomphe

TELEPHONE
43-80-01-85

FAX
40-53-94-62

MÉTRO
Charles-de-Gaulle Étoile, Argentine

CREDIT CARDS
MC, V

RATES
1–2 persons 345–385F, quad 500F

BREAKFAST
30F extra per person

HÔTEL EBER ★★★

18, rue Léon-Jost, 75017 (17th)

18 rooms, all with shower or bath and toilet

Travelers longing for peace and quiet have at their disposal a group of French hotels whose owners have taken a vow of silence. The Hôtel Eber is one of the 275 members of Relais du Silence, an association of individually owned hotels dedicated to providing a silent and calm atmosphere in which guests can feel at home. At the Eber, the entrance along a tiled walkway opens onto a beamed salon centered around a carved fireplace. To the left of the reception desk is an inviting bar and breakfast area with comfortable armchairs. In the back is a green patio with metal tables and chairs set out on warm days for alfresco breakfasts. The rooms tend to be small and are decorated in light beiges with good-looking art prints and posters on the walls. Many of the hotel

TELEPHONE
46-22-60-70

FAX
47-63-01-01

MÉTRO
Courcelles

CREDIT CARDS
AE, DC, MC, V

RATES
1–2 persons 630–700F, suite 1,100–1,400F

BREAKFAST
50F extra per person (served all day)

clientele are from the world of fashion or entertainment, not a group known for its introverted behavior. However, owner Jean-Marc Eber says that those who want excitement stay in St-Germain-de-Prés. In its other life years ago, the hotel was a bordello, so you can see things have improved drastically.

You will need public transportation for most things on a tourist agenda, but it might be interesting to walk by 25, rue de Chazelles, about two blocks away, and see where the Statue of Liberty was originally built.

English Spoken: Yes

Facilities and Services: Bar; direct-dial phone; hair dryer; elevator; mini-bar; radio; TV with international reception; office safe, no charge; room service from restaurants in the area

Nearest Tourist Attractions (Right Bank): Arc de Triomphe, Champs-Élysées

HÔTEL ÉTOILE PÉREIRE ★★

146, boulevard Péreire, 75017 (17th)

26 rooms, all with shower or bath and toilet

TELEPHONE
42-67-60-00

FAX
42-67-02-90

MÉTRO
Péreire

CREDIT CARDS
AE, DC, MC, V

RATES
Single 500–600F, double 700F, duplex 950F; no charge for extra bed

BREAKFAST
55F extra per person

The Étoile Péreire, a member of the Relais du Silence (see Hôtel Eber, page 183), is a sophisticated hotel offering modern luxury at affordable prices. Occupying a distinctive building which is hard to identify as a hotel, it benefited from a long-overdue remodeling project in 1987, when the 1900s' styles and bathtubs on feet were tossed out. Still, here is the tranquillity the location affords and the dedicated services of the staff headed for so many years by Ferruccio Pardi.

The crisp rooms offer guests a mixture of modern Italian furniture and country fabrics. The best selections are the two-story duplexes with ceiling fans, skylights, and soft watercolor paintings. M. Pardi prides himself on his breakfasts, which are served in a redecorated basement dining room. Diners have a choice of 40 jams, jellies, or honeys to accompany their croissants and fresh orange or grapefruit juice. If you want more, ham or bacon and eggs are available.

While hardly in the tourist mainstream, the hotel is close to Porte Maillot and the Air France air terminal. A large city park with tennis courts and plenty of picnic benches is across the street, as well as several old favorites listed in *Cheap Eats in Paris.*

English Spoken: Yes

Facilities and Services: Bar; direct-dial phone; hair dryer; elevator; mini-bar in all rooms except singles with showers; TV with French cable; office safe, no charge; room service from a restaurant delivery service

Nearest Tourist Attractions (Right Bank): None; must use public transportation

HÔTEL FLAUBERT ★★
19, rue Rennequin, 75017 (17th)
37 rooms, all with shower or bath and toilet

This garden hotel, designed and built by Christiane and Michel Niceron, opened its doors in January 1989. Warm toast tones and airy bamboo furniture set the stage in the lobby and mirrored breakfast room . . . both filled to capacity with green houseplants. A cage of colorful parakeets adds a tropical note. All this opens onto a lush outdoor garden overflowing with blooming hydrangeas, impatiens, and colorful seasonal plants. It is certainly clear that the Nicerons *love* to garden. Singles or couples with scanty luggage can reserve one of the rooms opening onto this garden. For more space and better lighting, I like a top-floor *chambre.* Mme. Niceron is a teacher, so not always at the hotel. M. Niceron *is* at the hotel full-time and works with his staff to provide pleasant stays for the guests. In addition, the rooms are perfectly clean, and the prices good for this part of Paris, which is not known for its budget anything.

English Spoken: Yes

Facilities and Services: Direct-dial phone; elevator; mini-bar; TV; no safe

Nearest Tourist Attractions (Right Bank): Ten-minute walk to Champs-Élysées and Arc de Triomphe

TELEPHONE
46-22-44-35

FAX
43-80-32-34

MÉTRO
Ternes

CREDIT CARDS
AE, DC, MC, V

RATES
Single 350–450F, double 470–675F, triple 775F

BREAKFAST
40F extra per person

HÔTEL NEVA ★★★
14, rue Brey, 75017 (17th)
31 rooms, all with shower or bath and toilet

For an upmarket choice by the Champs-Élysées, the Hôtel Neva delivers comfort and convenience, especially for guests who need to have business services close at hand, i.e., fax and conference room. Wood-paneled walls keep the mood warm, and the interesting collection of paintings and sculpture reminds you that this is, indeed, Paris. The mother of the owner is an acclaimed artist and is responsible for the five-person metal sculpture by the front entrance and many of the paintings that hang in the lobby, bar, and breakfast room.

TELEPHONE
43-80-28-26

FAX
47-63-00-22

MÉTRO
Charles-de-Gaulle-Étoile

CREDIT CARDS
AE, DC, MC, V

RATES
Single 630–680F, double 748–780F; extra bed 100F

BREAKFAST
45F extra per person

The rooms are uncluttered in a contemporary sort of way. The largest are on the first floor. One of the best of these is no. 5, overlooking the garden. It is a large accommodation, done in soft gray with a painting of Provence on one wall. Closet space is good and so is the tub and shower. No. 32 is a single on the back. Soft yellow walls give it a light look. While there is not much to beckon the visitor in the immediate neighborhood, the Champs-Élysées is close, and from there transportation to all *quartiers* is easy.

English Spoken: Yes

Facilities and Services: Air-conditioning; bar; direct-dial phone; hair dryer; elevator; mini-bar; fax and conference room; radio; TV with international reception; room safe, no charge

Nearest Tourist Attractions (Right Bank): Champs-Élysées, Arc de Triomphe

HÔTEL PALMA ★★
46, rue Brunel, 75017 (17th)
17 rooms, all with shower or bath and toilet

TELEPHONE
45-74-74-51

FAX
45-74-40-90

MÉTRO
Argentine

CREDIT CARDS
MC, V

RATES
Single 380–400F, double 400–430F, triple 500F

BREAKFAST
40F extra per person

If you want the most for your battered Yankee buck and don't mind being a bit far from the center of things, then the Palma is one of the best Cheap Sleep deals in the French capital. Its sensational value, coupled with the quality and quantity of service, delights its many followers . . . who come from all budget backgrounds. Located in the leafy precincts of the upper-crust 17th arrondissement, it is within an easy walk to the Palais des Congrès exhibition center, the Air France terminal at Porte Maillot, and excellent public transportation links that will whisk you anyplace you want to be in less than 30 minutes.

The best thing about this treasure besides its value and the congenial owners, M. and Mme. Couderc, is that guests never have any feeling they are "budgeting" by staying here. Aside from random use of florals, patterns, and colors, nothing is torn or tattered; no carpets are frayed; everything that should be painted is; the furnishings are exceptionally nice; and every room has a nice bathroom and color television with international reception, including CNN. The rooms in highest demand are the blissfully quiet and cozy top-floor roosts with skylight views and slanting ceilings, and the two ground-floor rooms off the lobby.

English Spoken: Yes

Facilities and Services: Direct-dial phone; elevator; TV with international reception; office safe, no charge

Nearest Tourist Attractions (Right Bank): Arc de Triomphe, Champs-Élysées, Palais des Congrès

HÔTEL REGENT'S GARDEN ★★★
6, rue Pierre-Demours, 75017 (17th)
39 rooms, all with shower or bath and toilet

Originally built by Napoléon III for his personal physician, this building is now a refined garden hotel. Hidden behind a high brick wall, it seems a little far from the hub of activity, but, in fact, rue Pierre-Demours is only a few minutes' walk from the Champs-Élysées and the Arc de Triomphe.

The cavernous, high-ceilinged rooms have crystal chandeliers, decorative moldings, marble fireplaces, brass bedsteads, floor-to-ceiling mirrors, and authentic period furnishings. Many rooms connect for convenient family use, and several have large walk-in closets with built-in shelves and shoe racks. The bathrooms are thoroughly 20th century and luxuriously fitted with fluffy terry robes, scented bubble bath and soaps, and plenty of light for applying makeup. Most rooms overlook the garden, which is landscaped with large trees, stone statues, flowering walkways, and a terrace with tables for summer breakfasts or afternoon teas. Everyone who has ever stayed here, and I include myself, loves it and you will too. It offers affordable elegance with an ambiance of bygone days in Paris.

English Spoken: Yes

Facilities and Services: Bar; direct-dial phone; hair dryer; elevator; mini-bar; parking in front, 55F per space (first-come basis); radio; TV with international reception; office safe, no charge

Nearest Tourist Attractions (Right Bank): Champs-Élysées, Arc de Triomphe

TELEPHONE
45-74-07-30; toll-free in the U.S. and Canada 1-800-528-1234 (Best Western)

FAX
40-55-01-42

MÉTRO
Wagram, Ternes, Charles-de-Gaulle Étoile, exit rue Carnot

CREDIT CARDS
AE, DC, MC, V

RATES
Single 660–875F, double 730–975F

BREAKFAST
45F extra per person

LIBERTEL MONCEAU ★★★
7, rue Rennequin, 75017 (17th)
25 rooms, all with shower or bath and toilet

The Libertel hotel group is one of the best things to happen on the Paris hotel scene in some time. The group takes over run-down hotels and transforms them into smart two- and three-star winners. The Libertel Monceau is one of their best . . . certainly not short on style or charm. The theme is The Chase, or The Hunt. It is

TELEPHONE
46-63-07-52; central reservation number 44-70-24-24

FAX
47-66-84-44; central fax number 44-70-24-51

MÉTRO
Ternes

CREDIT CARDS
AE, DC, MC, V

RATES
Single 610–695F, double 720–775F; extra bed 220F

BREAKFAST
60F extra per person

carried out with the black-and-white hunting prints hung in the bar and the deep hunter's green used in the public areas. In addition, the use of leather and brass suggests a clublike atmosphere.

If you want twin beds, request no. 103, with blue and maroon fabrics complementing yellow walls. The bathroom is large with sweetly framed prints of children frolicking on the moon. If a double bed is better, no. 101 on the back is quiet, with the blank view softened by the latticework installed on the opposing gray wall.

The only blip is the windowless breakfast room, which looks like a roadside coffee stop and is stuffy besides. The hard metal chairs are certainly not conducive to a comfortable stay. Best to order breakfast sent to your room or go out and save over $10 per person. You can also save money during the happy hour in the upstairs bar, between 6:30 and 7:30 P.M., when your second drink will be free.

English Spoken: Yes

Facilities and Services: Bar; direct-dial phone; hair dryer; elevator; mini-bar; radio; TV with international reception; office safe, no charge

Nearest Tourist Attractions (Right Bank): Champs-Élysées, Arc de Triomphe

RÉSIDENCE LEVIS HÔTEL ★★
16, rue Lebouteux, 75017 (17th)
10 rooms, 3 with shower or bath and toilet; 6 with shower, no toilet; 1 with bath, no toilet

TELEPHONE
47-63-86-38

FAX
40-53-00-92

MÉTRO
Villiers

CREDIT CARDS
MC, V

RATES
1–2 persons 365–420F

BREAKFAST
35F extra per person

If location is not your first concern, but money is, the 10-room Résidence Levis is worth serious thought. It is in an area restfully free of other tourists and definitely more than a heartbeat or two away from much action. However, by Métro the hotel is only a few stops from all the bright lights and lowlife in Montmartre and Pigalle. Closer to home, shop hounds and camera buffs will enjoy looking in the animated shops and watching the hawkers lining rue de Levis. It is not the place for finding the latest fashions, but it is a slice of Parisian middle-class life worth experiencing. As for the hotel's rooms, they are large and their colors blend, although the decor includes large-patterned, vivid-colored wallpaper, 1950s-style furniture (*à la* chrome and laminated tops), and more than a fair dose of chenille. That said, there is always a bowl of hard candies in your room, which will be as clean as anything you will find. The owners, Richard and Gisele, are sweet and helpful. Between them they speak five languages, but they are obviously partial to Americans. They spend part of their vacation every year at the Sands in Las Vegas, where Richard hits the gaming tables and Gisele works on her tan. Let's face it, the bottom line for Cheap Sleepers is price, and here it is kind to most budgets, allowing guests to spend their sleeping money doing more interesting things in Paris.

English Spoken: Yes, and Portuguese, German, and Dutch

Facilities and Services: Bar; direct-dial phone; no elevator; TV in four rooms; office safe, no charge

Nearest Tourist Attractions (Right Bank): None; must use public transportation

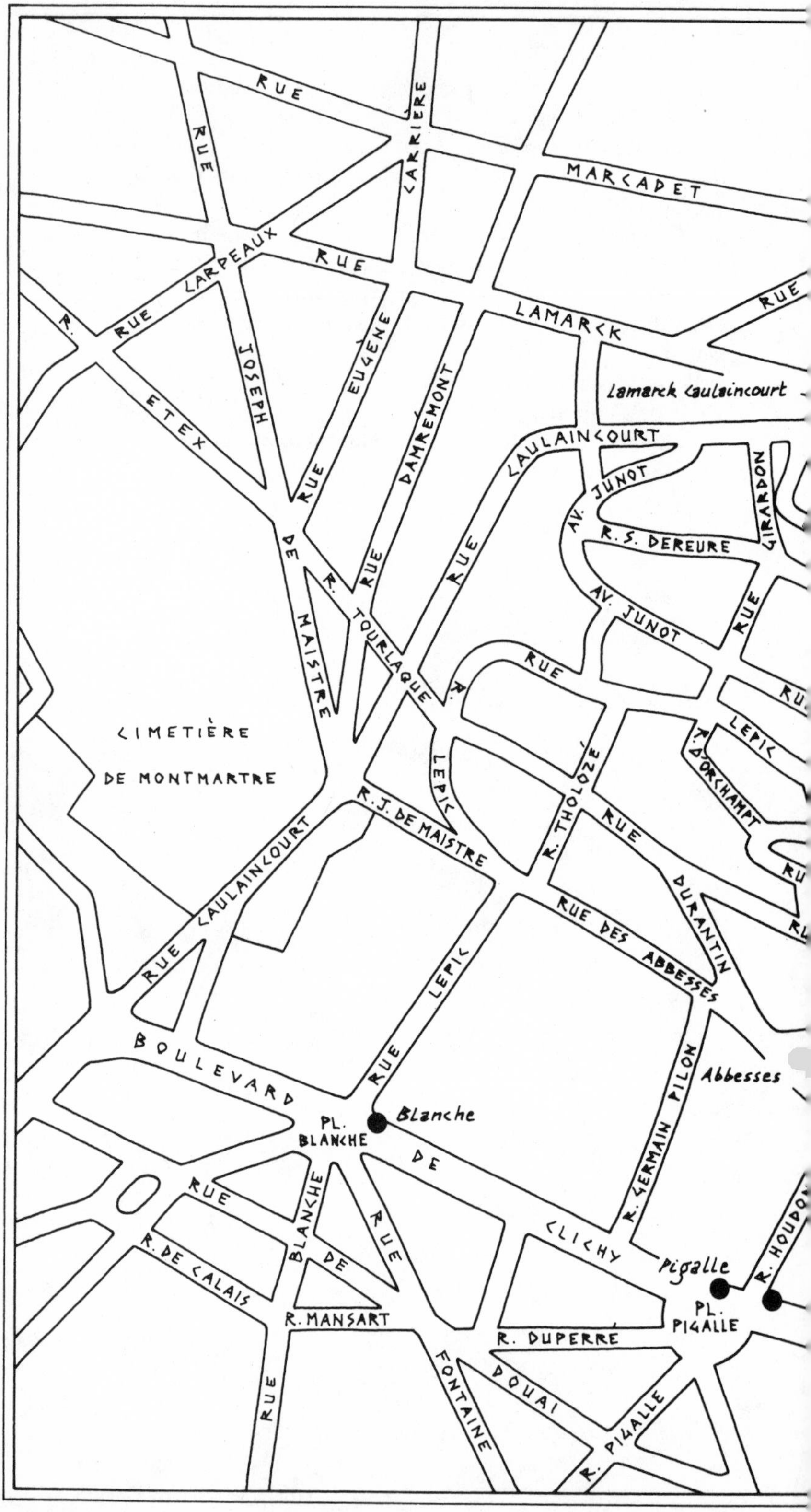

RUE
CARRIÈRE
RUE
MARCADET
RUE
LARPEAUX
RUE
RUE
LAMARCK
RUE
R.
RUE
JOSEPH
EUGÈNE
DAMREMONT
ETEX
Lamarck Caulaincourt
CAULAINCOURT
AV. JUNOT
GIRARDON
R. S. DEREURE
RUE
RUE
DE
MAISTRE
R.
TOURLAQUE
AV. JUNOT
RUE
RUE
R.
LEPIC
CIMETIÈRE
DE MONTMARTRE
LEPIC
R. D'ORCHAMPT
R. THOLOZÉ
R. J. DE MAISTRE
RUE
DURANTIN
RUE CAULAINCOURT
RUE DES ABBESSES
RUE LEPIC
BOULEVARD
Abbesses
R. GERMAIN PILON
Blanche
PL. BLANCHE
DE
CLICHY
RUE
BLANCHE
DE
RUE
R. DE CALAIS
R. MANSART
Pigalle
PL. PIGALLE
R. HOUDON
R. DUPERRE
RUE
FONTAINE
DOUAI
R. PIGALLE

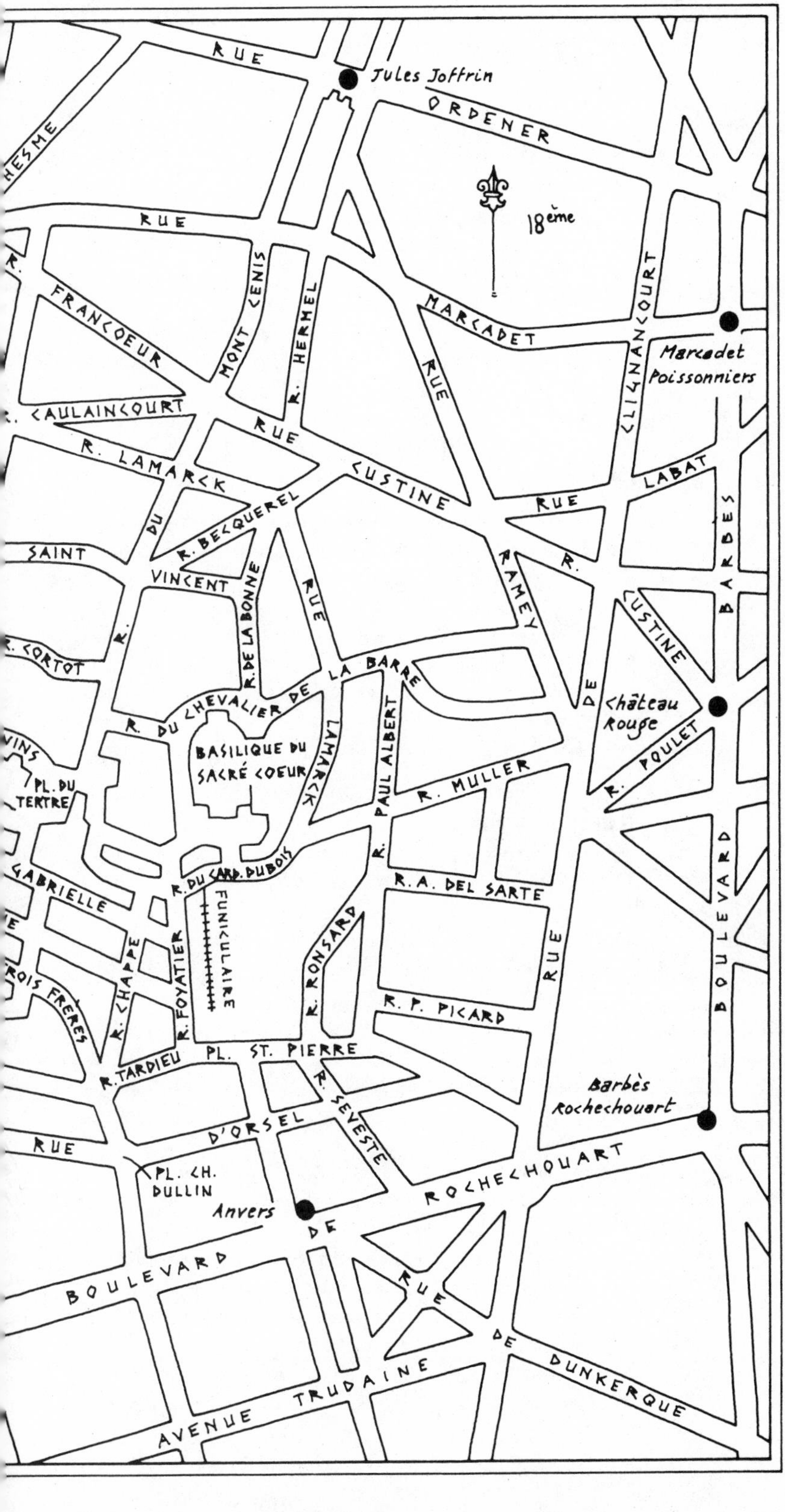

RUE
Jules Joffrin
ORDENER
18ème
RUE
FRANCOEUR
MONT CENIS
R. HERMEL
MARCADET
RUE
CLIGNANCOURT
Marcadet Poissonniers
CAULAINCOURT
RUE
R. LAMARCK
CUSTINE
RUE
LABAT
BARBES
DU
R. BECQUEREL
SAINT
VINCENT
R.
R. DE LA BONNE
RUE
RAMEY
R.
CUSTINE
CORTOT
R. DU CHEVALIER DE LA BARRE
DE
Château Rouge
BASILIQUE DU SACRÉ COEUR
LAMARCK
R. PAUL ALBERT
R. MULLER
R. POULET
PL. DU TERTRE
GABRIELLE
R. DU CARD. DUBOIS
FUNICULAIRE
R. A. DEL SARTE
BOULEVARD
RUE
R. RONSARD
R. CHAPPE
R. FOYATIER
R. P. PICARD
PL. ST. PIERRE
R. TARDIEU
R. SEVESTE
Barbès Rochechouart
D'ORSEL
RUE
PL. CH. DULLIN
ROCHECHOUART
Anvers
DE
BOULEVARD
RUE
DE
DUNKERQUE
TRUDAINE
AVENUE

Eighteenth Arrondissement

RIGHT BANK
Montmartre, Sacré-Coeur

Montmartre is a rambling *quartier* full of contrasts, combining picture-postcard quaintness and razzle-dazzle. It was here that Toulouse-Lautrec drew the cancan girls dancing at the Moulin Rouge and Picasso and Braque created cubism at the Bateau-Lavoir. The panoramic view from the steps of Sacré-Coeur at dawn or sunset, the many artists, and the intimate village atmosphere that prevails along the narrow streets—many of which are the same as when Utrillo painted them—continue to evoke the dynamic spirit and colorful past of this vibrant part of Paris. It is a must stop for anyone wanting to absorb the spirit of Paris, both present and past.

HOTELS IN THE EIGHTEENTH ARRONDISSEMENT

ERMITAGE HÔTEL ★★
24, rue Lamarck, 75018 (18th)
12 rooms, all with shower or bath and toilet

TELEPHONE
42-64-79-22

FAX
42-64-10-33

MÉTRO
Lamarck-Caulaincourt

CREDIT CARDS
None, cash only

RATES
Single 410F, double 460F, triple 590F, quad 700F

BREAKFAST
Included, cannot be deducted

Close your eyes and imagine being in Paris and waking up in an antiques-filled hotel high atop Montmartre with magical views over the entire city. Sound wonderful? It does, and it is all possible at the Ermitage, a poetic refuge run by the engaging Maggie Canipel and her husband. In the late 1970s the couple sold everything they had and bought the Ermitage. They updated the plumbing, filled the old mansion with their collection of fine furniture, and began welcoming guests, continually outdoing themselves to make everyone feel at home with their boundless energy and engaging smiles.

Any one of their rooms could steal your heart, but my favorites are nos. 6 and 10, on the top floor, with tall French windows opening onto the morning sun and views of all Paris, and nos. 11 and 12, which open onto their terrace garden. No. 2 is beautiful, with a magnificent set of antique bedroom furniture consisting of a carved bed, two side tables, and a mirrored armoire. A crystal chandelier completes the picture.

True, you will need strong legs and lungs to walk up the hill from the Métro, but once there you will be richly rewarded by being in the center of one of the most picturesque parts of Paris. You can wander the streets once painted by Utrillo, peek into artists' ateliers, and have your portrait painted by one of the pseudo-artists lining the touristy place du Theatre. Undiscovered restaurants in all price ranges are within easy walking distance (see *Cheap Eats in Paris*).

Note: Mme. Canipel prefers that all reservations be made by telephone, and she will confirm by fax.

English Spoken: Yes, also German and Italian

Facilities and Services: Direct dial phone; no elevator or TV; office safe, no charge

Nearest Tourist Attractions (Right Bank): Montmartre

HÔTEL DES ARTS ★★
5, rue Tholoze, 75018 (18th)
50 rooms, all with shower or bath and toilet

TELEPHONE
46-06-30-52

FAX
46-06-10-83

MÉTRO
Abbesses, Blanche

CREDIT CARDS
AE, MC, V

RATES
Single 350F, double 420–475F; extra bed 100F

BREAKFAST
35F extra per person

I first looked at the Hotel des Arts three years ago during the first week it reopened after being refurbished. Paint cans were still in the hallway and some of the furniture had not been placed. Still, I liked it . . . the owners were honest and hard-working and seemed intent on providing good value for money well spent, which is my bottom line. I am happy to report the hotel is now in full swing and living up to all its original promises.

There won't be lush fabrics, signed paintings, fancy mini-bar contents, or CNN television programs to keep you amused. You will be able to depend on the simple rooms in gray, peach, or beige providing a clean, comfortable place for a short stay in one of the most visited sectors of Paris. Sixth-floor rooms have rooftop views to the white tip of Sacré-Coeur. No. 12, on the street, is a large choice with built-in furniture giving the illusion of more space. The street is quiet, so you won't be listening to wild partying at all hours. I would not want to spend any time in no. 15, with its dull view. The bright breakfast room has stone walls and little bistro chairs set against paintings of Montmartre. It is a happy place to get ready for the day ahead of you in beautiful Paris.

English Spoken: Not on the weekends

Facilities and Services: Direct dial phone; elevator to fifth floor; TV; office safe, no charge

Nearest Tourist Attractions (Right Bank): Montmartre

HÔTEL LE BOUQUET DE MONTMARTRE ★★

1, rue Durantin, 75018 (18th)

36 rooms, all with shower, 22 with bath and toilet

TELEPHONE
46-06-87-54

FAX
46-06-09-09

MÉTRO
Abbesses

CREDIT CARDS
MC, V

RATES
1–2 persons 330–360F, triple 410–450F, quad 480F; extra bed at 10 percent of the cost of the room

BREAKFAST
35F extra per person

If you are a committed Cheap Sleeper with a fondness for Montmartre, and you want to experience the fun and the village atmosphere of the area and still stay under budget, the Bouquet de Montmartre is a little honey of a hotel. Its second-floor lobby may be difficult to find, but the search is worth it.

The Gibergues family works hard to keep their Victorian hotel as nice as it is for the price. They are on duty from Monday to Saturday, 9 A.M.–6 P.M., so when calling for reservations, bear this in mind. If you can wear blinders or dark glasses in your room, or do not mind living in a kaleidoscope of colors, then read on. Most of the bedrooms fall into the "cute and confusing" category. Lacy curtains, velvet chairs with plastic covers, floral rugs, and busy wallpaper march along with brightly tiled bathrooms in purple, lavender, royal blue, and aqua. All are positively spotless and tear-free. Breakfast is served in an ornate dining room with red velvet chairs, lacquered furniture, and globe lights . . . all serving to remind you that this *is* Montmartre, after all.

From the hotel you can stroll in any direction and see something interesting. You can climb up to Sacré-Coeur or crawl down the hill and view the underside of Paris on full display in Pigalle. For longer trips, jump on the Montmartobus, a minibus service that plies the winding streets snaking around the Butte. You can ride from the bottom at Pigalle to the end of the line at Métro Jules Joffrin. Stop along the route if something intrigues you and get back on . . . it will be one of the most pleasurable rides you will take in Paris.

English Spoken: Limited

Facilities and Services: Direct dial phone; office safe, no charge; no elevator or TV

Nearest Tourist Attractions (Right Bank): Montmartre

HÔTEL PRIMA-LEPIC ★★
29, rue Lepic, 75018 (18th)
38 rooms, all with shower or bath and toilet

The Prima-Lepic is a century-old Montmartre building that still has its ornate ceiling moldings, marble fireplaces, and a corner cherub or two for good measure. Appealing to a young European crowd on slim budgets, the hotel is a good base for exploring Montmartre.

It looks nice from the outside—painted white with balconies overlooking the busy market street that runs the length of rue Lepic. The welcoming entry overlooks a trompe l'oeil English garden that sets the floral theme for the main floor of the hotel. The beamed breakfast area has a fabulous mural depicting life in Montmartre and floral prints by Monet.

When reserving, request any room that faces front on the third, fourth, or fifth floor, because they have balconies and more light. Nos. 15 and 55 are two of the best, and so is no. 56, done in pale lavender with an Oriental throw rug and a 1930s-style lamp for accent pieces. The country-style furniture gives it a slightly romantic flavor. These rooms all have one thing in common: noise. Better pack earplugs because Montmartre jumps all night long, especially on the weekends. In a room on the back, you will get more space, but less light and no view at all. These are, of course, the quieter choices. The apartments are spacious enough, but not recommended because they are dark and gloomy and have depressing views on the back side of the building.

English Spoken: Yes

Facilities and Services: Direct dial phone; hair dryer; elevator to five floors; TV; office safe, no charge

Nearest Tourist Attractions (Right Bank): Montmartre

TELEPHONE
46-06-44-64

FAX
46-06-66-11

MÉTRO
Abbesses

CREDIT CARDS
MC, V

RATES
Single 375F, double 400–425F, triple 475F, apartment 725F

BREAKFAST
45F extra per person

HÔTEL ROMA SACRÉ-COEUR ★★
101, rue Caulaincourt, 75018 (18th)
57 rooms, all with shower or bath and toilet

Mention that you are a devoted reader of *Cheap Sleeps in Paris* and receive a 10 percent discount on the already reasonable rates. Frankly, this is a bit of a gamble, because staying here puts you *out* of the mainstream and does require some walking up and down hills. Its cachet comes because room no. 701 was where Georges Braque had his studio when Montmartre was in its artistic

TELEPHONE
42-62-02-02

FAX
42-54-34-92

MÉTRO
Lamarck-Caulaincourt

CREDIT CARDS
AE, DC, MC, V

RATES
Single 310F, double 375F
BREAKFAST
Included, cannot be deducted

heyday in the 1920s. It is easy today to picture the artist standing on the wraparound balcony, gazing at Northern Paris on the horizon, and turning out his canvases. Other rooms of note are nos. 501 and 506, with cityscape views to Sacré-Coeur. Singles are meager and the outlooks discouraging, so if you are a lone voyager, pay a little more and get a small double. Rooms are in nonclashing colors of soft peach, simple browns, and white. Management is agreeable and the neighborhood is pretty in that it reflects a *real* part of Paris that is untouched by the maddening tourist crowds.

English Spoken: Yes

Facilities and Services: Direct dial phone; hair dryer; elevator to all but top floor; mini-bar; radio; TV; office safe, no charge

Nearest Tourist Attractions (Right Bank): Montmartre

Big Splurges

The following hotels fall into the Big Splurge category. They are higher priced and are included here because their location, amenities, ambiance, service, and overall appeal will suit those travelers with more demanding tastes and flexible budgets.

FIRST ARRONDISSEMENT

FIFTH ARRONDISSEMENT

SIXTH ARRONDISSEMENT

SEVENTH ARRONDISSEMENT

EIGHTH ARRONDISSEMENT

Other Options

If hotel life is not for you, there are other reasonable options available in Paris. Consider a return to nature . . . i.e., camping . . . or perhaps staying as a paying guest in a private home and experiencing the Parisians on their own turf. Another cost-saving possibility is renting your own studio or apartment. The benefits of this are numerous, from having more space to spread out to shopping and cooking your own food so that you can save on expensive restaurant meals. Another advantage of choosing an apartment is that it lets you feel more a part of Paris and allows you to interact with merchants and shopkeepers. Trust me, it is great. Finally, there are home exchanges and the myriad of options available to students from 15-years-old on up.

APARTMENT RENTALS

BED & BREAKFASTS

CAMPING OUT

HOME EXCHANGES

RESIDENCE HOTELS

STUDENT ACCOMMODATIONS

Apartment Rentals

CHEZ VOUS
220 Redwood Highway, Suite 129
Mill Valley, California 94941 USA

TELEPHONE
(415) 331-2535

FAX
(415) 331-5296

CREDIT CARDS
AE, MC, V

RATES
Starts at $190 per night for two people (three night minimum) and goes up. Better prices for longer stays.

BREAKFAST
Available in the bed and breakfast accommodations only

A stay in a Chez Vous accommodation will allow you to actually *live* in Paris, not just visit. These private homes and apartments are located in some of the best areas of Paris, not in marginal, out-of-the-way *quartiers* of the city that the apartment owners will try and convince you are interesting. The 30 Paris possibilities range from self-contained homes in the posh 16th arrondissement to studios around place des Vosges. Each place is lightly stocked with milk, coffee, dishwashing soap, paper products, and a bouquet of fresh flowers. Airport pickup can be arranged, but it will be extra, as are linens and a cleaning fee at the end of your stay. The catalog listing the Paris properties is called *Bonjour Paris!!!* If you are venturing outside of Paris, and this type of stay appeals to you, ask about their catalog of rental properties throughout France, called *At Home in France.* They also offer bed and breakfast accommodations in private farmhouses, manor homes, and chateaux throughout France, but not in Paris. The catalog for this is *Bed & Breakfast: French Style.*

English Spoken: Yes

Facilities and Services: Varies with each location

Nearest Tourist Attractions: Varies with each location

DE CIRCOURT ASSOCIATES
170, rue de Grenelle, 75007 (7th)

De Circourt Associates was founded by Marie de Circourt to aid those people moving to Paris, either for professional reasons or for stays of at least two months. She lists over 4,000 apartments and homes in Paris and the suburbs, all within easy access. Thanks to her sophisticated computerized search system, which fits the person to an accommodation according to their wishes and needs, she or one of her exceptionally competent English-speaking staff will find you the place of your dreams at a price you can afford. The possibilities range from a sixth-floor walk-up with a futon on the floor, to a zany artist's studio done in black and white with a bird-shaped chair, to the to-die-for apartment occupied by Robert Altman while he was on location in Paris filming *Prêt-à-Porter.* It is all up to you and your budget . . . whatever you want, chances are excellent Marie de Circourt will have it.

English Spoken: Yes
Facilities and Services: Varies
Nearest Tourist Attractions: Varies

TELEPHONE
47-53-86-38
FAX
45-51-75-77
CREDIT CARDS
None, cash only
RATES
Starts from around $900 per month and up. Minimum stay at least two months; prefer six-month lease or one year.
BREAKFAST
Not available

RENTAL DIRECTORIES INTERNATIONAL (HELEN LONDON)
2044 Rittenhouse Square
Philadelphia, PA 19103 USA

Today's travelers are more sophisticated and independent. There is a growing market of travelers interested in renting vacation apartments or homes abroad for a week to a year. Sometimes the red tape and expense, not to mention the hassle, of dealing with foreign real estate companies can take all the fun out of such a good idea. Rental Directories International, a Pennsylvania-based organization run by Americans, has a publication providing an avenue for renting apartments, homes, and villas directly from the owners, eliminating the costly agency fees and commissions. Currently four directories are available, covering France (and Paris, of course), Italy, Spain and Portugal, and the United Kingdom. Each publication lists over 150 different properties, with location, description, availability, price range, and how to contact the owner directly. The cost of the directory is $39.95. Directories are published annually and come out in the fall.

English Spoken: Yes
Facilities and Services: Varies with each property
Nearest Tourist Attractions: Varies with each location

TELEPHONE
(215) 985-4001
FAX
(215) 985-0323
CREDIT CARDS
MC, V accepted for the purchase of the directory only. All rentals in cash only.
RATES
Depends on the owner

ROTHRAY
10, rue Nicolas-Flamel, 75004 (4th)

TELEPHONE
48-87-13-37

FAX
40-26-34-33

MÉTRO
Châtelet

CREDIT CARDS
None; cash or personal checks in your currency

RATES
From 575–1,200F per day; less by month. Prices vary according to size and location of apartment, as well as length of stay. Minimum stay 7 days.

BREAKFAST
Not available

Anyone who has ever stayed in one of RothRay's lovely apartments says they are the best. Period. I agree, because after one stay, I vowed to always let competent Ray Lampard and his capable partner Roth arrange my living accommodations anytime I am in Paris. Some short-term private apartment rentals in Paris can be potluck affairs that offer unwelcome surprises on arrival, and during a stay, force you to contend with strange decor, varying amenities and levels of cleanliness, and haphazard services by the agency in charge, who shows little interest in you after they have your money . . . up front. You will find none of these problems in any apartment rented through RothRay.

Their apartments are located in interesting *quartiers* where a stroll around a corner will put picturesque Paris at your fingertips. After a few days you will discover what fun it is to actually be a part of Paris, and probably spend a good deal of your time trying to make more permanent arrangements, or figuring out how to return again more often. It will be love at first sight when you walk into one of their tastefully furnished and beautifully equipped studios and apartments. In addition to attractive furnishings, most have cable televisions, stereo systems, washers and dryers, dishwashers, and American-style kitchens beautifully equipped with nice china, crystal, and utensils. You can only fully appreciate the quality of their kitchens if you have ever tried to prepare a meal in a French closet-style kitchen with a mish-mash of "rental" pots and pans and chipped, unmatched dishes for serving. Weekly maid service, linen changes, and a refrigerator stocked with fruit juices, wine, and beer are included. As one guest happily told me, "There is RothRay, and then everyone else, just trying to catch up." How very true it is.

English Spoken: Yes

Facilities and Services: The best, but vary with the apartment

Nearest Tourist Attractions: Varies by apartment

Bed & Breakfasts

BED & BREAKFAST 1 CONNECTION
73, rue Notre-Dame-des-Champs, 75006 (6th)

Live in Paris like a Parisian with Bed & Breakfast 1 Connection. This organization prides itself on matching visitors and their bed and breakfast hosts according to tastes, age levels, and lifestyles. There is a three-day minimum stay in these homes, which offer attractive guest rooms, not just a spare bed in a back room. Prices vary according to the type of accommodation and the location, which ranges from central Paris to the suburbs. Bed and breakfasts can also be booked for the Loire Valley, French Riviera, London, New York, and Canada. While it is always better to book ahead, you can also go to their Paris office and generally find something.

For the more independent traveler who may be staying longer, or who wants to spend less in restaurants and shop for food like a real Parisian, they offer fully equipped apartments from the simple to the luxurious. Because Pascal LeFebvre and his able assistant Marie-Christine Bourgeois are so busy, they do not always have time to check up on housekeeping. Before renting an apartment, if you can't look at it, please try to have someone you know check it out. A two-week minimum stay is generally required. There is a 30–50 percent discount after one month and a deposit equaling the entire price of your stay is required up front. As with most foreign apartment rentals, refunds are complex, so be sure to invest in a cancellation policy.

Both bed and breakfast and apartment reservations require a 50F reservation fee per person. However, if you mention *Cheap Sleeps in Paris* when reserving, the fee will be reduced to 50F for two or more persons.

English Spoken: In office for bookings; depends on bed and breakfast

Facilities and Services: Varies with each accommodation

Nearest Tourist Attractions: Varies with each accommodation

TELEPHONE
43-25-70-39

FAX
40-47-69-20

MÉTRO
Vavin

CREDIT CARDS
AE, MC, V

RATES
Bed and breakfast: single from 275F up, depending on quality of room; double from 325F up, depending on quality of room. Apartments: from 375–825F per day, 30–50 percent discount after one month.

BREAKFAST
Included with bed and breakfast stay

Camping Out

LES CAMPINGS DU BOIS DE BOULOGNE
Allée du Bord de l'Eau, 75016 (16th)

TELEPHONE
45-24-30-00

FAX
45-24-30-00 (same as telephone number)

MÉTRO
Porte-Maillot (exit is 4 km from campground). Take bus no. 244 from Porte-Maillot Métro stop, get off at route des Moulins, and walk down path to right. Do not follow misleading signs to left on main road. Free camp bus in July and August; other bus service from April–October only.

CREDIT CARDS
No credit cards; cash only

RATES
Tent (two people) 70F per night (no electricity), 145F per night (with electricity); RV hookups 100F; mobile home 475F first three nights, after three nights 400F. Lower prices September–June.

BREAKFAST
Not available

While Coleman stoves, tents, inflatable mattresses, and citronella candles are not on everyone's packing list for a trip to Paris, they might be on yours if you are a camper. Yes, it *is* possible to pitch a tent in Paris! Les Campings in the Bois de Boulogne is on the far edge of the park and provides the only true rustic opportunity for Cheap Sleeps in Paris. Geared to students and hearty international travelers, or those with RVs, the campground is located four kilometers away from the nearest Métro, making it almost essential that you have your own set of wheels, or that you don't mind walking if the camp bus schedule does not correspond with your plans to go into Paris or return later in the day. The bus service exists only from April to October and is free in July and August. A convenience store, money changer, hot showers, a coin-operated washer and dryer, and a restaurant are open to campers. The office is open from 6 A.M. until 2 A.M. and accepts *no* reservations for campsites, but does accept them for mobile home bookings and large camping groups. Everything is always on a first-come, first-served basis.

English Spoken: Limited

Facilities and Services: Convenience store; money changer; information office; coin-operated washing machines and dryers; free hot showers; bus service and restaurant from April–October

Nearest Tourist Attractions: None

Home Exchanges

Home exchanges have been around for a long time. It is really quite simple and the price is right: free. You trade your home and all its contents, often including pets and cars (sorry, not the children), for someone else's in a part of the world you want to visit. The exchange is negotiated by the parties involved, not by the organization publishing the directory. To avoid problems, it pays to be very specific about your needs and desires for your own home, as well as for the one you want to live in. The following companies publish directories you must purchase to take part in a home exchange. In some cases, rentals are possible, but that is not the focus of this type of accommodation.

HOMELINK USA
P.O. Box 650, Key West, FL 33041; tel: 1-800-638-3841, outside the U.S. 305-294-3720, fax: 305-294-1448

INTERVAC U.S./INTERNATIONAL HOME EXCHANGE
P.O. Box 590504, San Francisco, CA 94159; tel: 415-435-3497, fax: 415-386-6853

WORLDWIDE HOME EXCHANGE CLUB
806 Brantford Avenue, Silver Springs, MD 20904; tel: 301-680-8950
London: 50 Hans Crescent, London SW1X ONA, England; tel: 071-589-6055

Residence Hotels

CITADINES TROCADÉRO ★★★
29 bis, rue Saint-Didier, 75016 (16th)
97 accommodations, ranging from studettes to full-size apartments, all with shower, bath, and toilet

The Citadines residence-hotel group offers several locations in Paris. I like the Trocadéro site best because of the neighborhood and its proximity to more on a tourist's agenda. The others tend to be far from much on my list, but their offbeat locations may appeal to some.

At Citadines Trocadéro there are several types of accommodations, ranging from a studette to an apartment. Frankly, the studettes and unrenovated studios are just too miniscule for any degree of long-term comfort. The best deals are the studios in the new wing, which rent for the same price as the older ones. The new ones integrate Art Deco design with the latest in bathrooms and room layout. All types of facilities are furnished with equipped kitchenettes, a full bath with shelf space, a color TV with international reception, weekly linen changes, and a direct dial telephone. You must do your own housekeeping, unless you opt for a maid, which is extra. Baby beds, an iron and ironing board, and vacuum cleaner are provided free of charge. There is a coin-operated washing machine and dryer in the base-

TELEPHONE
44-34-73-73; central reservation service 47-25-54-54

FAX
47-04-50-07

MÉTRO
Victor Hugo

CREDIT CARDS
AE, DC, MC, V

RATES
Accommodations: studettes, studios, 1–3 bedroom apartments; studette 600F per night; 1,700F per night for a 3-bedroom apartment; weekly and monthly rates available, as well as off-season rates

BREAKFAST
40F extra per person

ment. Enclosed, private parking is also available. Stays can range from a night to several months, but the longer the stay, the lower the price, especially during the off-season. Just a block away is one of the best indoor supermarket complexes in Paris. After one trip through the aisles of this market, you will be inspired to use your kitchen.

Note: Other Citadines locations: Citadines Paris Opéra (2nd); Haussmann (8th); Mal herbes (8th); République (3rd); Lyon Bastille (12th); Austerlitz (13th); Didot Plaisance (14th); Montparnasse (14th)

English Spoken: Yes

Facilities and Services: Direct dial phone; elevator; baby bed; iron and ironing board; vacuum cleaner; sauna; TV with international reception; dishwasher in all but studettes; coin-operated washer and dryer; enclosed private parking, 50F per day; office safe, 90F per week

Nearest Tourist Attractions (Right Bank): Shopping on avenue Victor Hugo, Arc de Triomphe, Champs-Élysées

HOME PLAZZA RÉSIDENCE HÔTELS: BASTILLE AND SAINT-ANTOINE

Home Plazza Bastille

TELEPHONE
Central reservations 40-21-22-23; reception 40-21-22-00

FAX
47-00-82-40

MÉTRO
St-Sebastien-Froissart

CREDIT CARDS
AE, DC, MC, V

RATES
Residence plan: starts at 740F for one and goes to 2,180F for 6 persons per day; hotel plan: 840F for one to 2,280F for 6 persons per day; rates in both plans vary with length of stay

BREAKFAST
65F extra per person

The two Home Plazza residences are located in a part of Paris that until a few years ago was considered a tourist wilderness. Now they are close to the thick of things in the 11th arrondissement. The two residence hotels offer equipped studios and flats furnished in a modern style that holds up well under hard use. There are two plans: the Résidence Plan, with cleaning and linen changed once a week, or the Hoteliere Plan, where there is daily cleaning and towel change, but the bed linens are changed every three days. In both plans, the longer you stay, the less you pay. One of the benefits of staying here is all the extras available to the guest. While the Bastille résidence has the edge on location and amenities offered, the Saint-Antoine site seems less impersonal.

HOME PLAZZA BASTILLE ★★★
74, rue Amelot, 75011 (11th)
289 studios and apartments, fully furnished with equipped kitchens

English Spoken: Yes

Facilities and Services: Bar; conference room; direct dial phone; elevator; iron; hair dryer; parking, 100F per day; room safe, no charge; TV with video and international reception; restaurant; sauna; Jacuzzi; gym

Nearest Tourist Attractions (Right Bank): Marais, Bastille

Home Plazza Saint-Antoine

TELEPHONE
40-09-40-00

FAX
40-09-11-55

MÉTRO
Nation

CREDIT CARDS
AE, DC, MC, V

RATES
Residence plan: starts at 740F for one and goes to 2,180F for 6 persons per day;
hoteliere plan: starts at 840F for one and goes to 2,280F for 6 persons per day; both plans have varying rates according to length of stay

BREAKFAST
65F extra per person

HOME PLAZZA SAINT-ANTOINE ★★★

289 bis, rue de Faubour St-Antoine, 75011 (11th)

90 studios and apartments, fully furnished with equipped kitchens

English Spoken: Yes

Facilities and Services: Conference room; direct dial phone; elevator; hair dryer; iron; parking, 100F per day; room safe, no charge; radio; TV with international reception and videos

Nearest Tourist Attractions (Right Bank): Nothing; must use public transportation

PIERRE & VACANCES: RÉSIDENCE CHARLES DULLIN ★★★

10, place Charles Dullin, 75018 (18th)

76 studios and apartments with equipped kitchens, shower or bath, and toilet

TELEPHONE
42-57-14-55

FAX
42-54-48-87

MÉTRO
Abbesses, Anvers

CREDIT CARDS
AE, DC, MC, V

RATES
Lowest rates start at 550F for a studio in low season and go to 1,250F per night for a 3-room apartment sleeping 6; weekly, monthly, and seasonal rates available

BREAKFAST
50F extra per person

During two extended stays in Paris, the Résidence Charles Dullin was my *pied à terre.* I continue to recommend it as a home away from home for those who want to explore Paris from a typical neighborhood. This part of Montmartre is full of contrasts. By day, it is interesting for its many colorful local characters who wander the streets and sit and reminisce in the cafés. In the evening, the atmosphere changes and it becomes young and alive until the wee hours, with Parisians and tourists eating and drinking in the many bistros and restaurants that offer ever kind of cuisine from African couscous to health burgers and Spanish tapas.

From a practical standpoint, everything you will need to set up short- or long-term housekeeping is within an easy five- or ten-minute walk; small supermarkets, banks, a main post office, pharmacies, dry cleaners, a shoe repair shop, a photo store, pungent cheese shops, tempting *boulangeries,* colorful fish and meat markets, *charcuteries* brimming with beautiful, ready-made food (if cooking isn't up your alley), and finally, one of the best shopping streets in this part of Paris, rue Lepic.

The 76 studios and apartments are for the most part spacious and livable. All have kitchens and a uniformity of services and facilities. Weekly maid service *is* included, as are linen and towel changes twice weekly. If you want more frequent maid service, there is an hourly rate. The best part is, the longer you stay, the lower the price, especially in the low season.

English Spoken: Yes

Facilities and Services: Direct dial phone; dishwasher in most units; elevator; dry cleaning service; parking, 100F per day; TV; office safe, no charge

Nearest Tourist Attractions (Right Bank): Montmartre

RÉSIDENCE HÔTELIÈRE TROUSSEAU ★★
13, rue Trousseau, 75011 (11th)
66 studios and suites, all with fully fitted kitchens, bath, shower, and toilet

TELEPHONE
48-05-55-55

FAX
48-05-83-97

MÉTRO
Ledru-Rollin

CREDIT CARDS
AE, MC, V

RATES
Hotel plan: studio 510–780F per night, apartment or suite 930–1,300F per night; daily cleaning and linen change; sheets changed every two days. Residence plan (minimum stay 3 nights): 3–7 nights, 426F; weekly maid, sheet and towels. The longer you stay, the better the price. Prices vary according to the season in both plans.

BREAKFAST
45F extra per person

To tell you the truth, I never expected to find such a nice residence hotel a 15-minute walk *east* of the Bastille. If it was almost anyplace else in Paris, it would be almost twice the price and jam-packed year-round. It is part of a small chain that deals mainly in four-star addresses in Paris and along the French Riviera, so demanding, exacting guests are nothing new to management. Sixty-six studio flats and duplex suites have fully equipped kitchens with microwaves and satellite television reception. Disciples of Sister Parish and Billy Baldwin were not called upon to be decorating consultants, but the no-surprise rooms have excellent bathrooms with lots of shelf space, a medicine cabinet, and a drying rack. Just so you know, in the studios the sofa doubles as the bed and the closets have no doors. The overall popularity of this selection is due in no small measure to the list of amenities offered: private car parking, conference room, office space, fax capabilities, a golf practice cage—no kidding!—along with coin-operated laundries and shopping carts in the garage to help you lug your loot.

The proprietors own wineries in Bordeaux and sell their wines at this hotel. To go with your bottle of wine, you can order a light meal almost any time of day.

English Spoken: Yes

Facilities and Services: Bar; conference room; office rooms; fax services; direct dial phone; hair dryer; elevator; fitted kitchen; private parking, 60F per day; TV with international reception; office safe, no charge; coin-operated laundry; golf range; weekly or daily maid service, depending on accommodation; light meals served (mostly frozen)

Nearest Tourist Attractions (Right Bank): None; must use public transportation

TIMES SQUARE MONTPARNASSE ★★★

121, boulevard du Montparnasse, 75006 (6th)

52 apartments, all with fitted kitchenette, shower, bath, and toilet

For affordable quality in a Montparnasse residence hotel, this polished choice is just steps away from a kir or an espresso at Le Dôme and a leisurely stroll to many recommended Cheap Eats in Paris. Once inside there is a vaguely Philippe Starck look to its minimalistic lobby and sleek, chrome-furnished breakfast room. The apartments offer the latest in soft lighting, excellent space execution, and top-of-the-line marble baths. You won't be inspired to cook a Thanksgiving dinner here, but the kitchenettes, with two burners and a microwave, will allow you to shop with purpose at any of Paris's colorful outdoor *marchés.* Best sites are those on the back or overlooking the inner courtyard garden. Prices are quoted by the day, but reductions for long-term stays are always negotiable.

English Spoken: Yes

Facilities and Services: Air-conditioning; bar; conference room; direct dial phone; some hair dryers; elevator; fitted kitchenette; TV with international reception; safe in office, no charge

Nearest Tourist Attractions (Left Bank): Montparnasse, Luxembourg Gardens

TELEPHONE
43-35-46-35

FAX
40-47-43-01

MÉTRO
Vavin

CREDIT CARDS
AE, DC, MC, V

RATES
1–2 persons: per day, 775F; per week, 675F per day; per month, 570F per day

BREAKFAST
60F extra per person

Student Accommodations

There are more than 10,000 student beds in Paris. The following list of organizations offers help in finding low-cost accommodations year-round. It is critically important to remember that *only* cash is accepted and that in many cases, you must belong to a group to qualify (e.g., student, youth hostel, etc.).

Any student can take advantage of the French government–run and/or subsidized student lodgings in Paris. In most cases you will be required to show proof of full-time student status, in addition to your university or college ID. The International Student Identity Card (ISIC) not only identifies you as a student but entitles you to savings of up to 40 percent on museum entry fees, transportation, meals at certain student dining halls, and, of course, lodgings. If you purchase your ISIC card in the U.S., you will receive medical, accident, and hospital insurance. For more information about this important bargain, contact the Council on International Education Exchange (CIEE), 205 East 42nd Street, 16th floor, New York, NY 10017; tel: 212-661-1414 or 1-800-438-2643. You can also buy the card in Paris, but you won't receive the medical benefits. Go to 119, rue St-Martin (4th), Métro Rambuteau; open Monday–Friday, 9:30 A.M.–6 P.M. The new International Teacher Identity Card (ITIC) offers teachers the same discounts and is available at the same locations.

If you are not a student but are under 26 years old, the Federation of International Youth Travel Organization (FIYTO) issues an International Youth Card, or the GO 25 Card. This card is recognized internationally and gives the holder access to thousands of discounts on everything from transportation and accommodations, to restaurants, cultural activities, and tours. In the U.S. the card is available from CIEE (see address and telephone number above) and at any of their Paris offices.

Another option for saving money, whether or not you have student status, is to be a member of Hosteling International. You should become a member of the American Hosteling organization before you leave. If you show up at a hostel without a membership card, there will be a 20F supplement per night for six nights, then you will be a member. For more information, write or call the American Youth Hostel at P.O. Box 37163, Washington, D.C. 20013, or call 202-783-6161. For their address in Paris for central reservations, see page 211.

Finally, if none of the above work, try the Office du Tourisme at 127, Champs-Élysées, 75008, Métro Charles-de-Gaulle-Étoile, 47-23-61-72, open daily, 9 A.M.–6 P.M. Lines are long and selections not always the cheapest. Count on paying a supplement for the reservation service.

Listed below are organizations in Paris that specialize in student accommodations. In many of the locations (none of which are listed here, only the main office where you must go to make a reservation) there is a cafeteria serving low-cost food that you purchase through meal tickets. Cash is king. Forget the credit cards and personal checks. Most have a minimum stay in the summer, but in some you can move in for a year. Curfews are not uncommon. All will give you the rules of the road before you get your bed, so there will be no excuses.

La Centrale de Reservations (FUAJ-HI), run by Hosteling International, is the best place to get a cheap student bed in Paris. A trip to their office will provide you with a same-day reservation in any of their affiliated hostels or budget hotels. Not only can you book a bed, but you can make on-going travel arrangements by bus, boat, or air; book tours to other parts of the world; or nail down an excursion in Paris. There will be a reservation fee, payable at the time of booking, but it is deducted from the cost of your bed.

HOSTELING INTERNATIONAL
La Centrale de Reservations (FUAJ-HI)
4, bd. Jules Ferry, 75011 (11th)

Open daily 8 A.M.–10 P.M.

English Spoken: Yes

Facilities and Services: Reservations for other hostels and travel arrangements

Nearest Tourist Attractions: Varies with each location

TELEPHONE
43-57-02-60

FAX
Fax reservations taken for groups of 10 or more: 40-21-79-92

MÉTRO
République

CREDIT CARDS
None, cash only

RATES
120F per person, double; 110F per person in dorm (4–6 beds); showers are free; towels 15F; paper sheets 14F; MUST purchase card: 19F per night, 115F per year

BREAKFAST
Included

Foyers (residence halls) do not belong to an international organization and may not require membership. UCRIF (Union des Centres de Rencontres Internationales de France) has nine lodging places in Paris. For the complete listing, contact the Maison de L'UCRIF, 4, rue Jean-Jacques Rousseau (1st), Métro Louvre, 42-60-42-40; open Monday–Friday 9 A.M.–6 P.M. Arrive early for best selection.

Another foyer group is the Accueil des Jeunes in France (AJF), at 119, rue St-Martin (4th), Métro Rambuteau, 42-77-87-80; open Monday–Saturday, 9 P.M.–6 P.M. For best results arrive before 10 A.M., especially during the summer. Some of their lodgings are in historic, centrally located buildings; others are on the fringes, with long Métro commutes. Wherever you land, you will be required to pay in advance and won't be able to see the room ahead of time. Breakfast is included, showers are free, and no written reservations are accepted. The age limit of 18–30 is sometimes overlooked in the off-season. No curfews are enforced, and there are one to eight beds per room. If you are traveling elsewhere in France, ask for their thick book detailing a multitude of student accommodations throughout the country.

ALOHA HOSTEL

1, rue Borromée, opposite 243, rue de Vaugirard, 75015 (15th)

33 beds, 8 rooms with showers, none with toilets

TELEPHONE
42-73-03-03
FAX
42-73-14-14
MÉTRO
Volontaires
CREDIT CARDS
None, cash only
RATES
94F per person per night, 580F per person per week; must pay for your room for *next* day by 10 P.M. on previous day
BREAKFAST
Not served

The Aloha Hostel, the Young and Happy Hostel (Y & H Hostel), and the 3 Ducks Hostel appeal to travelers with youth on their side. In all of these lodgings, management spares no effort to cut corners in order to keep the prices at the rock-bottom level. At the Aloha Hostel guests can mingle in the backpack-laden reception area, comparing cheap travel tips gleaned from years of surviving on the edge. There are no single or triple rooms; doubles are reserved for couples; others get a bunk in a quad. There is no age limit (only stamina), and in the summer you can stay one week. Everything is payable in advance by 10 P.M. the previous day. Office and rooms are closed and all guests must vacate the premises between 11 A.M. and 5 P.M. BYO towels and sheets, or plan on spending 15F apiece. Showers are free, and so is the hot plate in the communal kitchen. The working-class neighborhood is full of bakeries, supermarkets, banks, and other survival-type shopping. Otherwise, it's at least 20 minutes to tourist destinations.

English Spoken: Yes

Facilities and Services: Safe in office, no charge

Nearest Tourist Attractions (Left Bank): None; must use public transportation

ASSOCIATION DES ÉTUDIANTS PROTESTANTS DE PARIS

46, rue Vaugirard, 75006, Métro Luxembourg, 43-33-23-30

Open to people from 18–26. No advance booking. Maximum stay five weeks. 10F membership.

CITÉ UNIVERSITAIRE

15, bd. Jourdan, 75014, Métro Cité Universitaire, 45-89-35-79

The Cité Universitaire is a vast maze of 40 international student residences located on the edge of the city next to the Parc Montsouris. Both advance and short-notice reservations are possible, depending on the residence. Foreign students and teachers are accepted from

July 1 to September 30. Minimum stay is 7–15 days, depending on residence. There are more than 4,500 rooms, so getting something should not be difficult. Open Monday–Friday 8 A.M.–7 P.M.

CROUS ACADÉMIE DE PARIS
39, avenue Georges-Bernanos, 95005, Métro Port-Royal, 40-51-36-00

This organization is in charge of all university student accommodations in Paris and has beds available during university vacations.

MAISON INTERNATIONALE DES JEUNES
4, rue Titon, 75011, Métro Faidherbe-Chaligny, 43-71-99-21

For anyone 18–30.

PALAIS DE LA FEMME—FOR WOMEN ONLY
94, rue de Charonne, 75011, Métro Charonne or Faidherbe-Chaligny, 43-71-11-27

Salvation Army hostel. Book in advance, in writing.

3 DUCKS HOSTEL (no stars)
6, place Étienne Pernet, 75015 (15th) (To the right side of Jean Baptiste de Grenelle Church at the end of rue de Commerce)
80 beds in shared rooms with 2–6 beds per room; 6 rooms have showers only, all others are without shower, bath, or toilet

One of the Cheapest Sleeps in Paris is found at the rugged 3 Ducks Hostel. This youthful hangout appeals to backpackers and other wanderers who value camaraderie along with wild and ribald fun over aesthetics or a peaceful night's rest. This is the sort of place where you must bring your own sheets and towels, or pay 12F rental the first night for a sheet and 12F to buy a towel. The laid-back management requires shirts and shoes to be worn at all times and provides cooking facilities, hot showers, summer barbecues, a TV lounge, casual bar with cheap beer, and rooms for two, three, or four persons. There are no lockers, nor is there any minimum or maximum stay. There is, however, a strict 1 A.M. curfew. Future guests should remember that cash is all that is accepted, and they probably should not send their parents by to check the place out first.

Note: The great Mountain Bike trips in Paris start here every day at 11 A.M. The price (120F) includes a

TELEPHONE
48-42-04-05

FAX
None

MÉTRO
Commerce

CREDIT CARDS
None, cash only

RATES
95F per person in a shared room; 580F per person per week in shared room; free showers 24 hours a day

BREAKFAST
Not provided

fully guided tour in four languages (request yours in advance), insurance, and the bike. You travel from the Latin Quarter to the Bastille, to Notre Dame and the Champs-Élysées. It is wonderful fun, and you don't have to be an Olympic athlete to enjoy it. For more information, call 48-42-57-87.

English Spoken: Yes

Facilities and Services: Bar with beer and soft drinks; TV in lounge; office safe, no charge; kitchen privileges

Nearest Tourist Attractions (Left Bank): Far from everything; must use public transportation

YOUNG & HAPPY HOSTEL (Y & H HOSTEL)

(no stars)

80, rue Mouffetard, 75005 (5th)

54 beds, none with private shower, bath, or toilet

TELEPHONE
45-35-09-53

FAX
47-07-22-24

MÉTRO
Monge, Censier-Daubenton

CREDIT CARDS
None, cash only

RATES
95F per person in shared room; showers are free

BREAKFAST
Included

Called the Young & Happy Hostel because this place is friendly and everyone who stays here has such a good time. It is located on rue Mouffetard, a famous *marché* street with loads of Cheap Eats serving everything from crêpes and croissants to pizza slices and dripping Greek sandwiches. Reception is open daily from 8–11 A.M. and from 5 P.M.–1 A.M. Showers and breakfast are included in the rate. You can reserve with a one-night advance deposit or arrive when they open and hope for the best. There is no age limit, but you will have to deal with a lockout from 11 A.M.–5 P.M. and a 1 A.M. curfew.

English Spoken: Yes

Facilities and Services: None

Nearest Tourist Attractions (Left Bank): Rue Mouffetard, Jardin des Plantes

Shopping: Cheap Chic

Paris is wrenchingly beautiful, and so are many of its people. If you use your eyes and take in everything, you can learn more about true style in a weekend than in a lifetime's perusal of fashion magazines . . .

Lucia Van der Post

A museum is a museum, but a bargain is forever . . .

Suzy K. Gershman, Born to Shop Paris

Paris is a shopper's dreamworld. Even those who claim to dislike shopping are bound to be attracted by the unending selection of shops with beautiful window displays. The haute couture, open-air *marchés* overflowing with beautiful foods, extravagant toy shops, and the dazzling displays of jewelry, antiques, and collectibles tempt everyone from the serious buyer to the casual browser. However, most of us cannot afford to pay the astronomically high prices that come with this glorious merchandise. What to do? Become a Parisian smart shopper.

There has always been something very stylish about the French. Just the addition of the word *French* to everyday objects such as jeans, silk, bread, and toast lifts them above the ordinary. After you have been in Paris for a day or so, you will realize that the French do not just get dressed, they get turned out. You will no doubt wonder how a modest shop girl manages to look so elegant, considering her low wages and the high price tags on clothing. The answer is simple: savvy Parisian shoppers know where to go for the best quality and value, and they *never* pay full price.

As a life-long, dedicated discount shopper with a black belt in the art, I know that bargain shopping can be both frustrating and exhausting until you find that fabulous designer suit in your size and favorite color for half price. This type of discount shopping in Paris takes a good eye, limitless patience, endurance, and comfortable shoes. In Paris, of all places, it should be more than just a quest to track down the cheapest items available . . . it should be fun. Finding something *très a la mode* at below retail in Paris is not that difficult once you know how. The trick is in knowing when and where to shop to get the most for your money. That is what Cheap Chic will help you to do: transform your T-shirt into a significant outfit, with just the right pair of pants, a sassy jacket, and perfect accessories for the moment . . . all for reduced prices and, more importantly, for less than you would pay at home.

With all discount shopping, the selections will vary from day to day and season to season. Shops also come and go. What is here today and very "in" may be gone tomorrow. Not all shops take credit cards, so be prepared with extra francs. The comfort of the customer is seldom a top priority. As a result, many places do not have proper dressing rooms, most are jammed with merchandise, there is limited individual attention, and in many cases only fragmented English is spoken. And never mind the icy salesperson who has an innate knack for sizing you up and pricing everything you are wearing in one glance. Believe me, it is all worth it, because nothing is more satisfying than being clad in designer labels at knockdown prices. Armed with Cheap Chic, you are bound to find great buys, save money, and come home with things your friends will die over. *Bon Chance!* And please, if you discover something wonderful, let me know.

Cheap Chic Shopping Tips

1. Know the prices at home so you will be able to spot a bargain when you see it.
2. To get a rough idea of how much something costs, double the francs and add a decimal (e.g., 100F = $20.00; 80F = $16.00). To be precise, carry a calculator.
3. If you like something, can get it home, and can afford it, buy it when you see it. If you wait until later, it probably will not be there when you go back, or you will see it when you get home for twice the price.
4. Look for these signs in the windows—they mean lower prices:

Soldes	a sale in progress (see page 241 for Parisian sales)
Fin de Séries	end of collection
Dégriffés	labels cut out
Stock	overstock
Dêpot Vente	resale
Fripes	used clothing

5. Nothing is returnable. Be sure when you buy something that it does not have flaws and that it fits.
6. *Never* change money at a shop. The rate will not be in your favor. Go instead to a bank or use a credit card.
7. If you are shopping at one of the flea markets, be sure to bargain. The asking price is not the price you are expected to pay. You should be able to bargain the price down by 15–30 percent. Also, bring cash: plastic is not part of a bargaining discussion, and most sellers do not take credit cards of any type.
8. Pharmacies marked with a green cross on a white background are upscale and expensive. They are the places to go if you need a prescription filled or advice on cold remedies. Buy toiletries, cosmetics, and basic over-the-counter drugs in supermarkets or at Monoprix or Prisunic. Pharmacy prices are at least double.

9. Pack an empty, soft-folding suitcase in your luggage so you can transport your treasures without the extra hassle and expense of mailing. An extra bag on an airline will cost less than $100, and that will be far less than you will have to pay at the store or at the post office to have it sent.

10. Take the time to do all the *détaxe,* and remember to turn it in to the customs officials at the airport *before* you relinquish your luggage or go through customs or passport control (see *Détaxe,* below).

11. Each person is entitled to bring back $400 worth of duty-free goods acquired abroad, even a week-old baby, so you can use what your husband and children do not. After the $400 point, there will be a 10 percent charge on the next $1,000, and more as the amount increases. If you ship things back home, any package worth *less* than $50 is considered an unsolicited gift and can be sent duty-free. If your package worth exceeds $50, you will pay duty.

12. Generally speaking, shop hours are Monday through Saturday from 10 A.M. to 7 P.M. Large department stores are open one night a week. Small shops often close Monday mornings and for lunch. Everything is closed on Sundays and holidays.

13. When you enter a store, you will be greeted with "Bonjour Madame" (or "Monsieur"), and when you leave, "Au revoir Madame" (or "Monsieur"). Please respond . . . "Bonjour Mademoiselle," etc. It is considered extremely bad form not to acknowledge the salespeople when entering or leaving a store.

Tax Refund: *Détaxe*

Every tourist visiting France is entitled to a *détaxe* (tax rebate) for purchases totalling 2,000F or more in one store. The refund averages about 13 percent. If shopping with a friend, combine your purchases to reach the total and share the proceeds when they arrive. The simple paperwork is filled out by you and the store. You will need to have your passport available for identification. On the *détaxe* form, you will be asked to state whether you want the refund mailed to you in a French-franc check (not recommended because it is hard to deal with in the U.S. and getting it can take forever) or to have it credited to your credit card. This last option is the best because your credit card company will credit the refund to you in U.S. dollars. Expect a delay of two to three months. For items shipped directly from the store, the *détaxe* is automatically deducted without any paperwork. At your point of exit from France, a customs official will stamp your documents, which you then mail back to the store in the self-addressed, stamped envelope they gave you at the time of purchase. That's it. Sometimes an eager official will ask to see your purchases, so keep them handy, just in case. At the airport, look for the window that says *douane de détaxe* and allow an extra half-hour to accomplish the mission. Generally, you must *ask* for the *détaxe* forms because most smaller shopkeepers do not volunteer the information. In the large department stores there are special offices that take care of the paperwork. Yes, it all does take some extra time and effort, but the savings do add up, so persevere.

Vocabulary for Cheap Chic Shoppers

à la mode	in style
atelier	workshop
bas	stockings
bleus de travail	blue cotton worker's uniform
brocanteur	second-hand dealer
caleçons	boxer shorts
Carte Bleu	VISA charge card
ceinture	belt
chaussures	shoes
cravate	tie
dégriffés	labels cut out
dépôt vente	resale shop
détaxe	tax refund
duvet	down comforter
écharpe	scarf
Eurocard	MasterCard charge card
faience	hand-painted pottery
fermé	closed
fin de series	end of the collection
fripes	secondhand clothes (à la thrift shops)
gant	glove
grand magasin	large department store
jupe	skirt
manteau	coat
marché	market
marché aux puces	flea market
ouvert	open
pantalons	pants
prêt-a-porter	ready-to-wear
pull	sweater
rez-de-chausée	ground floor (we call it the first floor)
sac	purse
stock	overstock
tablier	apron

taille	size
Ca coute combien?	How much does this cost?
Acceptez-vous les cartes de credit?	Do you accept credit cards?

Consignment Shops

CATHERINE BARIL
14–16, rue de la Tour, 75016 (16th)

All the biggies from Chanel to Yves St. Laurent to Cardin and Ricci . . . but they are previously owned. A nice staff, fair prices, a super selection of clothing in apple-pie condition. This is one of the favorites of smart French discount denizens.

Telephone: 45-20-95-21
Métro: Passy
Credit Cards: MC, V
Hours: Monday 2–7 P.M., Tuesday–Saturday 10 A.M.–7 P.M., closed August

DÉPÔT-VENTE DE PASSY
25, rue de la Tour, 75016 (16th)

Inexpensive, new (without the labels), and used menswear at bargain prices. It is all mixed together, but except for the shoes, it is hard to tell the old from the new.

Telephone: 45-27-11-46
Métro: Passy
Credit Cards: MC, V
Hours: Monday 2–7 P.M., Tuesday–Saturday 10 A.M.–7 P.M., closed August

RÉCIPROQUE
89, 92, 93, 95, 97, 101, 123, rue de la Pompe, 75016 (16th)

The Rolls-Royce of formerly worn designer duds for a fraction of their original retail price. Consignments of everything from gifts and antiques to estate jewelry, shoes, bags, clothes, furs, evening wear, and menswear and children's wear. Allow plenty of time if this type of *haute* thrift shopping is your *forte.* The staff is helpful.

Telephone: 47-04-30-28
Métro: Pompe
Credit Cards: MC, V
Hours: Tuesday–Saturday 10:30 A.M.–7 P.M., closed Mondays and last week of July to last week of August

Conversion Charts

French and American clothing sizes

Women's dresses: To change French dress size to U.S. sizes, subtract 28 from the French dress size.

To change U.S. dress size to French, add 28 to the U.S. dress size.

French	32	34	36	38	40	42	44
U.S.	4	6	8	10	12	14	16

Women's sweaters and blouses: To change French sizes to U.S., subtract 8 from the French blouse or sweater size.

To change U.S. sizes to French sweater or blouse sizes, add 8 to the U.S. blouse or sweater size.

French	38	40	42	44	46	48	50
U.S.	30	32	34	36	38	40	42

Men's suits: To change French suit size to U.S. sizes, subtract 10 from the French suit size.

To change U.S. suit size to French, add 10 to the U.S. size.

French	46	48	50	52	54	56	58
U.S.	36	38	40	42	44	46	48

Men's shirts: To change French shirt size to U.S. shirt size, subtract 8 from the French size and divide by 2.

To change U.S. shirt size to French, multiply the U.S. size by 2 and add 8.

French	36	37	38	39	40	41	42	43
U.S.	14	14.5	15	15.5	16	16.5	17	17.5

Shoes: To change French shoe size to U.S., subtract 32 from the French size.

To change U.S. shoe size to French shoe size, add 32 to the U.S. shoe size.

French	36	37	38	39	40	41	42	43	44
U.S.	4	5	6	7	8	9	10	11	12

Children's clothing: French children's clothes are sized according to the age of the child: 2m means 2 months, 16m means 16 months, etc. 2a means 2 years, 6a means 6 years (*a* stands for *ans,* which in French means *years*).

How much is that in miles, feet, pounds, or degrees?

Kilometers–Miles: To change kilometers to miles, multiply the kilometers by .621. To change miles to kilometers, multiply the miles by 1.61.

Meters–Feet: To change meters to feet, multiply the meters by 3.28. To change feet to meters, multiply the feet by .305.

Kilograms–Pounds: To change kilograms to pounds, multiply the kilograms by 2.20. To change pounds to kilograms, multiply the pounds by .453.

Celsius–Fahrenheit: Double the Celsius figure and add 30. If the Celsius figure is below zero, double the subzero number and subtract it from 32.

Cosmetics and Perfumes

CATHERINE PERFUMES AND COSMETICS
6, rue de Castiglione, 75001 (1st)

Jacques Levy and his daughter Patricia run this wonderful boutique on rue de Castiglione. They offer an excellent selection of perfumes, cosmetics, scarves, umbrellas, hair ornaments, jewelry, and ties. They give a tax-free price of 40 percent off if you purchase 2,000F or more worth of merchandise, and 25–30 percent off if you buy less. There is no hard sell. For mail orders, the same discounts are offered. Fax your order to 42-61-02-35

Telephone: 42-61-02-89
Métro: Tuileries
Credit Cards: AE, DC, MC, V
Hours: Monday–Saturday 9:30 A.M.–7 P.M.

FREDDY
10, rue Auber, 75009 (9th) (through the courtyard, up two flights of stairs)

Freddy specializes in perfumes. Forty percent is taken off if you spend the required 2,000F; if you spend less, you will get a 30 percent discount. Prices are marked *with* the discount already taken off.

Telephone: 47-42-63-41
Métro: Opéra
Credit Cards: AE, MC, V
Hours: Monday–Friday 9 A.M.–6:30 P.M.

L'OCCITANE
26, rue Vavin, 75006 (6th)

For the best in natural cosmetics which are all vegetable based, go to l'Occitane. All the products are from Aix-en-Provence and include soaps, creams, perfumes, and bath accessories. It is worth a trip to the shop just to smell the aromas and admire the beautiful displays.

Telephone: 43-25-07-71
Métro: Vavin
Credit Cards: MC, V
Hours: Daily 10 A.M.–8 P.M.

MICHEL SWISS
16, rue de la Paix, 2nd floor, 75002 (2nd)

Michel Swiss is in business to sell perfumes, cosmetics, and accessories, and sell them they do, at an almost frenzied pace. There is no shortage of clerks, all speaking four or five languages in order to sell you as much as possible. For male shopping companions, there are chairs. First off, you will get a 25 percent discount with almost no minimum purchase. If you spend 2,000F *after* the 25 percent discount has been deducted, then you get a 15 percent *détaxe.* The merchandise is varied, and all your faves are here, from Celine to Chanel (only a 12 percent discount on Chanel). Quality very good.

Telephone: 42-61-61-11
Métro: Opéra
Credit Cards: AE, DC, MC, V
Hours: Monday–Saturday 9 A.M.–6:30 P.M.

SEPHORA
50, rue de Passy, 75016 (16th)

An absolutely mind-boggling collection of cosmetics, perfumes, and miscellaneous accessories. They carry all the lines, including Bourjois. No *détaxe,* but competitive prices make them worth a look. No air-conditioning, so avoid on hot days.

Other addresses: 66, rue Chausse-d'Antin, 75009 (9th); Métro: Chausee-d'Antin; and Forum des Halles, 75001 (1st); Métro: Les Halles
Telephone: Not available
Métro: Passy
Credit Cards: MC, V
Hours: Monday–Saturday 10 A.M.–7 P.M.

Department Stores

AU PRINTEMPS
64, boulevard Haussmann, 75009 (9th)

Métro: Havre-Caumartin
Credit Cards: AE, MC, V
Hours: Monday–Saturday 10 A.M.–7 P.M.

Known as "The Most Parisian Department Store." Famous designer boutiques, a separate men's store, and an excellent leather and cosmetic department on the ground floor. Go to the Welcome Desk for a 10 percent discount card upon presentation of your passport.

BAZAAR DE L'HÔTEL DE VILLE (BHV)
52, rue de Rivoli, 75004 (4th)

A shopping experience no do-it-yourselfer should miss. Vast kitchen, hardware, and automotive departments.

Métro: Hôtel-de-Ville

Credit Cards: AE, MC, V

Hours: Monday, Tuesday, Thursday, Saturday 9 A.M.–6:30 P.M.; Wednesday 9 A.M.–10 P.M.

BON MARCHÉ
38, rue de Sèvres and rue du Bac, 75007 (7th)

The first department store in Paris, and still my favorite. It is a showplace store, with Gustave Eiffel–designed balustrades and balconies. It combines the elegant and the practical. Be sure and see their excellent grocery and fresh food stores—a fairyland for the gourmet.

Métro: Sèvres-Babylone

Credit Cards: AE, MC, V

Hours: Monday–Saturday 9:30 A.M.–6:30 P.M.

FRANCK ET FILS
80, avenue Paul Doumer, 75016 (16th)

A small, elegant department store catering primarily to the women of Passy, one of Paris's most expensive neighborhoods. Clothing and accessories only. Super sales in January and July.

Métro: Muette

Credit Cards: MC, V

Hours: Monday–Saturday 10 A.M.–7 P.M.

GALERIES LAFAYETTE
40, boulevard Haussmann, 75009 (9th)

Top names in fashion. Gourmets and gourmands will want to spend time in their grocery department. This store borders on the inspirational, with its dazzling array of delicacies featuring everything a gastronome could possibly want, including food stations where you can stop for a plate of just-made pasta, a sampling of sushi, a quick cappuccino, or a pastry (see *Cheap Eats in Paris*). Even dedicated noncooks will want to see this beautiful part of Galeries Lafayette. Be sure to stop by the Welcome Desk on the ground floor to get a 10 percent tourist discount card upon presentation of your passport.

Other branch: Centre Commercial Montparnasse; Métro: Montparnasse

Métro: Havre-Caumartin

Credit Cards: AE, MC, V

Hours: Monday–Saturday 9:30 A.M.–6:30 P.M.

LA SAMARITAINE
19, rue de la Monnaie, 75001 (1st)

Don't miss the panoramic view of Paris from the top floor. This is a good place to buy Parisian-style work clothes as worn by waiters, chefs, butchers, etc.

Métro: Pont Neuf

Credit Cards: AE, MC, V

Hours: Monday, Thursday, Saturday 9:30 A.M.–7 P.M.; Tuesday and Friday 9:30 A.M.–8:30 P.M.; Wednesday 9:30 A.M.–10 P.M.

MARKS & SPENCER
35, boulevard Haussmann, 75009 (9th)

Parisian branch of the London standby. A good selection of basic clothes that are *not* in the trendy fast track. The silk lingerie is well priced. The food hall in the basement is a good place to pick up prepared snacks or a jar of real English bitter marmalade.

Other branch: 88, rue de Rivoli (1st); Métro: Hôtel-de-Ville, Châtelet

Métro: Havre-Caumartin

Credit Cards: AE, MC, V

Hours: Monday–Saturday 10 A.M.–6:30 P.M.

MONOPRIX
Boulevard Haussmann between Au Printemps and Galeries Lafayette, 75009 (9th)

A notch or two above Prisunic. This chain is ever-present in Paris, but this is one of their biggest stores. The grocery departments are very good places to pick up jars of fancy mustard, jams, jellies, and good cheap wine. It is the place to stock up on your Bourjois cosmetics, which all savvy Cheap Chic shoppers know is the prototype for Chanel, at a fraction of the designer cost. You probably won't consider either Prisunic or Monoprix for your seasonal wardrobe, but they do have cute outfits that are "fashionably correct" at reasonable prices. If you like Target and Mervyn's, stop by Monoprix.

Métro: Havre-Caumartin

Credit Cards: MC, V

Hours: Monday–Saturday 9:30 A.M.–6:30 P.M.

PRISUNIC
52, avenue des Champs-Élysées, 75008 (8th)

Similar to Target and K-Mart, this chain of low-priced stores is good to keep in mind for children's clothes, cotton underwear, fashion accessories of the moment, housewares, groceries, and the tourist corner. There are several stores in Paris, but this is the one most visitors will see. This link in the chain serves an impressive 9,000 tourists and locals each day. Because of the inadequate ratio of cash registers to shoppers, you may feel as if you are in line behind all 9,000.

Telephone: 42-25-27-60

Métro: Franklin D. Roosevelt

Credit Cards: V

Hours: Daily 9:45 A.M.–midnight

TATI DEPARTMENT STORES
4–30, boulevard Rouchechouart, 75018 (18th)

If you love swap meets, garage sales, and basement fire sales, then Tati is for you. The crowds are impossible, especially on Saturdays, but for truly amazing bargains hidden among some real junk, join the diverse crowd at a Tati. Prices defy the competition, but be sure to check each item carefully because quality control is not a priority where this much volume is concerned, and *returns do not exist.* Warning: watch out for pickpockets, especially children, at the boulevard Rochechouart store. If this is a new sort of shopping trip for you, best go to the shop on rue de Rennes.

Métro: Anvers
Credit Cards: None, cash only
Hours: Monday–Saturday 10 A.M.–6 P.M.
Other locations: 140, rue de Rennes, 75006 (6th); Métro: Montparnasse, St-Placide; and 13, place de la République, 75003 (3rd); Métro: République

Discount Shopping Shops

ADECTA . . . ACCESSORIES
(sign over door says: MANUFACTURE DE CHAPEAUX)
6–8, rue du Grenier-Saint-Lazare, 75003 (3rd)

This is really a wholesale operation featuring children's accessories, but if you are tactful and don't ask questions, they will let you buy. Prices are at the give-away level. You can find baby hats here for 10F that sell for three and four times the price in baby shops. They also have a hat store next door with the same low prices.

Telephone: 42-72-79-88, 42-77-31-33
Métro: Rambuteau, exit rue du Grenier-St-Lazare
Credit Cards: None, cash only
Hours: Monday–Friday 8 A.M.–12:30 P.M., 1:30–6 P.M.; closed Saturday, Sunday, holidays, 22 July–22 August

ANDRÉ COURRÈGES
7, rue de Turbigo, 75001 (1st)

A good selection of the designer's last season's clothing that did not sell. The shop is located upstairs. Look for the name by the entrance.

Telephone: 42-33-03-57
Métro: Étienne-Marcel, Les Halles
Credit Cards: None, cash only
Hours: Monday–Saturday 10 A.M.–6 P.M., closed all holidays

ANNA LOWE
35, avenue Matignon, 75008 (8th)

All the top-name designers, including Chanel, at reduced prices. All labels left in; a fabulous selection of evening wear. Sensational July and mid-December sales and fast alterations.

Telephone: 43-59-96-61
Métro: Miromesnil, St-Phillippe-de-Roule
Credit Cards: AE, DC, MC, V
Hours: Monday–Saturday 10:30 A.M.–7 P.M.

ANNEXE DES CRÉATEURS
19, rue Godot-de-Mauroy, 75009 (9th)

No Chanel or Yves St. Laurent, but last season's clothes from French, Italian, and Japanese manufacturers. Labels are left in. There are two shops next to each other, one for dressy, the other for sportswear and separates. They also have hats, jewelry, coats, bags, and wedding gowns. Sales are in January and July.

Telephone: 42-65-46-40
Métro: Madeleine
Credit Cards: AE, MC, V
Hours: Monday–Saturday 11 A.M.–7 P.M.

BAB'S
89, bis avenue des Ternes, 75017 (17th)

Bab's used to work at Christian Dior and knows her clothes. Her shop stocks some of the best clothing and accessories found in discount shops in Paris. The items are not *haute haute,* but they are of long-lasting quality. The dressing rooms are nice, and the staff helpful and friendly, including the house cat Bebert, who usually sits by the door.

Telephone: 45-74-02-74
Métro: Pte Maillot or bus 43 or 92
Credit Cards: AE, DC, MC, V
Hours: Monday–Saturday 9 A.M.–7 P.M.

BETTY
10, place d'Aligre, 75012 (12th)

Probably the best time to hit Betty's is early Sunday morning and combine it with a trip to the flea market at place d'Aligre. Betty's is not worth a separate journey, but it is worth a quick look. They say they have designer labels, but not any on most top-ten lists. The prices are low, and if you want something *French* and don't care about famous designer labels, this could be interesting.

Telephone: 43-07-40-64
Métro: Ledru-Rollin
Credit Cards: None, cash only
Hours: Tuesday–Sunday 9 A.M.–12:30 P.M., Thursday and Saturday 2:30–7 P.M.

DAVID SCHIFF CLUB DES DIX
13, rue Royale, 75008 (8th)

Not a cheap store, but an extremely good value with an excellent selection. Beautiful women's fashions for ladies who lunch or go to corporate board meetings. English-speaking staff and the added bonus of being open on Sundays and most holidays.

Telephone: 42-66-43-61
Métro: Concorde
Credit Cards: MC, V
Hours: Daily, 10 A.M.–6 P.M.

Other location: G.H.S. Le Petit Club; 18, rue Boccador, 75008 (8th); Men's clothing and accessories only; Telephone: 47-20-99-34; Métro: Alma-Marceau; Hours: Tuesday–Saturday 10 A.M.–6 P.M.

OLIVER B
21, rue Pierre Lescot, 75001 (1st)

Oliver B is omnipresent in Paris. This is one of their biggest and best shops with bargains galore. You will find inexpensive separates that are easy to wear and inexpensive enough to toss out after a season or two. Lots of small sizes and nothing too far out.

Telephone: 40-26-26-26
Métro: Étienne-Marcel, Les Halles
Credit Cards: MC, V
Hours: Monday–Saturday 10:30 A.M.–7 P.M., Sunday 2–7 P.M.

HALLE BYS
60, rue de Richelieu, 75002 (2nd) (in the courtyard)

Everything from boots and underwear to suits, dresses, separates, and more for men, women, and children. The selection varies from good to just so-so. The best choices are upstairs. Not on the A-list for everyone, but for discount diggers, worth a look.

Telephone: 42-96-65-42
Métro: Bourse
Credit Cards: V
Hours: Monday–Saturday 10 A.M.–7 P.M.

JEAN-LOUIS SCHERRER STOCK
29, avenue Ledru-Rollin, 75012 (12th)

Two rooms of *haute couture* by Scherrer for the classy, elegant look of old money. Sales at the end of June. Other times, prices about half.

Telephone: 46-28-39-72
Métro: Gare de Lyon
Credit Cards: None, cash only
Hours: Monday–Friday 10 A.M.–6 P.M.

LE MOUTON À CINQ PATTES
18, rue Saint-Placide, 75006 (6th)

These bargain bin stores sell fashions from a variety of designers. The crowds are daunting and the places are piled high. Quality varies, but if you are persistent, something should turn up.

Telephone: 45-44-83-25
Métro: Sèvres-Babylone
Credit Cards: V
Hours: Tuesday–Saturday 11 A.M.–7 P.M., Monday 2–7 P.M.
Other locations: 8 & 14, rue Saint Placide, 75006 (6th); Telephone: 45-44-83-25; Métro: Sèvres-Babylone; Hours: Same hours as above

19, rue Grégoire-de-Tours, 75006 (6th); Telephone: 43-29-73-56; Métro: Odéon; Hours: Same hours as above

15, rue Vielle-du-Temple, 75004 (4th); Telephone: 42-74-86-30; Métro: St-Paul; Hours: Same hours as above

130, avenue Victor Hugo, 75016 (16th); Telephone: 47-55-42-25; Métro: Pompe; Hours: Same hours as above

MAGIC STOCK
38, rue de Rivoli, 75004 (4th)

Thirty percent off children's clothes makes these shops magnets for Cheap Chic shoppers with youngsters on their lists. As with most places like this, some looking is required and help is not always wonderful.

Telephone: 42-72-22-46
Métro: Hôtel-de-Ville
Credit Cards: MC, V
Hours: Tuesday–Saturday 10 A.M.–7 P.M., Monday noon–7 P.M.
Other locations: 60, rue Saint Placide, 75006 (6th); Telephone: 45-44-01-89; Métro: St-Placide

2, rue Joubert, angle Chaussée-d'Antin, 75009 (9th); Telephone: 48-74-74-10; Métro: Chaussée-d'Antin

47, avenue du Général-Leclerc, 75014 (14th); Telephone: 43-21-32-55; Métro: Mouton-Duvernet

16, rue de Levis, 75017 (17th); Telephone: 47-63-09-51; Métro: Villiers

MENDÈS-YSL (YVES ST-LAURENT)
65, rue Montmartre, 75002 (2nd)

Mendès sells Yves St-Laurent variations (first floor) and Rive Gauche lines (second floor) one season out of date and at bargain prices for this designer. Collections arrive in July and January, and in December and June they have a sale and take 20–30 percent more off. There are no dressing rooms, so you must change in public. Do not expect help from the ice maiden-*venduses.* If you hit this one right, it is a gold mine.

Telephone: 45-08-52-62, 42-36-83-32
Métro: Sentier

Credit Cards: V

Hours: Monday–Friday 9:30 A.M.–1 P.M., 2–5 P.M.; Saturday 9:30 A.M.–4 P.M.

MISS "GRIFFE'S"
19, rue de Penthièvre, 75008 (8th)

One of the best in the discount hunt for women's clothing, shoes, handbags, and accessories from all the top names, including Chanel and Valentino. The owner, Madame Vincent, has been here for 15 years and knows her business. Free alterations are ready in two days. A 10 percent discount will be given to readers who show her *Cheap Sleeps in Paris*.

Telephone: 42-65-10-00

Métro: Miromesnil

Credit Cards: AE, DC, MC, V

Hours: Monday–Friday 11 A.M.–6:30 P.M., Saturday 3–7 P.M.; closed middle two weeks in August

M.G.S
10, rue de Pont-aux-Choux, 75003 (3rd)

Cut-rate designer clothing for men. Many names most Americans will not recognize, but they do have Dior.

Telephone: 42-78-09-27

Métro: St-Sébastien-Froissart

Credit Cards: MC, V

Hours: Monday–Saturday 9 A.M.–7:30 P.M.

PWS (PRICES WITHOUT SURPRISE)
1, rue de Penthièvre, 75008 (8th)

Owner Claude Windisch got the idea for his men's discount store after visiting the United States and seeing all the cut-price stores. He stocks everything for men from top-name designers, and some no-name designer clothing for women that is best forgotten. Prices are 30 percent off *this* season's clothing.

Telephone: 47-42-64-30

Métro: Miromesnil

Credit Cards: V

Hours: Tuesday–Saturday 10 A.M.–7 P.M.

SODICLUB
57, rue Ste-Anne, 75002 (2nd)

Thirty percent off items not sold in the last year at airport boutiques.

Telephone: Not available

Métro: 4 Septembre

Credit Cards: MC, V

Hours: Monday–Saturday 10 A.M.–6 P.M.

SOIRÉE GOURMANDE
15, bd Richard Lenoir, 75011 (11th)

The motto of Soirée Gourmande is "Madeleine quality at Bastille prices." Those of you who know and love Fauchon and Héidard, both located at place de la Madeleine, know that prices at these two citadels of gourmet grocery shopping are fit for kings and nobles. Soirée Gourmande is for the smart shopper with Fauchon taste and style, but who does not want to pay the stratospheric prices. At Soirée Gourmande, you can buy the exact champagne bottled for Fauchon and the Ritz Hotel, but with the S.G. label instead. Goose liver pâté is 405F less, and so are their specialties of caviar, foie gras, chocolates, and Norwegian salmon. You can buy one or two items, a gift basket, or items by the case.

Telephone: 43-38-99-11
Métro: Voltaire, Bastille
Credit Cards: MC, V
Hours: Tuesday–Saturday 10 A.M.–7 P.M.

SOLDE TROIS
3, rue de Vienne, 75008 (8th)

Well worth the safari to the edge of things to check out the impressive selection of Lavin clothing for men and women that has not sold in the very high-priced boutique on rue St-Honoré. If you hit a sale, the bargains are even more exciting.

Telephone: Boutique for men: 42-94-99-67; Boutique for women: 42-94-93-34
Métro: Europe
Credit Cards: MC, V
Hours: Monday–Friday 10:30 A.M.–1:30 P.M., 4:30–6 P.M.; Saturday 10:30 A.M.–4:30 P.M.; closed first three weeks in August

SULMACO
13, rue de Trévise, 75009 (9th)

An excellent selection of designer men's fashion at below retail. Tailor-made suites from 6,000F, and the *détaxe* after any purchase of 2,000F.

Telephone: 48-24-89-00
Métro: Montmartre
Credit Cards: AE, MC, V
Hours: Monday–Saturday 10 A.M.–7 P.M., August noon–6:30 P.M.

Discount Shopping Streets

Just as Paris has its high-priced shopping streets, it also has its discount shopping streets. No certified Cheap Chic shopper will want to miss a trip to one of these streets where, if you are lucky, you will bring home something marvelous that your friends would kill for . . . even at three times the price *you* paid.

RUE D'ALÉSIA, 75014 (14th)

Both sides of rue d'Alésia are home to an assortment of outlet shops carrying last season's lines of designers you have heard of and some you never will. The best line of attack is to go up one side and down the other to get an overview, then come back to those that seem promising. Worst time to go is on Saturday. Some of the better shops are: Carré d'As, No. 62; SR (Sonya Rykiel), No. 64; Evolutif, No. 72; Dorothée Bis, No. 74; Stock & Stock II, No. 92–94; Stock System, No. 110–112; Kookai, No. 111; Cacharel, No. 114; Daniel Hechter, No. 116–118; Philippe Salvert, No. 122; Alésia Discounts, No. 139.

Métro: Alésia

Credit Cards: Varies by shop

Hours: Generally shops are open Monday afternoons, Tuesday–Saturday 10 A.M.–7 P.M.

RUE MESLAY, 75003 (3rd)

One entire street devoted to shoes—one store after the other—with everything from clodhoppers to 4-inch red-satin sling pumps. Prices are good. The best advice is to browse first, then go back and do serious buying. Finding the perfect pair of shoes takes time and energy, not to say patience. Don't try to squeeze this one in . . . allow time and leave nonshopping pals at the hotel. If all else fails here, you can run by Tati at 13, place de la République (see page 225).

Métro: République

Credit Cards: Varies with each shop

RUE SAINT-PLACIDE, 75006 (6th)

Bargain fever has hit Paris in a cluster of boutiques along the rue Saint-Placide. Start at Bon Marché department store and work both sides of the street. This is hard work if the crowds are out in force, especially at lunch time when the office girls surge through and on Saturdays when housewives leave *les enfants* at home and make the pilgrimage. Best buys are in casual sportswear and teenage "must-haves" of the moment. There are a limited number of top-name designers, but everything is *au courant.* Windows are often more appealing than the stuffy, cramped interiors. Sharpen your elbows for this.

Métro: Sèvres-Babylone

Credit Cards: Varies with each shop

Hours: Usually closed until 2 P.M. on Monday, open Monday afternoons until 7 P.M., Tuesday–Saturday 10 A.M.–7 P.M.

RUE ST-DOMINIQUE, 75007 (7th)

From avenue Bosquet to boulevard de Latour-Maubourg, shops sell clothing for men, women, and children from designer *dégriffés* (labels cut out) to bins of last season's T-shirts. Affordable.

Métro: Latour-Maubourg

Credit Cards: Varies with each shop

Hours: Some shops closed until 2 P.M. on Monday and in August; Monday afternoons 2–7 P.M., Tuesday–Saturday 10 P.M.–7 P.M.

RUE DE PARADIS, 75010 (10th)

The best area in Paris for china and crystal, in one crowded shop after another. Be sure to see Baccarat at 32, rue de Paradis; open Monday–Friday 9 A.M.–6 P.M., Saturday 10 A.M.–noon and 2–5 P.M. Another excellent choice is Limoges-Unic at 12, rue de Paradis; same hours as Baccarat. Staff at both shops speak English; the *détaxe* is available after spending 2,000F, and they ship.

Métro: Château-d'Eau

Credit Cards: Varies with each shop

Flea Markets—Les Marchés Aux Puces

What to do on a Saturday or Sunday morning? Go early to the flea market; wear old clothes and comfortable shoes, beware of pickpockets, and bring cash. You will have a good time even if you don't buy a thing. The days of finding a fabulous antique for a few *centimes* is gone, but you will probably find a keepsake or two. If you have nothing special on your list, just people-watch; the wildlife at the *puces* beats that at the zoo.

MARCHÉ D'ALIGRE
Place d'Aligre (12th)

This is a small, daily food and flea *marché,* good for little objects, antique buttons, bric-a-brac, and inexpensive clothes.

Métro: Ledru-Rollin

Hours: Tuesday–Sunday until 1 P.M.

MARCHÉ DE MONTREUIL
Porte de Montreuil (20th)

The huge market begins once you get through the long line of vendors hawking cheap trash on the bridge.

Métro: Porte de Montreuil

Hours: Saturday–Monday 9 A.M.–5 P.M.

MARCHÉ DE CLIGNANCOURT
Avenue Michelet at rue des Rossiers (18th)

Clignancourt is the largest flea market in the world—too big to conquer in only a day. Once you get past the piles of jeans and the Indians selling cheap beads, head for the Marché Biron on the corner of rue des Rossiers. It has the most expensive sellers, but also the most serious. The Paul Bert Marché, 16, rue Paul Bert, has an unusual collection of Art Deco pieces and antiques from the late 1890s. The Marché Jules-Valles, 17, rue Jules-Valles, has the least expensive items. For vintage clothing, the Marché Malik at 60, rue Jules-Valles, is the place.

Métro: Porte de Clignancourt

Hours: Saturday–Monday, dawn until 7 P.M.

MARCHÉ DE VANVES
Avenue Georges Lafenestre (14th)

If you like to bargain, walk along avenue Marc-Sangnier. The locals know to come before noon, when most of the serious sellers fold up their stalls. It is a good place for small antiques and collectibles that tuck easily into a suitcase. Every Sunday morning from March to October, the Square George-Lafenestre is an open-air art gallery where you can buy directly from the artists.

Métro: Porte de Vanves

Hours: Saturday and Sunday 9 A.M.–6:00 P.M.

Food Shopping Streets and Outdoor Roving Markets

There are two types of markets in Paris (in addition to the growing number of *supermarchés*): *rue commerçantes*—stationary indoor/outdoor markets open 6 days a week—and *marchés volants*—roving markets of independent merchants who move from one neighborhood to another on any given day. A visit to one of these markets will provide a real look at an old, unchanging way of daily Paris life. When you go, take your camera, don't touch the merchandise, and watch your wallet. I guarantee you that a trip or two to a Paris market will spoil you for your hometown supermarket. In Paris markets, fruits and vegetables of every variety are arranged with the skill and precision usually reserved for fine jewelry store windows. Equal care and attention is given to the displays of meats, fish, cheese, and fresh flowers. A few favorites are listed here. To locate the ones closest to your hotel, ask at the desk.

SHOPPING STREETS—*RUES COMMERÇANTES*

Generally open Tuesday–Sunday 8 A.M.–1 P.M. and 4:30–7 P.M. Closed Monday and Sunday afternoon.

RUE MONTORGEUIL (1st)

Métro: Étienne-Marcel

RUE MOUFFETARD (5th)
Métro: Censier-Daubenton, Monge

RUE DE SEINE & BUCI (6th)
Métro: Odéon

RUE CLER (7th)
Métro: École-Militaire

RUE DE LÉVIS (17th)
Métro: Villiers

RUE PONCELET (17th)
Métro: Ternes

RUE LEPIC (18th)
Métro: Abbesses, Blanche

ROVING MARKETS—*MARCHÉS VOLANTS*
Open: 7:30 A.M.–1:30 P.M.

CARMES (5th)
Place Maubert
Métro: Maubert-Mutualité
Open: Tuesday, Thursday, Saturday

MONGE (5th)
Place Monge
Métro: Monge
Open: Wednesday, Friday, Sunday

RASPAIL (6th)
Boulevard Raspail, between rue du Cherche-Midi and rue de Rennes
Métro: Rennes, Sèvres-Babylone
Open: Tuesday, Friday, and Sunday (organic)
Note: On Sundays there is an organic market, but the quality varies greatly.

RICHARD-LENOIR (11th)
Boulevard Richard-Lenoir at rue Amelot
Métro: Bastille, Richard-Lenoir
Open: Thursday, Sunday

DUPLEIX (15th)
Boulevard du Grenelle between rue Lourmel and rue de Commerce

Métro: Dupleix, La Motte-Piquet-Grenelle
Open: Wednesday, Sunday

COURS DE LA REINE (16th)
Avenue Président Wilson

Métro: Alma Marceau or Iéna
Open: Wednesday, Saturday

Gifts and Handicrafts

ARTISINAT MONASTIQUE
68, bis avenue Denfert-Rochereau, 75014 (14th)

What a find for handicrafts, embroidered linens, cosmetics, food products, and beautiful robes and nightgowns . . . all made by French priests and nuns in monastaries throughout France. The quality is beautiful, and whatever you buy will show the name of who made it. A volunteer staff of sweet, gray-haired ladies will assist you, wrap your purchase, and graciously take your money. Even if you only buy a candle or a bar of soap, it is worth a visit.

Telephone: 43-35-15-76
Métro: Denfert-Rochereau
Credit Cards: None, cash only
Hours: Monday–Saturday 1:45–7 P.M.; closed holidays and August

BAÏKAL
15, East Lacharrière, 75011 (11th)

Michael Monlaü's shop is on a quiet park in a neighborhood most tourists never see. He stocks one-of-a-kind gifts you will want for friends and yourself. Michael loves Americans, speaks perfect English, and is willing to take the time to help you select just the right item. Prices are within all budgets.

Telephone: 48-06-00-37
Métro: St-Ambroise
Credit Cards: AE, MC, V
Hours: Monday 2–8 P.M., Tuesday–Saturday 10 A.M.–8 P.M.

CALLISTO
16, rue de Elzevir, 75003 (3rd)

Colette Ferrandis has one of the most unusual shops in the Marais. Everything is a work of art and an original quality design. Expect to find beautiful jewelry, hand knits, handmade purses, winter gloves with matching bags, sweaters, and more. Plan to spend time just looking. A bonus is that Colette speaks wonderful English.

Telephone: 42-78-36-56
Métro: St-Paul, Chemin Vert
Credit Cards: AE, MC, V
Hours: Wednesday–Monday 11 A.M.–1:30 P.M., 3–7 P.M.; closed Tuesday

LA DAME BLANCHE
186, rue de Rivoli, 75001 (1st)

You will soon become dizzy and confused walking along the tourist trail that leads from place de la Concorde down rue de Rivoli. The area has one of the highest concentrations of tourist merchandise in the city. You know the type: plastic Eiffel Towers, T-shirts with the Mona Lisa and a smart saying, gaudy scarves, and wild ties that will make your husband blush. However, dedicated shophounds know that with a little digging, treasures are here. Where? At Michael and Suzanne's La Dame Blanche. The windows of their side-by-side shops are jam-packed with Limoges boxes, leather gloves, authentic berets, silk scarves, Haviland china, hand-painted plates, and more. Do not let this confusing clutter deter you from exploring the best shop along this stretch. Not only is the selection the best, so are the prices. If you want a special Limoges box, ask Michael and he can have it made for you. Both Michael and his sister Suzanne speak English, offer excellent service, and are delightful besides. They give a 15 percent discount if you spend 2,000F or more and they ship all over the world.

Telephone: 42-60-67-12, 42-96-31-56
Métro: Palais-Royal
Credit Cards: AE, DC, MC, V
Hours: Monday–Saturday 10 A.M.–6 P.M.

Hairdresser

FRANCK FANN COIFFURE (FOR MEN AND WOMEN)
5, rue d'Ormesson, 75004 (4th)

Where to get your hair cut? It is always a problem in a strange city, especially if you cannot communicate very well. Relax, now you have Franck to do your hair. He is wonderful at cutting both men and women's hair. I have never had any of the other operators, and my advice to you is to stick with Franck and tell him I sent you. In French salons, all services are individually priced, from the shampoo to the blow dry. At Franck's, it should run around 200F, and that is very reasonable. Appointments are suggested, especially for Franck.

Telephone: 48-04-50-62
Métro: St-Paul
Credit Cards: MC, V
Hours: Monday–Saturday 10 A.M.–7 P.M.

Jewelry

ALLIX
6, rue de Surène, 75008 (8th)

For 10 years the two owners have been making simple, well-priced handbags and unusual jewelry.

Telephone: 42-65-10-79
Métro: Madeleine
Credit Cards: MC, V
Hours: Monday–Friday 11 A.M.–2:30 P.M., 3–6 P.M.; closed Saturday and August

BIJOUX BURMA
72, rue du Faubourg St-Honoré, 75008 (8th)

The best *faux* jewelry in Paris at affordable prices. Stores are located throughout Paris.

Telephone: 42-65-44-90
Métro: Madeleine, Concorde
Credit Cards: AE, DC, MC, V
Hours: Monday–Saturday 10 A.M.–6:30 P.M.

DE GUSTIBUS
14, rue Princesse, 75006 (6th)

"Where did you find that pin?" or "Your necklace is so unusual, where did you get it?" Admittedly I have a wonderful job—traveling, shopping, eating out, visiting hotels, and getting paid to do it! One of the other benefits is finding unusual bits of this and that to add to my wardrobe. One of the best places to do this is at De Gustibus on the Left Bank. They stock different jewelry, amusing hats, umbrellas, a few pieces of clothing, and gloves. Prices are quite reasonable for most of the items, so if you are close, stop by.

Telephone: 40-51-01-08
Métro: St-Germain-de-Prés or Mabillor
Credit Cards: AE, V
Hours: Tuesday–Saturday 1–8 P.M.; closed Monday and August

MATIÈRE PREMIERE
12, rue de Sévigné, 75004 (4th)

Baubles, bangles, and beads . . . either assemble your own or buy ready-made necklaces, earrings, and pins at decent prices. No English and not much help either, but if you like this sort of thing, you will enjoy looking at this shop.

Telephone: 42-78-40-87
Métro: St-Paul
Credit Cards: MC, V
Hours: Monday–Saturday 10 A.M.–7 P.M.

Passages

Long before anyone heard of shopping malls, Paris had *galeries* and passages—skylighted, decorated, tiled, and beautiful. Tucked away off major commercial streets, mainly in the second and ninth arrondissements, they are easy to miss if you are not looking for them. It is fun to stroll through one or two if only to see a sampling of the old-fashioned shops still selling handmade dolls, fancy pipes, old books, 78-rpm records, model trains, and toys.

GALERIE COLBERT
6, rue des Petits-Champs, 75002 (2nd)

Next to the Biblioteque Nationale and restored to all of its 19th-century glory.

Métro: Bourse

GALERIE VIVIENNE
4, rue des Petits-Champs, 75002 (2nd)

The most beautiful passage of all.

Métro: Bourse

PASSAGE JOUFFROY
12, boulevard Montmartre, 75009 (9th)

The oldest passage, opened in 1800.

Métro: Montmartre

PASSAGE DES PANORAMAS
11, boulevard Montmartre, 75009 (9th)

Métro: Montmartre

PASSAGE VERDEAU
31, bis rue du Faubourg-Montmartre, 75009 (9th)

Shops feature collectibles: books, records, etc.

Métro: Montmartre

Premier Paris Shopping Areas (Cost is not *an object)*

AVENUE GEORGE V, AVENUE MARCEAU, AVENUE MONTAIGNE, FAUBOURG ST-HONORÉ, AND RUE FRANÇOIS 1er (1st and 8th)

For window-shopping and dreaming of the highest order, these five premier shopping streets are to designer fashion and *haute couture* as the Louvre is to priceless art. The boutiques and shops are not to be missed, even if you only stroll by the elegant window displays.

LE FORUM DES HALLES (1st)

The ultramodern, multilevel complex on the site of the old Les Halles market attracts more than 40 million visitors per year. In this covered shopping wonderland, there are over 200 shops displaying the latest fashion fads, scores of fast-food joints, walk-in hair salons offering sculpted cuts or dye jobs in glowing green or blue, and several cinemas. The largest Métro station in the world lies under it (and it is not considered by Parisians to be safe at night). It is fun to be part of the strolling crowds, if only for the experience of the entertaining people-watching.

MARAIS (3rd and 4th)

The kosher food shops along rue des Rosiers, the trendy boutiques along rue Francs Bourgeois, and the avant-garde designers make shopping in the Marais an excellent offbeat adventure. Be sure to include a stroll by the lovely place des Vosges and sit in one of the cafés (see *Cheap Eats in Paris*).

PLACES DES VICTOIRES (1st)

A wonderful shopping trip nestled behind Palais-Royal. After going around the place des Victoires, branch out down the side streets. This is an area of many fashion innovators and well worth serious time just to see what you will be wearing two years from now. The prices are not in the bargain department, unless you happen to hit a sale.

ST-GERMAIN-DES-PRÉS (6th and 7th)

Sensational shopping can be found on the rue de Sèvres, rue Bonaparte, rue de Four, rue St-Sulpice, rue Jacob, and the rue de Seine, to mention only a few of the streets that line this *quartier,* which is literally packed with fashion boutiques, antique shops, art galleries, and bookshops. In fact, if you have only a short time to devote to shopping and browsing, this is where you should go.

CHAMPS-ÉLYSÉES (8th)

While the Champs-Élysées used to be the finest address a retailer could have, today there are waves of tourists flowing up one side and down the other. Movie theaters, airline offices, banks, car dealers, outdoor cafés, and minimalls charging top francs for everything line each side of the famous avenue. Pickpockets work both sides of the street and are pros . . . watch out! Reserve your time on the Champs-Élysées for sipping an afternoon drink at a café and for fascinating people-watching. Do your shopping elsewhere.

RUE DE PASSY AND AVENUE VICTOR-HUGO (16th)

Walking down either of these streets in the 16th arrondissement will give you an idea of what it is like to be in the upper middle-class and live in Paris. You will see few tourists, no razor-shaved haircuts, and certainly no hawkers waving T-shirts or plastic replicas of the Eiffel Tower. This is the land of the BCBG's (French yuppies), old money, and tradition. There are several cafés if someone in your party would rather sit and have a beer while watching the world wander by.

Rent an Outfit

L'AFFAIR D'UN SOIR
147, rue de la Pompe, 75016 (16th)

If you have been invited for dinner at the Élysée Palace and "haven't a *thing* to wear," don't worry. Silk dresses, ball gowns, hats, and elegant accessories are available here for all *soirée* goers. Sophie de Mestier designs two original collections each year for rent. Many customers rent an outfit and cannot bear to part with it, so they end up buying it. The shop is located in one of the posh neighborhoods of Paris, so this tells you another secret of the well-dressed French woman . . . maybe she leases! Prices for rentals are from 700–750F. To rent something, you *must* make an appointment.

Telephone: 47-27-37-50
Métro: Victor-Hugo
Credit Cards: MC, V
Hours: Tuesday–Saturday 10:30 A.M.–1 P.M. and 2–7 P.M.; closed 12–24 August

Sales (Soldes)

During most of the year, when you venture into one of the designer shops, they are quiet enough for you to hear the rustle of money being spent by affluent customers. However, we less-affluent mortals also have a chance. For the first three weeks in January and July, Paris is *on sale.* In addition, Galeries Lafayette and Au Printemps have sales in March and October. The crowds of shoppers move with dizzying swiftness, all zeroing in on the considerable savings. If you can brave these shopping pros, this is the time to go to the designer boutiques and pick up a little number for about one-third the U.S. retail price. In October, Hèrmes has its once-yearly sale. The line forms the night before, with shoppers eager to pay 50 percent less for the famous signature scarves (currently retailing for over $200), ties, leather goods, and conservative line of clothing. Again, if you do not mind standing in line and fighting crowds packed in ten-deep, then this sale is a must for Hèrmes fans.

Shoes

BALLY SHOES
156, rue de Rivoli, at corner of rue du Louvre, 75001 (1st)

Enter on the rue du Louvre side for the bargains in Bally Shoes for men, women, and children. The front section of the store sells shoes at full price, but the back section is where the sale items are.

Telephone: 42-60-22-46
Métro: Louvre
Credit Cards: MC, V
Hours: Monday–Saturday 10 A.M.–7 P.M.

FRANCHI CHAUSSURES
15, rue de la Pépinière, 75008 (8th)

Lots of Charles Jourdan shoes at half-price, but the styles are sometimes a bit dated (e.g., stiletto heels). End-of-series shoes and Italian designs, but no place to really sit to try on unless you count the one stool by the door. Remember, this is discount and comfort is not part of the package.

Telephone: 42-94-28-88
Métro: Saint-Augustin
Credit Cards: AE, DC, MC, V
Hours: Monday–Saturday 10:30 A.M.–7 P.M.
Other locations: 10, rue du Rome, 75008 (8th); Telephone: 43-87-42-59; Métro: Saint-Lazare

30, bd de Vaugirard, 75015 (15th); Telephone: 43-21-90-67; Métro: Falguière, Montparnasse

TIZIANO
7, rue Notre-Dame des Champs, 75006 (6th)

Last year's collection of beautiful Italian shoes for men and women, at 30 percent off and more. One of the best selections of wearable footwear in Paris. I *never* miss shopping here on every trip to Paris, and I have yet to come away empty-handed. They also have a few handbags, but you are here for the shoes. Not to be missed.

Telephone: 42-22-74-20
Métro: St-Placide
Credit Cards: AE, MC, V
Hours: Monday noon–7 P.M.; Tuesday–Friday 10 P.M.–7 P.M.; Saturday 10 A.M.–12:30 P.M., 2–7 P.M.

Shopping Malls

FORUM DES HALLES
Main entry: rue Pierre Lescott or rue Rambuteau, 75001 (1st)

This is the result of filling the hole left after the wholesale food market Les Halles was moved to Rungis. The Forum des Halles is the largest commercial project in France and has the largest Métro station under it all. The shops sell fashions of the moment, aimed at a hip, slim crowd, all under thirty . . . at least in spirit. If you don't feel like shopping, you can watch a film, grab a snack or meal, swim, or just hang out. Warning: not considered a safe place to be late at night.

Telephone: 40-39-38-74
Métro: Les Halles
Credit Cards: Depends on each shop
Hours: 10:30 A.M.–7:30 P.M. for the shops

PASSY PLAZA
Corner rue Jean Bologne and rue de Passy, 75016 (16th)

Middle-of-the-road boutiques with lots of clothes for the junior set or for something to knock around in and still feel fashionable. Also a very good supermarket.

Métro: Passy
Credit Cards: Varies with each shop
Hours: Shops: Monday–Saturday 10 A.M.–7 P.M.; Supermarché: Monday–Saturday 8:30 A.M.–8 P.M.

LES TROIS QUARTIERS
23, boulevard de la Madeleine, 75008 (8th)

Seventy-five boutiques including Kenzo, Yves St-Laurent, Dorothée Bis, and Givenchy. Prices are high, but stroll through anyway to get an idea of how much you will save by shopping at the Cheap Chic shops listed in this book. The quality is better than at Forum des Halles, but the spirit is really dead.

Telephone: 42-97-80-12
Métro: Madeleine
Credit Cards: Depends on the boutique
Hours: Monday–Saturday 10 A.M.–7 P.M.

Silk

CHRISTIAN LU
95, rue de Bac, 75007 (7th)

Silk blouses, dresses, suits, ties—either off-the-rack or custom-made. Prices and styles are good.

Telephone: 42-22-42-19
Métro: Sèvres-Babylone
Credit Cards: AE, DC, MC, V
Hours: Monday noon–7 P.M., Tuesday–Saturday 10:30 A.M.–7 P.M.
Other locations: 1–3, rue du Plat d'Étain (behind MacDonald's), 75001 (1st); Telephone: 42-21-35-60; Métro: Châtelet

86, rue Vaugirard, 75006 (6th); Telephone: 45-44-93-37; Métro: Falguière

85, rue de Provence, 75009 (9th); Telephone: 48-74-16-13; Métro: Havre-Caumartin

GIANNI D'ARNO PUR RÈVE DE SOIE
17, rue St-Marc, 75002 (2nd)

The best-priced silk blouses in Paris in a rainbow of colors and styles. No Chinese imports . . . all French or Italian silk. Scarves by Erre, the same quality as Hermès at much less.

CLOSED

Telephone: 42-36-98-73
Métro: Richelieu-Drouot
Credit Cards: None, cash only
Hours: Monday–Saturday 9:30 A.M.–6:30 P.M.

Sweaters

CACHEMIRE FIRST
9, rue Richepance, 75008 (8th)

Cashmere sweaters for men and women in more than 25 colors and in traditional styles. Also, men's and women's cashmere blazers, scarves, socks, and gloves. Sales in February, July, and August, when 30 percent is taken off.

Telephone: 42-60-12-78
Métro: Madeleine, Concorde
Credit Cards: AE, DC, MC, V
Hours: Monday–Saturday 9:30 A.M.–7 P.M.

ORIGINAL DAMOUR/L'ESPACE CASHMERE DAMOUR CREATION
101, rue Reaumur, corner rue de Clery, 75002 (2nd)

You will not see this fine quality of cashmeres anywhere . . . and that includes most of Scotland. Sales around the 15th of June make it even more appealing.

Telephone: 42-36-91-63
Métro: Sentier
Credit Cards: MC, V
Hours: Monday–Saturday 10 A.M.–6 P.M.; closed in August

PIERRE VIVREZ
6, rue des Saussaies, 75008 (8th)

A large collection of traditional pure wool sweaters for men and women. Also cotton T-shirts, jackets, and skirts for summer. Everything is guaranteed washable.

Telephone: 42-65-26-54
Métro: Champs-Élysées Clemanceau
Credit Cards: MC, V
Hours: Monday–Saturday 10 A.M.–7 P.M.
Other location: 75, rue Michel-Ange, 75016 (16th); Telephone: 46-51-63-14; Métro: Michel-Ange-Molitor

Used Books

TEA & TATTERED PAGES
24, rue Mayet, 75006 (6th)

A visit to Tea & Tattered Pages offers more than just browsing through more than 10,000 used books. Run by vivacious American expatriate Kristi Chavane, the store also sells gifts, fantasy teapots, cards, coffee from J.B Loucks, and serves meals, including brunch on Sundays (see *Cheap Eats in Paris*). Kristi and her staff are friendly and plugged into the Paris scene, and I guarantee you will not regret a visit to her two-level shop.

Telephone: 40-65-94-35
Métro: Falguière
Credit Cards: None, cash only
Hours: Monday–Saturday 10 P.M.–7 P.M., Sunday 11 A.M.–5 P.M. (spring and summer)

Watches

CAPION
9, rue Auber, 75009 (9th)

Watches for everyone on your list at prices starting at 60F.

Telephone: Not available
Métro: Opéra
Credit Cards: AE, MC, V
Hours: Monday–Saturday 9:30 A.M.–7 P.M.

Readers' Comments

While every effort has been taken to provide accurate information in this guide, the publisher and author cannot be held responsible for changes in any of the listings due to rate increases, inflation, the rise and fall of the dollar, the passage of time, or management changes.

Cheap Sleeps in Paris is updated and revised on a regular basis. If you find a change before I do, or make an important discovery you want to pass along to me, please send a note stating the name and address of the hotel or shop, the date of your visit, and a description of your findings. Your comments are very important to me, and I follow through on every letter I receive. Thank you very much.

Send your letters to Sandra A. Gustafson *(Cheap Sleeps in Paris),* c/o Chronicle Books, ~~275 Fifth Street~~, San Francisco, CA ~~94103.~~ 94105-3441
85 2ND ST, 6TH FLOOR

Index of Accommodations

H